# Global Challenges for Business
## Custom Edition

Custom Edition for University of Edinburgh Business School

ISBN 13: 9781307080407

McGraw-Hill Custom Publishing

http://create.mheducation.com/uk/

Published by McGraw-Hill Education, 2 Penn Plaza, New York, NY 10121.

Cover image: ©iStock

ISBN: 9781307080407

# Global Challenges for Business
### CUSTOM EDITION

# Contents

# Credits

# 1

# Don't Believe Everything You Think

A little before noon on December 14, 2015, a man wearing a black stocking cap, black gloves, and a green sweat shirt with a four-leaf clover and the words "Get Lucky" printed on the front entered the Sterling State Bank in Rochester, Minnesota.* He demanded cash and gave the teller a note saying he was armed. Police officers arrived and followed the man's tracks in the snow to the parking lot of a Comfort Inn nearby, but by then the man had driven off in a car.

The next day, a reporter from KIMT-TV had set up in front of the bank to update the story, and right then and there the same man tried to rob the same bank again. When the teller saw the man he yelled out, "That's the robber!" and the reporter called the police. This time when the police followed the suspect's footprints they spotted his vehicle and apprehended him.

Now, educators will disagree about what exactly critical thinking is, but there will be no disputing that, whatever it is, "Get Lucky" wasn't doing it. First of all, robbing banks isn't necessarily the best way to make a living. But if you insist on robbing a bank, then probably you don't want to leave footprints to your car, and probably you don't want to try to rob the bank when a TV crew is filming it. Among other things, critical thinking involves considering the possible outcomes of an action.

*http://www.postbulletin.com/news/crime/robber-hits-rochester-bank-a-second-time-arrested-at-gunpoint/article_c0f55ab9-97b5-5a52-95d7-484ef2b6fcc9.html.

## Students will learn to . . .

1. Define critical thinking

2. Explain the role of beliefs and claims in critical thinking

3. Identify issues in real-world situations

4. Recognize an argument

5. Define and identify the common cognitive biases that affect critical thinking

6. Understand the terms "truth" and "knowledge" as used in this book

Among what other things? Speaking generally, if we just think or do stuff, that's not thinking critically. Critical thinking kicks in when we *evaluate* beliefs and actions—when we critique them. On the one hand, there is good, old-fashioned thinking. That's what we do when we form opinions, make judgments, arrive at decisions, develop plans, come to conclusions, offer hypotheses, and the like. On the other hand, there is *critical* thinking. That's what we do when we *rationally evaluate* the first kind of thinking. *Critical thinking is thinking that critiques.* It involves critiquing opinions, judgments, decisions, plans, conclusions, and reasoning in general. We engage in it when we consider whether our thinking (or someone else's) abides by the criteria of good sense and logic.

If you are taking other courses, chances are your *instructor* will think critically about the work you turn in. He or she will offer critical commentary on what you submit. If you want to think critically, you have to do this yourself to your own work. Try to leave your instructor with nothing to say except, "Good job!"

It can be the same in the workplace or in the military. You might perhaps be asked to solve a problem or troubleshoot a situation or come up with a recommendation, or any number of other things that involve arriving at conclusions. Your colleagues or friends or supervisors may give you feedback or commentary. They are thinking critically about your reasoning.

Of course, if you are so brilliant that you never err in your thinking, then you may not need feedback from others. Unfortunately, there is evidence that people who think they are experts are more likely to believe they know things they don't really know.* Anyway, almost everyone makes mistakes. We overlook important considerations, ignore viewpoints that conflict with our own, or in other ways don't think as clearly as we might. Most of us benefit from a little critical commentary, and this includes commentary that comes from ourselves. The chances of reaching defensible conclusions improve if we don't simply conclude willy-nilly, but reflect on our reasoning and try to make certain it is sound.

Being able to think critically can be useful in another way. Others try to influence what we think and do. There is much to be said for being able to critically evaluate a sales pitch, whether it comes from a stranger or a friend, or is about kitchen gadgets or for whom to vote for president. Critical thinking helps us recognize a scam when we see it.

Some educators equate critical thinking with problem solving or innovative thinking ("thinking outside the box"). This is fine, though at a certain point proposed solutions and possible innovations have to be tested. That's where critical thinking comes in.

This is a book in *critical* thinking because it offers guidance about *critiquing* thinking. The book and the course you are using it in, if you are, explain the minimum criteria of good reasoning—the requirements a piece of reasoning must meet if it is worth paying attention to, *no matter what the context.* Along the way we will explore the most common and important obstacles to good reasoning, as well as some of the most common mistakes people make when coming to conclusions. Other courses you take offer refinements. In them you will learn what considerations are important from the perspective of individual disciplines. But in no course anywhere, at least in no course that involves arriving at conclusions, will thinking that violates the standards set forth in this book be accepted.

If it does nothing else, what you read here and learn in your critical thinking course should help you avoid at least a few of the more egregious common errors people make when they reason. If you would have otherwise made these mistakes, you will have become smarter. Not smarter in some particular subject, mind you, but

---

*Scientific American Mind*, January/February 2016, p. 13.

smarter in general. The things you learn from this book (and from the course you may be reading it for) apply to nearly any subject people can talk or think or write about.

To a certain extent, questions we should ask when critiquing our own—or someone else's—thinking depend on what is at issue. Deciding whom to vote for, whether to buy a house, whether a mathematical proof is sound, which toothpaste to buy, or what kind of dog to get involve different considerations. In all cases, however, we should want to avoid making or accepting weak and invalid arguments. We should also avoid being distracted by irrelevancies or ruled by emotion, succumbing to fallacies or bias, and being influenced by dubious authority or half-baked speculation. These are not the only criteria by which reasoning might be evaluated, but they are central and important, and they provide the main focus of this book.

## Critical Thinking, the Long Version

The Collegiate Learning Assessment (CLA) Project of the Council for Aid to Education has come up with a list of skills that covers almost everything your authors believe is important in critical thinking. If you achieve mastery over all these or even a significant majority of them, you'll be well ahead of most of your peers—and your fellow citizens. In question form, here is what the council came up with:

How well does the student

- determine what information is or is not pertinent;
- distinguish between rational claims and emotional ones;
- separate fact from opinion;
- recognize the ways in which evidence might be limited or compromised;
- spot deception and holes in the arguments of others;
- present his/her own analysis of the data or information;
- recognize logical flaws in arguments;
- draw connections between discrete sources of data and information;
- attend to contradictory, inadequate, or ambiguous information;
- construct cogent arguments rooted in data rather than opinion;
- select the strongest set of supporting data;
- avoid overstated conclusions;
- identify holes in the evidence and suggest additional information to collect;
- recognize that a problem may have no clear answer or single solution;
- propose other options and weigh them in the decision;
- consider all stakeholders or affected parties in suggesting a course of action;
- articulate the argument and the context for that argument;
- correctly and precisely use evidence to defend the argument;
- logically and cohesively organize the argument;
- avoid extraneous elements in an argument's development;
- present evidence in an order that contributes to a persuasive argument?

www.aacu.org/peerreview/pr_sp07_analysis1.cfm.

■ The judges on *The Voice* critique singers, but that doesn't automatically qualify as thinking critically.

## BELIEFS AND CLAIMS

Why bother thinking critically? The ultimate objective in thinking critically is to come to conclusions that are correct and to make decisions that are wise. Because our decisions reflect our conclusions, we can simplify things by saying that *the purpose of thinking critically is to come to correct conclusions.* The method used to achieve this objective is to evaluate our thinking by the standards of rationality. Of course, we can also evaluate someone else's thinking, though the objective there might simply be to help the person.

When we come to a conclusion, we have a belief. Concluding involves believing. If you *conclude* the battery is dead, you *believe* the battery is dead. Keeping this in mind, let's define a few key terms.

A belief is, obviously, something you believe. It is important to understand that a belief is *propositional,* which means it can be expressed in a declarative sentence—a sentence that is either true or false. A good bit of muddleheaded thinking can be avoided if you understand that beliefs are propositional entities, but more on this later.

As we use these words, *beliefs* are the same as *judgments* and *opinions.* When we express a belief (or judgment or opinion) in a declarative sentence, the result is a *statement* or *claim* or *assertion,* and for our purposes these are the same thing. Claims can be used for other purposes than to state beliefs, but this is the use we're primarily concerned with.

> Beliefs and claims are *propositional:* they can be expressed in true-or-false declarative sentences.

### Objective Claims and Subjective Claims

Before we say something more about conclusions, we should make a distinction between objective and subjective claims. An **objective claim** has this characteristic:

whether it is true or false is independent of whether people think it is true or false. "There is life on Mars" is thus an objective claim, because whether or not life exists there doesn't depend on whether people think it does. If everyone suddenly believed there is life on Mars, that doesn't mean that suddenly there would be life on Mars. Likewise, "God exists" is an objective claim because whether it is true doesn't depend on whether people think it is true.

Although objective claims are either true or false, we may not know which a given claim is. "Portland, Oregon, is closer to the North Pole than to the equator" is a true objective claim. "Portland, Oregon, is closer to the equator than to the North Pole" is a false objective claim. "More stamp collectors live in Portland, Oregon, than in Portland, Maine" is an objective claim whose truth or falsity is not known, at least not by us.

 That could be you under the snow if you don't think critically.

Not every claim is objective, of course. "Bruno Mars has swag" is not objective, for it lacks the characteristic mentioned previously. That is, whether or not someone has swag *does* depend on whether people think he does. If nobody thinks Bruno Mars has swag, then he doesn't. If Parker thinks he does and Moore doesn't, you will say that Parker and Moore are each entitled to their opinions. Whether someone has swag is in the eyes of the beholder.

Claims of this variety are **subjective.** Whether a subjective claim is true or false is not independent of whether people think it is true or false. Examples of subjective claims would be judgments of taste, such as "Rice vinegar is too sweet." Is rice vinegar too sweet? It depends on what you think. Some kinds of comparisons also are subjective. Is snowboarding more fun than skiing? Again, it depends on what you think, and there is no further "truth" to consider. However, many statements contain both objective and nonobjective elements, as in "Somebody stole our nifty concrete lawn duck." Whether the lawn duck is *concrete* is an objective question; whether it is *our* lawn duck is an objective question; and whether it was *stolen* is an objective question. But whether the stolen concrete lawn duck is *nifty* is a subjective question.

## Fact and Opinion

Sometimes people talk about the difference between "fact" and "opinion," having in mind the notion that *all* opinions are subjective. But some opinions are not subjective, because their truth or falsity is independent of what people think. Again, in this book "opinion" is just another word for "belief." If you believe that Portland, Oregon, is closer to the North Pole than to the equator, that opinion happens to be true, and would continue to be true even if you change your mind. You can refer to objective opinions as *factual* opinions or beliefs, if you want—*but that doesn't mean factual opinions are all true.* "Portland, Oregon, is closer to the equator than to the North Pole" is a factual opinion that is false.

Factual opinion/belief/claim = objective opinion/belief/claim = opinion/belief/claim whose truth is independent of whether anyone thinks it is true.

## Thinking About Thinking

Remember, an *objective* statement is not made true by someone thinking it is true. "Wait a minute," you might say. "Isn't the statement 'Joanie is thinking about Frank' made true by her thinking that it is true?" The answer is no! It is made true by her *thinking about Frank*.

### Relativism

**Relativism** is the idea that truth is relative to the standards of a given culture. More precisely, relativism holds that if your culture and some other culture have different standards of truth or evidence, there is no independent "God's-eye view" by which one culture's standards can be seen to be more correct than the others'.

Whatever may be said of this as an abstract philosophical doctrine, it cannot possibly mean that an objective statement could be made true by a culture's thinking that it is true. If it is universally believed in some culture that "water" is not $H_2O$, then either the people in that culture are mistaken or their word "water" does not refer to water.

### Moral Subjectivism

**Moral subjectivism** is the idea that moral opinions, such as "Bullfighting is morally wrong" or "Jason shouldn't lie to his parents," are subjective. It is the idea, in other words, that if you think bullfighting is morally wrong, then it is morally wrong for you and you don't need to consider any further truth. It is the idea expressed by Hamlet in the famous passage, "There is nothing either good or bad, but that thinking makes it so."

You should be wary of Hamlet's dictum. Ask yourself this: If someone actually believed there is nothing wrong with torturing donkeys or stoning women to death for adultery, would you say, well, if that's what he thinks, then it's fine for him to torture donkeys or stone women to death? Of course you wouldn't. Those ideas can't be made true by thinking they are true anymore than drinking battery acid can be made good for you by thinking it is.

### ISSUES

An **issue,** as we employ that concept in this book, is simply a question. Is Moore taller than Parker? When we ask that question, we raise the issue as to *whether* Moore is taller than Parker. To put it differently, we are considering whether the claim "Moore is taller than Parker" is true. Let us note in passing that as with claims, some issues are objective. Is Moore taller than Parker? Whether he is or isn't doesn't depend on whether we think he is, so this is an objective issue (question).

Other issues, such as whether P. Diddy dresses well, are subjective, in the sense explained previously.

*The first order of business* when it comes to thinking critically about an issue is to determine what, exactly, the issue *is*. Unfortunately, in many real-life situations, it is difficult to identify exactly what the issue is—meaning it is difficult to identify exactly what claim is in question. This happens for lots of reasons, from purposeful obfuscation to ambiguous terminology to plain muddleheaded thinking. In his inaugural address President Warren G. Harding said,

> We have mistaken unpreparedness to embrace it to be a challenge of the reality and due concern for making all citizens fit for participation will give added strength of citizenship and magnify our achievement.

This is formidable. Do you understand what issue Harding is addressing? Neither does anyone else, because his statement is perfectly meaningless. (American satirist H. L. Mencken described it as a "sonorous nonsense driven home with gestures."*) Understanding what is meant by a claim has so many aspects that we'll devote a large part of Chapter 3 to the subject.

However, if you have absolutely no clue as to what an issue actually is, there isn't much point in considering it further—you don't know what "it" is. There also isn't much point in considering it further if you have no idea as to what would count toward settling it. For example, suppose someone asks, "Is there an identical you in a different dimension?" What sort of evidence would support saying either there is or isn't? Nobody has any idea. (Almost any question about different "dimensions" or "planes" or "universes" would be apt to suffer from the same problem unless, possibly, it were to be raised from someone well educated in physics who used those concepts in a technical way.) "Is everything really one?" would also qualify as something you couldn't begin to settle, as would wondering if "the entire universe was created instantly five minutes ago with all false memories and fictitious records."**

Obscure issues aren't always as metaphysical as the preceding examples. Listen carefully and you may hear more than one politician say something like, "It is human nature to desire freedom." Oh, really? This sounds good, but if you look at it closely it's hard to know exactly what sort of data would support the remark.

This isn't to imply that only issues that can be settled through scientific test or via the experimental method are worth considering. Moral issues cannot be settled in that way, for example. Mathematical and historical questions are not answered by experiment, and neither are important philosophical questions. Does God exist? Is there free will? What difference does it make if he does or doesn't or there is or isn't? Legal questions, questions of aesthetics—the list of important questions not subject to purely scientific resolution is very long. The point here is merely that if a question is to be taken seriously, or if you want others to take it seriously, or if you want others who can think critically to take it seriously, you must have *some* idea as to what considerations bear on the answer.

## ARGUMENTS

In our experience, lots of college students seriously contemplate getting a dog or cat. But they are conflicted. On the one hand, it would be sweet to have a nice pet; but on the other, it would be extra work and cost money, and they aren't sure what to do with the animal if they take a trip.

If you are such a student, you weigh the arguments pro and con. An **argument** presents a consideration for accepting a claim. For example, this is an argument:

> A dog would keep me company; so I should get one.

*Reported on NBC News, *Meet the Press*, January 16, 2005.
**This famous example comes from philosopher Bertrand Russell.

## Are You Good at Reasoning?

Are you the kind of person who reasons well? Some people are. Unfortunately, maybe people who *aren't* very good at reasoning are the most likely to overestimate their reasoning ability.*

---

*See Justin Kruger and David Dunning, "Unskilled and Unaware of It: How Difficulties in Recognizing One's Own Incompetence Lead to Inflated Self-Assessments," *Psychology* 1 (2009): 30–46.

And so is this:

> My landlord will raise my rent; so I shouldn't get one.

The first example is an argument for getting a dog. The second is an argument for not getting one.

As you can see from these two examples, an argument consists of two parts. One part gives a reason for accepting the other part. The part that provides the reason is called the **premise** of the argument,* though an argument may have more than one premise. The other part is called the conclusion. The **conclusion** of an argument is what the premise supposedly supports or demonstrates.

You should always think of the conclusion of an argument as stating a position on an issue, and of the premise or premises as giving reasons for taking that position.

Want an example? Look at the two arguments previously shown. They both address the issue of *whether I should get a dog*. The premise of the first example ("A dog would keep me company") gives a reason for saying I *should* get a dog. The premise of the second example ("My landlord will raise my rent") gives a reason for saying I *should not* get a dog.

What does this have to do with critical thinking? Everything. You want to make the best decision on an important issue—in this case, whether to get a dog. You evaluate the arguments pro and con. Being able to do this intelligently may not be the sum total of critical thinking, but it is an essential part of it.

A large part of this book is devoted to understanding how to evaluate arguments, and all this will begin in Chapter 2. However, right now, two minor points about arguments are worth noticing:

1. The two arguments given as examples are not very long or complicated. Some arguments can be very long and complicated. Einstein's revolutionary theory that $E = mc^2$ was based on complex mathematical reasoning, and that reasoning was his argument for saying that $E = mc^2$.

2. Not every issue requires an argument for resolution. Is your throat sore? You can just tell directly, and no argument is necessary.

We will now offer you a few exercises to help you understand these fundamental concepts. In the next section we will look at psychological factors that impede clear thought.

---

*Unfortunately, sometimes people use the word "argument" to refer only to the premise or premises of an argument.

Answer the questions based on your reading to this point, including the boxes.          Exercise 1-1

▲ —See the answers section at the back of the book.

▲ 1. What is an argument?

2. T or F: A claim is what you use to state an opinion or a belief.

3. T or F: Critical thinking consists in attacking other people's ideas.

▲ 4. T or F: Whether a passage contains an argument depends on how long it is.

5. T or F: When a question has been asked, an issue has been raised.

6. T or F: All arguments have a premise.

▲ 7. T or F: All arguments have a conclusion.

8. T or F: You can reach a conclusion without believing it is true.

9. T or F: Beliefs, judgments, and opinions are the same thing.

▲ 10. T or F: All opinions are subjective.

11. T or F: All factual claims are true.

12. "There is nothing either good or bad but that thinking makes it so" expresses a doctrine known as _____.

▲ 13. The first order of business when it comes to thinking critically about an issue is (a) to determine whether the issue is subjective or objective, (b) to determine whether the issue can be resolved, or (c) to determine what exactly the issue is.

14. T or F: The conclusion of an argument states a position on an issue.

15. T or F: Issues can be resolved only through scientific testing.

▲ 16. T or F: Statements, claims, and assertions are the same thing.

17. T or F: The claim "Death Valley is an eyesore" expresses a subjective opinion.

18. T or F: Every issue requires an argument for a resolution.

▲ 19. T or F: Relativism is the idea that if the standards of evidence or truth are different for two cultures, there is no independent way of saying which standards are the correct ones.

20. T or F: It is not possible to reason correctly if you do not think critically.

On the basis of a distinction covered so far, divide these items into two groups of five items each such that all the items in one group have a feature that none of the items in the second group have. Describe the feature on which you based your classifications. The items that belong in one group are listed at the back of the book.          Exercise 1-2

▲ 1. You shouldn't buy that car because it is ugly.

2. That car is ugly, and it costs more than $25,000, too.

3. Rainbows have seven colors, although it's not always easy to see them all.

▲ 4. Walking is the best exercise. It places the least stress on your joints.

■ Can bears and other animals think critically? Find out by checking the answers section at the back of the book.

5. The ocean on the central coast is the most beautiful shade of sky blue, but it gets greener as you go north.

6. Her favorite color is yellow because it is the color of the sun.

▲ 7. Pooh is my favorite cartoon character because he has lots of personality.

8. You must turn off the lights when you leave the room. They cost a lot of money to run, and you don't need them during the day.

9. Television programs have too much violence and immoral behavior. Hundreds of killings are portrayed every month.

▲ 10. You'll be able to find a calendar on sale after the first of the year, so it is a good idea to wait until then to buy one.

**Exercise 1-3**  Which of the following claims are objective?

▲ 1. Nicki Minaj can fake a great English accent.

2. On a baseball field, the center of the pitcher's mound is 59 feet from home plate.

3. Staring at the sun will damage your eyes.

▲ 4. Green is the most pleasant color to look at.

5. Yellow is Jennifer's favorite color.

6. With enough experience, a person who doesn't like opera can come to appreciate it.

▲ 7. Opera would be easier to listen to if they'd leave out the singing.

8. Sailing is much more soothing than sputtering about in a motorboat.

9. Driving while drowsy is dangerous.

▲ 10. Pit vipers can strike a warm-blooded animal even when it is pitch dark.

11. P. Diddy is totally bink.

12. P. Diddy is totally bink to me.

**Exercise 1-4**  Which of the following are subjective?

▲ 1. Fallon tells better jokes than Colbert.

2. In 2013 Miguel Cabrera hit the most home runs on a 3–0 count.

3. Your teacher will complain if you text in class.

▲ 4. Your teacher would be crazy not to complain if you text in class.

5. There is life on Mars.

6. Golf wastes time.

▲ 7. *Warcraft* scared the you-know-what out of my sister.

8. *Warcraft* is lousy. A total letdown.

9. Movies like *Warcraft* lack redeeming social value. [*Hint:* An assertion might have more than one subjective element.]

▲ 10. Donald Trump has unusual hair.

**Exercise 1-5**  Some of these items are arguments, and some are not. Which are which?

▲ 1. Tipsarevic is unlikely to win the U.S. Open this year. He has a nagging leg injury, plus he doesn't have the drive he once had.

2. Hey there, Marco! Don't go giving that cat top sirloin. What's the matter with you? You got no brains?

3. If you've ever met a pet bird, you know they are busy creatures.

▲ 4. Everybody is saying the president earned the Nobel Prize. What a stupid idea! She hasn't earned it at all. There's not a lick of truth in that notion.

5. "Is the author really entitled to assert that there is a degree of unity among these essays which makes this a book rather than a congeries? I am inclined to say that he is justified in this claim, but articulating this justification is a somewhat complex task."

*—From a book review by Stanley Bates*

6. As a long-time customer, you're already taking advantage of our money management expertise and variety of investment choices. That's a good reason for consolidating your other eligible assets into an IRA with us.

▲ 7. PROFESSOR X: Well, I see where the new chancellor wants to increase class sizes.

PROFESSOR Y: Yeah, another of his bright ideas.

PROFESSOR X: Actually, I don't think it hurts to have one or two extra people in class.

PROFESSOR Y: What? Of course it hurts. Whatever are you thinking?

PROFESSOR X: Well, I just think there are good reasons for increasing the class size a bit.

8. Yes, I charge a little more than other dentists. But I feel I give better service. So my billing practices are justified.

9. Since you want to purchase the house, you should exercise your option before June 30, 2018. Otherwise, you will forfeit the option price.

▲ 10. John Montgomery has been the Eastern Baseball League's best closer this season. Unfortunately, when a closer gets shelled, as Montgomery did last night, it takes him a while to recover. Nobody will say he is the best closer after that performance.

Determine which of the following passages contain arguments. For any that do, identify the argument's conclusion. There aren't hard-and-fast rules for identifying arguments, so you'll have to read closely and think carefully about some of these.

Exercise 1-6

▲ 1. The Directory of Intentional Communities lists more than 200 groups across the country organized around a variety of purposes, including environmentally aware living.

2. Carl would like to help out, but he won't be in town. We'll have to find someone else who owns a truck.

3. Once upon a time Washington, DC, passed an ordinance prohibiting private ownership of firearms. After that, Washington's murder rate shot up 121 percent. Bans on firearms are clearly counterproductive.

▲ 4. Computers will never be able to converse intelligently through speech. A simple example proves this. The sentences "How do you recognize speech?" and "How do you wreck a nice beach?" have different meanings, but they sound similar enough that a computer could not distinguish between the two.

■ Think you are welcome?
Think again and think
critically.

5. *The Carrie Diaries* isn't very good. It's just a repackage of *Sex and the City*.

6. "Like short-term memory, long-term memory retains information that is encoded in terms of sense modality and in terms of links with information that was learned earlier (that is, meaning)."

*—Neil R. Carlson*

▲ 7. Fears that chemicals in teething rings and soft plastic toys may cause cancer may be justified. Last week, the Consumer Product Safety Commission issued a report confirming that low amounts of DEHP, known to cause liver cancer in lab animals, may be absorbed from certain infant products.

8. "It may be true that people, not guns, kill people. But people with guns kill more people than people without guns. As long as the number of lethal weapons in the hands of the American people continues to grow, so will the murder rate."

*—Susan Mish'alani*

9. Then: A Miami man gets thirty days in the stockade for wearing a flag patch on the seat of his trousers. Now: Miami department stores sell boxer trunks made up to look like an American flag. Times have changed.

▲ 10. Dockers are still in style, but skinny legs are no longer trending.

**Exercise 1-7**

For each numbered passage, identify which lettered item best states the primary issue discussed in the passage. Be prepared to say why you think your choice is the correct one.

▲ 1. Let me tell you why Hank ought not to take that math course. First, it's too hard, and he'll probably flunk it. Second, he's going to spend the whole term in a state of frustration. Third, he'll probably get depressed and do poorly in all the rest of his courses.

a. whether Hank ought to take the math course
b. whether Hank would flunk the math course
c. whether Hank will spend the whole term in a state of frustration
d. whether Hank will get depressed and do poorly in all the rest of his courses

2. The county has cut the library budget for salaried library workers, and there will not be enough volunteers to make up for the lack of paid workers. Therefore, the library will have to be open fewer hours next year.

a. whether the library will have to be open fewer hours next year
b. whether there will be enough volunteers to make up for the lack of paid workers

3. Pollution of the waters of the Everglades and of Florida Bay is due to multiple causes. These include cattle farming, dairy farming, industry, tourism, and urban development. So it is simply not true that the sugar industry is completely responsible for the pollution of these waters.

   a. whether pollution of the waters of the Everglades and Florida Bay is due to multiple causes
   b. whether pollution is caused by cattle farming, dairy farming, industry, tourism, and urban development
   c. whether the sugar industry is partly responsible for the pollution of these waters
   d. whether the sugar industry is completely responsible for the pollution of these waters

▲ 4. It's clear that the mainstream media have lost interest in classical music. For example, the NBC network used to have its own classical orchestra conducted by Arturo Toscanini, but no such orchestra exists now. One newspaper, the no-longer-existent *Washington Star*, used to have thirteen classical music reviewers; that's more than twice as many as *The New York Times* has now. H. L. Mencken and other columnists used to devote considerable space to classical music; nowadays, you almost never see it mentioned in a major column.

   a. whether popular taste has turned away from classical music
   b. whether newspapers are employing fewer writers on classical music
   c. whether the mainstream media have lost interest in classical music

5. This year's National Football League draft lists a large number of quarterbacks among its highest-ranking candidates. Furthermore, quite a number of teams do not have first-class quarterbacks. It's therefore likely that an unusually large number of quarterbacks will be drafted early in this year's draft.

   a. whether teams without first-class quarterbacks will choose quarterbacks in the draft
   b. whether this year's NFL draft includes a large number of quarterbacks
   c. whether an unusually large number of quarterbacks will be drafted early in this year's draft

6. An animal that will walk out into a rainstorm and stare up at the clouds until water runs into its nostrils and it drowns—well, that's what I call the world's dumbest animal. And that's exactly what young domestic turkeys do.

   a. whether young domestic turkeys will drown themselves in the rain
   b. whether any animal is dumb enough to drown itself in the rain
   c. whether young domestic turkeys are the world's dumbest animal

▲ 7. The defeat of the school voucher initiative was a bad thing for the country because now public schools won't have any incentive to clean up their act. Furthermore, the defeat perpetuates the private-school-for-the-rich, public-school-for-the-poor syndrome.

   a. whether public schools now have any incentive to clean up their act
   b. whether the defeat of the school voucher initiative was bad for the country
   c. whether public schools now have any incentive to clean up their act and whether the private-school-for-the-rich, public-school-for-the-poor syndrome will be perpetuated (issues are equally stressed)

8. From an editorial in a newspaper outside Southern California: "The people in Southern California who lost a fortune in the wildfires last year could have

bought insurance that would have covered their houses and practically every-thing in them. And anybody with any foresight would have made sure there were no brush and no trees near the houses so that there would be a buffer zone between the house and any fire, as the Forest Service recommends. Finally, anybody living in a fire danger zone ought to know enough to have a fireproof or fire-resistant roof on the house. So, you see, most of the losses those people suffered were simply their own fault."

a. whether fire victims could have done anything to prevent their losses
b. whether insurance, fire buffer zones, and fire-resistant roofs could have prevented much of the loss
c. whether the losses people suffered in the fires were their own fault

9. "Whatever we believe, we think agreeable to reason, and, on that account, yield our assent to it. Whatever we disbelieve, we think contrary to reason, and, on that account, dissent from it. Reason, therefore, is allowed to be the principle by which our belief and opinions ought to be regulated."

—*Thomas Reid,* Essays on the Active Powers of Man

a. whether reason is the principle by which our beliefs and opinions ought to be regulated
b. whether what we believe is agreeable to reason
c. whether what we disbelieve is contrary to reason
d. both b and c

10. Most people you find on university faculties are people who are interested in ideas. And the most interesting ideas are usually new ideas. So most people you find on university faculties are interested in new ideas. Therefore, you are not going to find many conservatives on university faculties, because conservatives are not usually interested in new ideas.

a. whether conservatives are interested in new ideas
b. whether you'll find many conservatives on university faculties
c. whether people on university faculties are interested more in new ideas than in older ideas
d. whether most people are correct

## COGNITIVE BIASES

When a poll is really, really out of whack with what I want to happen, I do have a tendency to disregard it.

—Rush Limbaugh, recognizing his own confirmation bias

Unconscious features of psychology can affect human mental processes, sometimes in unexpected ways. Recent research suggests that donning formal business attire or a physician's white lab coat might improve a person's performance on a cognitive test.* Seeing a fast food logo (e.g., McDonald's golden arches) may make some individuals attempt to process information more hastily.** In one experiment, subjects being told that the expensive sunglasses they were asked to wear were fake increased their propensity to cheat on tests that involved cash payments for correct answers.[†] In another experiment, male subjects, if dressed in sweats, made less profitable deals in simulated negotiations than did subjects dressed in suits.

*Referenced in *Scientific American Mind,* January/February 2016, p. 13.
**Referenced in a posting dated April 13, 2010, by Christopher Peterson in *Psychology Today.* https://www.psychologytoday.com/blog/the-good-life/201004/fast-food-and-impatience.
†This and the experiment cited in the next sentence also are referenced in *Scientific American Mind,* January/February 2016, p. 13.

Were we entirely rational, our conclusions would be grounded in logic and based on evidence objectively weighed. The unconscious features of human psychology affecting belief formation that have been reasonably well established include several that are widely referred to as *cognitive biases*.* They skew our apprehension of reality and interfere with our ability to think clearly, process information accurately, and reason objectively.

For example, we tend to evaluate an argument based on whether we agree with it rather than on the criteria of logic. Is the following specimen good reasoning?

> All pit bulls are dogs.
> Some dogs bite.
> Therefore some pit bulls bite.

People will generally accept facts as truth only if the facts agree with what they already believe.

—Andy Rooney, nicely explaining belief bias

It isn't. You might as well conclude some pit bulls are fox terriers. After all, all pit bulls are dogs and some dogs are fox terriers. If it took you a moment to see that the first argument is illogical, it's because its conclusion is something you know is true.

The tendency to evaluate reasoning by the believability of its conclusion is known as **belief bias.** A closely related cognitive bias is **confirmation bias,** which refers to the tendency to attach more weight to evidence that supports our viewpoint. If you are a Democrat, you may view evidence that Fox News is biased as overwhelming; if you are a Republican you may regard the same evidence as weak and unconvincing. In science, good experiments are designed to ensure that experimenters can't "cherry-pick" evidence, that is, search for evidence that supports the hypothesis they think is true while ignoring evidence to the contrary.

There isn't any hard-and-fast difference between confirmation bias and belief bias; they are both unconscious expressions of the human tendency to think our side of an issue must be the correct side. Thinking critically means being especially critical of arguments that support our own points of view.

Some cognitive biases involve **heuristics,** general rules we unconsciously follow in estimating probabilities. An example is the **availability heuristic,** which involves unconsciously assigning a probability to a type of event on the basis of how often one thinks of events of that type. After watching multiple news reports of an earthquake or an airplane crash or a case of child abuse, thoughts of earthquakes and airplane crashes and child abuse will be in the front of one's mind. Accordingly, one may overestimate their probability. True, if the probability of airplane crashes were to increase, then one might well think about airplane crashes more often; but it does not follow that if one thinks about them more often, their probability has increased.

The availability heuristic may explain how easy it is to make the mistake known as generalizing from anecdote, a logical fallacy

■ Bad-mouthing someone is not the same as thinking critically about what he or she says.

we discuss later in the book. Generalizing from anecdote happens when one accepts a sweeping generalization based on a single vivid report. The availability heuristic is also probably related to the **false consensus effect,** which refers to the inclination we may have to assume that our attitudes and those held by people around us are shared by society at large.*

Another source of skewed belief is the **bandwagon effect,** which refers to an unconscious tendency to align one's thinking with that of other people. The bandwagon effect is potentially a powerful source of cognitive distortion. In famous experiments, psychologist Solomon Asch found that what other people say *they* see may actually alter what we think *we* see.** We—the authors—have students take tests and quizzes using smartphones and clickers, with software that instantly displays the opinion of the class in a bar graph projected on a screen. Not infrequently it happens that, if opinion begins to build for one answer, almost everyone switches to that option—even if it is incorrect or illogical.

If you have wondered why consumer products are routinely advertised as bestsellers, you now know the answer. Marketers understand the bandwagon effect. They know that getting people to believe that a product is popular generates further sales.

Political propagandists also know we have an unconscious need to align our beliefs with the opinions of other people. Thus, they try to increase support for a measure by asserting that everyone likes it, or—and this is even more effective—by asserting that *nobody* likes whatever the opposition has proposed. Given alternative measures X and Y, "Nobody wants X!" is even more likely to generate support for Y than is "Everyone wants Y!" This is because of **negativity bias,** the tendency people have to weight negative information more heavily than positive information when evaluating things. Negativity bias is hard-wired into us: the brain displays more neural activity in response to negative information than to positive information.† A corollary to negativity bias from economics is that people generally are more strongly motivated to avoid a loss than to accrue a gain, a bias known as **loss aversion.**

It also should come as no surprise that we find it easier to form negative opinions of people who don't belong to our club, church, party, nationality, or other group. This is a part of **in-group bias,** another cognitive factor that may color perception and distort judgment. We may well perceive the members of our own group as exhibiting more variety and individuality than the members of this or that outgroup, who we may view as indistinguishable from one another and as conforming to stereotypes. We may attribute the achievements of members of our own group to gumption and hard work and our failures to bad luck, whereas we may attribute *their* failures—those of the members of out-groups—to their personal shortcomings, while grudgingly discounting their achievements as mere good luck. The tendency to not appreciate that others' behavior is as much constrained by events and circumstances as our own would be if we were in their position is known as the **fundamental attribution error.**††

Experiments suggest that people find it extraordinarily easy to forge group identities. When assigned to a group on the basis of something as trivial as a coin

*See L. Ross, "The 'False Consensus Effect': An Egocentric Bias in Social Perception and Attribution Processes," *Journal of Experimental Social Psychology* 13, no. 3 (May 1977): 279–301.

**A copy of Asch's own summary of his experiments can be found at www.panarchy.org/asch/social.pressure.1955.html.

†See Tiffany A. Ito, et al., "Negative Information Weighs More Heavily on the Brain," *Journal of Personality and Social Psychology* 75, no. 4 (1998): 887–900.

††E. E. Jones and V. A. Harris, "The Attribution of Attitudes," *Journal of Experimental Social Psychology* 3 (1967): 1–24. For in-group biases, see Henri Tajfel, *Human Groups and Social Categories* (Cambridge, England: Cambridge University Press, 1981).

## Rational Choice?

Critical thinking is aimed at coming to correct conclusions and making wise choices or decisions. We know from everyday experience that desires, fears, personal objectives, and various emotions affect choices. As explained in the text, experimental psychologists have discovered other, more unexpected and surprising, influences on our thinking.

■ In a recent experiment, researchers at Yale and Harvard Universities asked subjects to evaluate a job candidate by reading an applicant's résumé, which had been attached to a clipboard. Some of the clipboards weighed ¾ pound; the others weighed 4½ pounds. Subjects holding the heavier clipboard rated the applicant as better overall. Evidently a "rational evaluation" of a person's qualifications may be affected by irrelevant physical cues.*

*Reported by Randolph E. Schmid of the Associated Press, in *The Sacramento Bee*, June 23, 2010.

flip, subjects will immediately begin exhibiting in-group and attribution biases.* In a famous experiment in social psychology, the Robber's Cave Experiment, twenty-two 12-year-old boys who previously hadn't known each other were divided *arbitrarily* into two groups. When the two groups were forced to compete, the members of each group instantly exhibited hostility and other indicators of in-group bias toward the members of the other group.**

People make snap judgments about who is and who is not a member of their group. Students transferring into a new high school are branded swiftly. Once, one of the authors and his wife were walking their dogs, not necessarily the world's best-behaved pooches, along a street in Carmel, an affluent town on California's central coast. When the author fell a few paces behind his wife, a well-dressed woman walked by and glanced disapprovingly at the dogs. "Did you see that woman?" she asked indignantly, unaware that she was referring to the wife of the man she was addressing. "You can tell she isn't from around here," she said. She seems to have assumed that the author was from the Carmel in-group, simply because he wasn't connected to the misbehaving dogs.

In a series of famous experiments in the 1960s regarding **obedience to authority,** psychologist Stanley Milgram discovered that a frightening percentage of ordinary men and women will administer apparently lethal electrical shocks to innocent people, when told to do so by an experimenter in a white coat.† The findings are subject to multiple interpretations and explanations, but the tendency of humans to obey authority simply for the sake of doing so hardly needs experimental confirmation. Not long ago French researchers created a fake TV game show that was much like the Milgram experiment. The host instructed contestants to deliver electrical shocks to an individual who was said to be just another contestant, but who in reality was an actor. The contestants complied—and delivered shocks right up to a level that (if the shock was really being delivered) might execute the man. Whether the subjects were blindly following the instructions of an authority or were responding to some other impulse isn't completely clear, but

*Tajfel, *Human Groups and Social Categories*.
**A report of the Robber's Cave experiment is available online at http://psychclassics.yorku.ca/Sherif/.
†Milgram discusses his experiments in *Obedience to Authority: An Experimental View* (New York: HarperCollins, 1974).

■ Does Kanye West dress well? The issue is *subjective,* or, as some people say, "a matter of opinion."

it is impossible to think that good judgment or rational thought would lead them to such excess.*

Yet another possible source of psychological distortion is the **overconfidence effect,** one of several self-deception biases that may be found in a variety of contexts.** If a person estimates the percentage of his or her correct answers on a subject, the estimate will likely err on the high side—at least if the questions are difficult or the subject matter is unfamiliar.[†] Perhaps some manifestation of the overconfidence effect explains why, in the early stages of the *American Idol* competition, many contestants appear totally convinced they will be crowned the next American Idol—and are speechless when the judges inform them they cannot so much as carry a tune.[††]

Closely related to the overconfidence effect is the **better-than-average illusion.** The illusion crops up when most of a group rate themselves as better than most of the group relative to some desirable characteristic, such as resourcefulness or driving ability. The classic illustration is the 1976 survey of SAT takers, in which well over 50 percent of the respondents rated themselves as better than 50 percent of other SAT takers with respect to such qualities as leadership ability.[‡] The same effect has been observed when people estimate how their intelligence, memory, or job performance stacks up with the intelligence, memory, and job performances of other members of their profession or workplace. In our own informal surveys, more than 80 percent of our students rate themselves in the top 10 percent of their class with respect to their ability to think critically.

Unfortunately, evidence indicates that even when they are informed about the better-than-average illusion, people may *still* rate themselves as better than most in their ability to not be subject to it.[‡‡]

That beliefs are generated as much by psychology and impulse as by evidence should come as no surprise. The new car that was well beyond our means yesterday seems entirely affordable today—though our finances haven't changed. If someone invited us to The Olive Garden we'd expect decent fare; but if they suggested we

---

*Jamey Keaton, Associated Press. Reported in *The Sacramento Bee,* Thursday, March 18, 2010. Did the subjects suspect the shocks weren't real? Their statements afterward don't rule out the possibility but certainly seem to suggest they believed they truly were administering painful electrical shocks to the actor.

**However, a universal tendency among humans to irrationally exaggerate their own competencies hasn't been established. For an online quiz purportedly showing the overconfidence effect, see www.tim-richardson.net/joomla15/finance-articles-profmenu-70/73-over-confidence-test.html.

[†]See Sarah Lichtenstein and other authors, "Calibration of Probabilities: The State of the Art to 1980," in Daniel Kahneman, Paul Slovic, and Amos Tversky, *Judgment under Uncertainty: Heuristics and Biases* (Cambridge, England: Cambridge University Press, 1982), 306–34.

[††]This possibility was proposed by Gad Saad, *Psychology Today,* www.psychologytoday.com/blog/homo-consumericus/200901/self-deception-american-idol-is-it-adaptive.

[‡]See Mark D. Alicke and other authors in "The Better-Than-Average Effect," in Mark D. Alicke and others, *The Self in Social Judgment: Studies in Self and Identity* (New York: Psychology Press, 2005), 85–106. The better-than-average illusion is sometimes called the Lake Wobegon effect, in reference to Garrison Keillor's story about the fictitious Minnesota town "where all the children are above average."

[‡‡]http://weblamp.princeton.edu/~psych/FACULTY/Articles/Pronin/The%20Bias%20Blind.PDF. The better-than-average bias has not been found to hold for all positive traits. In some things, people underestimate their abilities. The moral is that for many abilities, we are probably not the best judges of how we compare to others. And this includes our ability to avoid being subject to biasing influences.

try dining at, say, The Lung Garden, we'd hesitate—even if we were told the food is identical. People will go out of their way to save $10 when buying a $25 pen, but won't do the same to save the same amount buying a $500 suit.* Programmed into our psyches are features that distort our perception, color our judgment, and impair our ability to think objectively.

The best defense? Making it a habit to think critically—and to be especially critical of arguments and evidence that seem to accord with what we already believe.

The following exercises may help you understand the cognitive biases discussed in the previous section.

The following questions are for thought or discussion. Your instructor may ask you to write a brief essay addressing one or more of them.     Exercise 1-8

 1. Which of the cognitive biases discussed in this section do you think you might be most subject to? Why?

2. Can you think of other psychological tendencies you have that might interfere with the objectivity of your thinking? For example, are you unusually generous or selfish?

3. Think again about a student (or anyone) contemplating getting a pet. Is there a cognitive bias a person in that position might be especially prone to, when weighing the arguments on both sides?

4. Explain belief bias (or confirmation bias) in your own words, and give an example of a time when you may have been subject to it.

5. What might you do to compensate for a bias factor you listed in questions 1 or 2 in this exercise?

For each of the following attributes, rate yourself in comparison with other students in your class. Are you     Exercise 1-9

a. in the top 10 percent?
b. in the top 50 to 89 percent?
c. in the lower 25 to 49 percent?
d. below the top 75 percent?

▪ ability to think clearly
▪ ability to think logically
▪ ability to think critically
▪ ability to be objective
▪ ability to think creatively
▪ ability to read with comprehension
▪ ability to spot political bias in the evening news
▪ IQ

If you answered (a) or (b) about one of the preceding abilities, would you change your mind if you learned that most of the class also answered (a) or (b) about that ability? Why or why not?

---

*Daniel Ariely, *Predictably Irrational* (New York: HarperCollins, 2008), 19–20.

**Exercise 1-10**

Select one of the following claims you are inclined to strongly agree or disagree with. Then produce the best argument you can think of for the opposing side. When you are finished, ask someone to read your argument and tell you honestly whether he or she thinks you have been fair and objective.

- "There is (is not) a God."
- "Illegal immigrants should (should not) be eligible for health care benefits."
- "Handgun owners should (should not) be required to register each handgun they own."
- "The words 'under God' should (should not) be removed from the Pledge of Allegiance."
- "Sex education should (should not) be taught in public schools."

## TRUTH AND KNOWLEDGE

At the end of the day, when we are ready to turn out the lights and go to bed, we want the conclusions we have reached through painstaking critical thinking to be *true*—and we want to *know* they are true. However, what are truth and knowledge? Through the years, many competing theories have been offered to account for their real nature, but fortunately for you, we can tell you what you need to know for this discussion without getting mired in those controversies.

As for truth, the most important thing is to understand that an objective belief or claim is either true or false in the normal, commonsense way. Truth and falsity are properties of propositional entities like beliefs, opinions, judgments, statements, claims, and the like. As mentioned previously, when any of those entities is objective, whether it is true or false does not depend on whether we think it is true or false.

You can assert a claim's truth in a number of ways. In normal conversation, we'd take each of the following as making the same statement:

> A book is on the table.
> It is true a book is on the table.
> It is a fact a book is on the table.
> Yes, a book is on the table.

The concept of knowledge is another that philosophers have contested at a deep, theoretical level despite a general agreement that in everyday life, we understand well enough what we mean when we say we know something.

Ordinarily, you are entitled to say you *know* a book is on the table, provided that (1) you believe a book is on the table, (2) you have justification for this belief in the form of an argument beyond a reasonable doubt that a book is on the table, and (3) you have no reason to suspect you are mistaken, such as that you haven't slept for several nights or have recently taken hallucinogenic drugs. Skeptics may say it is impossible to know anything, though one wonders how they know that. Presumably, they'd have to say they're just guessing.

## WHAT CRITICAL THINKING CAN AND CAN'T DO

We think critically when we evaluate the reasoning we and others use in coming to conclusions. Perhaps this remark strikes you as restricted and narrow. A composer, for example, thinks critically when he or she tries to find the right instrumentation to introduce a musical theme. A general thinks critically when he or she defines a military objective and weighs various strategies for achieving it. Dentists think critically when they weigh the likely duration of alternative dental repairs against a patient's life expectancy. Mechanics think critically when they attempt to diagnose mechanical problems by listening to the sound of an engine. People in each walk of life examine considerations that are unique to them.

Yet every discipline, every walk of life, every enterprise without exception involves the two kinds of reasoning we will begin examining in the next chapter. And critical thinking anywhere can be waylaid by emotion, self-interest, wishful thinking, desire to be accepted, confirmation bias, and various other psychological propensities that come with being a human being, and that also will be considered in this book.

Thinking critically won't necessarily tell you whether you should get a dog or whom to vote for or whether there is global warming or why your car won't start. It can, however, help you spot bad reasoning about all these things.

## A WORD ABOUT THE EXERCISES

To get good at tennis, golf, playing a musical instrument, or most other skills, you have to practice, practice, and practice more. It's the same way with critical thinking, and that's why we provide so many exercises. For some exercises in this book, there is no such thing as only one correct answer, just as there is no such thing as only one correct way to serve a tennis ball. Some answers, however—just like tennis serves—are better than others, and that is where your instructor comes in. In many exercises, answers you give that are different from your instructor's are not necessarily incorrect. Still, your instructor's answers will be well thought out, reliable, and worth your attention. We recommend taking advantage of his or her experience to improve your ability to think critically.

Answers to questions marked with a triangle are found in the answers section at the back of the book.

We think critically when we evaluate reasoning used in coming to conclusions. Conclusions are beliefs; when they are expressed using true-or-false declarative sentences, they are claims (or statements or assertions). A belief (or opinion or claim or statement, etc.) whose truth is independent of whether people think it is true is objective.

**Recap**

An issue is simply a question. One uses an argument to establish a position on an issue; the position is the conclusion of the argument. Evaluation of arguments can be skewed by emotion, wishful thinking, self-interest, confirmation bias, and other psychological impediments to objectivity.

What follows is a more complete list of ideas explored in this chapter.

- **Claim:** When a belief (judgment, opinion) is asserted in a declarative sentence, the result is a claim, statement, or assertion.
- **Objective claim vs. subjective claim:** An objective claim is true or false regardless of whether people think it is true or false. Claims that lack this property are said to be subjective.

- **"Fact vs. opinion":** People sometimes refer to true objective claims as "facts," and use the word "opinion" to designate any claim that is subjective.
- **"Factual claim":** An objective claim. Saying that a claim is "factual" is not the same as saying it is true. A factual claim is simply a claim whose truth does not depend on our thinking it is true.
- **Moral subjectivism:** Moral subjectivism is the idea that moral judgments are subjective. "There is nothing either good or bad but that thinking makes it so."
- **Issue:** A question.
- **Argument:** An argument consists of two parts—one part of which (the premise or premises) is intended to provide a reason for accepting the other part (the conclusion).
- **"Argument":** People sometimes use this word to refer just to an argument's premise.
- **Arguments and issues:** The conclusion of an argument states a position on the issue under consideration.
- **Cognitive bias:** A feature of human psychology that skews belief formation. The ones discussed in this chapter include the following:
  - **Belief bias:** Evaluating reasoning by how believable its conclusion is.
  - **Confirmation bias:** A tendency to attach more weight to considerations that support our views.
  - **Availability heuristic:** Assigning a probability to an event based on how easily or frequently it is thought of.
  - **False consensus effect:** Assuming our opinions and those held by people around us are shared by society at large.
  - **Bandwagon effect:** The tendency to align our beliefs with those of other people.
  - **Negativity bias:** Attaching more weight to negative information than to positive information.
  - **Loss aversion:** Being more strongly motivated to avoid a loss than to accrue a gain.
  - **In-group bias:** A set of cognitive biases that make us view people who belong to our group differently from people who don't.
  - **Fundamental attribution error:** Having one understanding of the behavior of people in the in-group and another for people not in the in-group.
  - **Obedience to authority:** A tendency to comply with instructions from an authority.
  - **Overconfidence effect:** A cognitive bias that leads us to overestimate what percentage of our answers on a subject are correct.
  - **Better-than-average illusion:** A self-deception cognitive bias that leads us to overestimate our own abilities relative to those of others.
- **Truth:** A claim is true if it is free from error.
- **Knowledge:** If you believe something, have an argument beyond a reasonable doubt that it is so, and have no reason to think you are mistaken, you can claim you know it.

Here are more exercises to help you identify objective and subjective claims, recognize arguments, identify issues, and tell when two people are addressing the same issue. In addition, you will find writing exercises as well as an exercise that will give you practice in identifying the purpose of a claim.

## Additional Exercises

### Exercise 1-11

Identify the conclusion of any arguments contained in the following passages.

1. There is trouble in the Middle East, there is a recession at home, and all economic indicators are trending downward. It seems likely, then, that the only way the stock market can go is down.

2. Lucy is too short to reach the bottom of the sign.

3. "Can it be established that genetic humanity is sufficient for moral humanity? I think there are very good reasons for not defining the moral community in this way."

   —*Mary Anne Warren*

4. Pornography often depicts women as servants or slaves or as otherwise inferior to men. In light of that, it seems reasonable to expect to find more women than men who are upset by pornography.

5. "My folks, who were Russian immigrants, loved the chance to vote. That's probably why I decided that I was going to vote whenever I got the chance. I'm not sure [whom I'll vote for], but I am going to vote. And I don't understand people who don't."

   —*Mike Wallace*

6. "Dynamism is a function of change. On some campuses, change is effected through nonviolent or even violent means. Although we too have had our demonstrations, change here is usually a product of discussion in the decision-making process."

   —*Hillary Clinton, while a student at Wellesley College in the 1960s*

7. What does it take to make a good soap? You need good guys and bad guys, sex, babies, passion, infidelity, jealousy, hatred, and suspense. And it must all be believable. Believability is the key.

8. We need to make clear that sexual preference, whether chosen or genetically determined, is a private matter. It has nothing to do with an individual's ability to make a positive contribution to society.

9. The report card on charter schools is mixed. Some show better results than public schools, others show worse. Charter schools have this advantage when it comes to test scores: the kids attending them are more apt to have involved parents.

10. *American Idol* is history, but when you remember whose careers were launched by *AI*, you know it was the best talent show on TV.

### Exercise 1-12

For each numbered passage in this exercise, identify which lettered item best states the primary issue discussed in the passage. Be prepared to say why you think your choice is the correct one.

1. In pre-civil war Spain, the influence of the Catholic Church must have been much stronger on women than on men. You can determine this by looking at the number of religious communities, such as monasteries, nunneries, and so forth. A total of about 5,000 such communities existed in 1931; 4,000 of them were female, whereas only 1,000 of them were male. This proves my point about the Church's influence on the sexes.

   a. whether the Catholic Church's influence was stronger on women than on men in pre-civil war Spain
   b. whether the speaker's statistics really prove his point about the Church's influence
   c. whether the figures about religious communities really have anything to do with the overall influence of the Catholic Church in Spain

2. *Breaking Bad* might have been a good series without all the profanity. But without the profanity, it would not have been believable. Those people just talk that way. If you have them speaking Shakespearean English, nobody will pay attention. Yes, like many programs with offensive features—whether it's bad language, sex, or whatever—it will never appeal to the squeamish.

   a. whether movies with offensive features can appeal to the squeamish
   b. whether *Breaking Bad* would have been entertaining without the bad language
   c. whether *Breaking Bad* would have been believable without the profanity
   d. whether believable programs must always have offensive features

3. Siri is great, but it isn't an encyclopedia. It will tell you where the nearest Round Table is, but right now it won't tell you how late the place is open.

   a. whether Siri is great
   b. whether Siri has encyclopedic knowledge
   c. whether Siri will have encyclopedic knowledge
   d. whether Siri knows a lot about Round Table

4. From the way it tastes, you might think French roast has more caffeine in it than regular coffee, but it has less. The darker the roast, the less caffeine there is in it. I read this in *Consumer Reports*.

   a. whether *Consumer Reports* is a good source of information about coffee
   b. whether French roast has more caffeine than regular coffee
   c. whether most people think French roast has more caffeine than regular coffee

5. In Miami–Dade County, Florida, schools superintendent Rudy Crew was inundated with complaints after a police officer used a stun gun on a six-year-old student. As a result, Crew asked the Miami–Dade police to ban the use of stun guns on elementary school children. Crew did the right thing. More than 100 deaths have been linked to tasers.

   a. whether a police officer used a stun gun on a six-year-old student
   b. whether the superintendent did the right thing by asking the police to ban the use of stun guns on elementary school children

   c. whether 100 deaths have been linked to tasers

   d. whether the fact that 100 deaths have been linked to tasers shows that the superintendent did the right thing when he asked the police not to use tasers on children

6. Letting your children surf the net is like dropping them off downtown to spend the day doing whatever they want. They'll get in trouble.

   a. whether letting your children off downtown to spend the day doing whatever they want will lead them into trouble

   b. whether letting your children surf the net will lead them into trouble

   c. whether restrictions should be placed on children's activities

7. The winner of this year's spelling bee is a straight-A student whose favorite subject is science, which isn't surprising, since students interested in science learn to pay attention to details.

   a. whether the winner of this year's spelling bee is a straight-A student

   b. whether science students learn to pay attention to details

   c. whether learning science will improve a student's ability to spell

   d. whether learning science teaches a student to pay attention to details

   e. none of the above

8. Illinois state employees, both uniformed and nonuniformed, have been serving the state without a contract or cost-of-living pay increase for years, despite the fact that legislators and the governor have accepted hefty pay increases. All public employee unions should launch an initiative to amend the Illinois constitution so that it provides compulsory binding arbitration for all uniformed and nonuniformed public employees, under the supervision of the state supreme court.

   a. whether Illinois state employees have been serving the state without a contract or cost-of-living pay increase for years

   b. whether public employee unions should launch an initiative to amend the Illinois constitution so that it provides compulsory binding arbitration for all uniformed and nonuniformed public employees, under the supervision of the Illinois Supreme Court

   c. neither of the above

9. In 2007, the Dominican Republic banned the sale of two brands of Chinese toothpaste because they contained a toxic chemical responsible for dozens of poisoning deaths in Panama. The company that exported the toothpaste, the Danyang Household Chemical Company, defended its product. "Toothpaste is not something you'd swallow, but spit out, and so it's totally different from something you would eat," one company manager said. The company manager was taking a position on which issue?

   a. whether the Danyang Household Chemical Company included toxic chemicals in its toothpaste

   b. whether Danyang Household Chemical Company toothpaste prevents cavities

   c. whether the Danyang Household Chemical Company did anything wrong by exporting its toothpaste

   d. whether China should have better product safety controls

10. YOU: So, what do you think of the governor?

   YOUR FRIEND: Not much, actually.

   YOU: What do you mean? Don't you think she's been pretty good?

   YOUR FRIEND: Are you serious?

YOU: Well, yes. I think she's been doing a fine job.

YOUR FRIEND: Oh, come on. Weren't you complaining about her just a few days ago?

a. whether your friend thinks the governor has been a good governor
b. whether you think the governor has been a good governor
c. whether the governor has been a good governor
d. whether you have a good argument for thinking the governor has been a good governor

## Exercise 1-13

On what issue is the speaker taking a position in each of the following?

▲ 1. Police brutality does not happen very often. Otherwise, it would not make headlines when it does.

2. We have little choice but to concentrate crime-fighting efforts on enforcement because we don't have any idea what to do about the underlying causes of crime.

3. A lot of people think the gender of a Supreme Court justice doesn't matter. But with three women on the bench, cases dealing with women's issues are handled differently.

▲ 4. "The point is that the existence of an independent world explains our experiences better than any known alternative. We thus have good reason to believe that the world—which seems independent of our minds—really is essentially independent of our minds."

   —*Theodore W. Schick Jr. and Lewis Vaughn,* How to Think About Weird Things

5. Sure, some hot-doggers get good grades in Bubacz's class. But my guess is if Algernon takes it, all it'll get him is flunked out.

6. It's so dumb to think sales taxes hit poor people harder than rich people. The more money you have, the more you spend; and the more you spend, the more sales taxes you pay. And rich people spend more than poor people.

▲ 7. If you're going to buy a synthesizer, sign up for lessons on how to use the thing. A synthesizer won't work for you if you don't know how to make it work.

8. Intravenous drug use with nonsterile needles is one of the leading causes of the spread of AIDS. Many states passed legislation allowing officials to distribute clean needles in an effort to combat this method of infection. But in eleven states, including some of the most populous, possession of hypodermic syringes without a prescription is illegal. The laws in these foot-dragging states must be changed if we hope to end this epidemic.

9. The best way to avoid error is to suspend judgment about everything except what is certain. Because error leads to trouble, suspending judgment is the right thing to do.

▲ 10. "[Readers] may learn something about their own relationship to the earth from a people who were true conservationists. The Indians knew that life was equated with the earth and its resources, that America was a paradise, and they could not comprehend why the intruders from the East were determined to destroy all that was Indian as well as America itself."

—*Dee Brown*, Bury My Heart at Wounded Knee

## Exercise 1-14

Is the second person addressing the issue raised by the first person?

**Example**

ELMOP: Toilet paper looks better unwinding from the back of the spool.

MARWOOF: Get real! That is so stupid! It should unwind the other way.

**Analysis**

Marwoof addresses the issue raised by Elmop.

▲ 1. MR.: Next weekend, we go on standard time again. We have to set the clocks ahead.
MRS.: It isn't next weekend; it's the weekend after. And you set the clocks back an hour.

2. MOORE: Getting out of Afghanistan is only going to make us vulnerable to terrorism.
PARKER: Yeah, right. You're just saying that 'cause you don't like Obama.

3. SHE: You don't give me enough help around the house. Why, you hardly ever do anything!
HE: What??? I mowed the lawn on Saturday, and I washed both of the cars on Sunday. What's more, I clean up after dinner almost every night, and I hauled all that garden stuff to the dump. How can you say I don't do anything?
SHE: Well, you sure don't want to hear about what I do! I do a lot more than that!

▲ 4. HEEDLESS: When people complain about what we did in Afghanistan, they just encourage terrorists to think America won't fight. People who complain like that ought to just shut up.
CAUTIOUS: I disagree. Those people are reminding everyone it isn't in our interest to get involved in wars abroad.

5. MR. RJ: If you ask me, there are too many casinos around here already. We don't need more.
MR. JR: Yeah? Well that's a strange idea coming from you; you play the lottery all the time.

6. JOE FITNESS: Whoa, look at that! The chain on my bike is starting to jump around! If I don't fix it, it'll stop working.
COUCH POTATO: What you need is to stop worrying about it. You get too much exercise as it is.

▲ 7. YOUNG GUY: Baseball players are better now than they were forty years ago. They eat better, have better coaching, you name it.
OLD GUY: They aren't better at all. They just seem better because they get more publicity and play with juiced equipment.

8. STUDENT ONE: Studying is a waste of time. Half the time, I get better grades if I don't study.

   STUDENT TWO: I'd like to hear you say that in front of your parents.

9. PHILATELIST: Did you know that U.S. postage stamps are now being printed in Canada?

   PATRIOT: What an outrage! If there is one thing that ought to be made in the United States, it's U.S. postage stamps!

   PHILATELIST: Oh, c'mon. If American printing companies can't do the work, let the Canadians have it.

▲ 10. FIRST NEIGHBOR: See here, you have no right to make so much noise at night. I have to get up early for work.

   SECOND NEIGHBOR: Yeah? Well, if you have the right to let your idiot dog run loose all day long, I have the right to make noise at night.

11. STUDY PARTNER ONE: Let's knock off for a while and go get pizza. We'll function better if we eat something.

   STUDY PARTNER TWO: Not one of those pizzas you like! I can't stand anchovies.

12. FEMALE STUDENT: The Internet is overrated. It takes forever to find something you can actually use in an assignment.

   MALE STUDENT: Listen, it takes a lot longer to drive over to the library and find a place to park.

▲ 13. RAMON: Hey, this English course is a complete waste of time. You don't need to know how to write anymore.

   DEVON: That's ridiculous. You're just saying that because you're a PE major.

14. CULTURALLY CHALLENGED PERSON: A concert! You think I'm going to a concert when I can be home watching football?

   CULTURALLY CHALLENGED PERSON'S SPOUSE: Yes, if you want dinner this week.

15. REPUBLICAN: I don't think Obama's budget requests make sense.

   DEMOCRAT: You just can't stand more taxes, can you?

▲ 16. MOORE: I've seen the work of both Thomas Brothers and Vernon Construction, and I tell you, Thomas Brothers does a better job.

   PARKER: Listen, Thomas Brothers is the highest-priced company in the whole state. If you hire them, you'll pay double for every part of the job.

17. URBANITE: The new requirements will force people off septic tanks and make them hook up to the city sewer. That's the only way we'll ever get the nitrates and other pollutants out of the groundwater.

   SUBURBANITE: You call it a requirement, but I call it an outrage! They're going to charge us from five to fifteen thousand dollars each to make the hookups! That's more than anybody can afford!

18. CRITIC: I don't think it's proper to sell junk bonds without emphasizing the risk involved, but it's especially bad to sell them to older people who are investing their entire savings.

   ENTREPRENEUR: Oh, come on. There's nothing the matter with making money.

▲ 19. ONE HAND: What with the number of handguns and armed robberies these days, it's hard to feel safe in your own home.

   THE OTHER HAND: The reason you don't feel safe is you don't have a handgun yourself. Criminals would rather hit a house where there's no gun than a house where there is one.

20. ONE GUY: Would you look at the price they want for these computer tablets? They're making a fortune on every one of these things!
    ANOTHER: Don't give me that. I know how big a raise you got last year—you can afford a truckload of those things!

21. FED UP: This city is too cold in the winter, too hot in the summer, and too dangerous all the time. I'll be happier if I exercise my early retirement option and move to my place in Arkansas.
    FRIEND: You're nuts. You'll be miserable if you don't work, and if you move, you'll be back in six months.

▲ 22. KATIE: Hey Jennifer, I hate to say this, but you would be better off riding a bike to school.
    JENNIFER: What, this from someone who drives everywhere she goes?

23. DEZRA: What are you thinking, mowing the lawn in your bare feet? That's totally unsafe.
    KEN: Like you never did anything you could get hurt doing?

24. YAO: Nice thing about an iMac. It never gets viruses.
    MAO: Of course you would say that; you own one.

▲ 25. HERR ÜBERALLES: We spend too much on heating. We must show more fortitude.
    FRAU ÜBERALLES: But you know I get cold easily.

## Exercise 1-15

Which of the following claims pertain to right/wrong, good/bad, or should/shouldn't?

▲ 1. We did the right thing getting rid of Saddam. He was a sadistic tyrant.

2. That guy is the smartest person I know.

3. Contributing to the Humane Society is good to do.

▲ 4. It's time you start thinking about somebody other than yourself!

5. Your first duty is to your family; after that, to God and country, in that order.

6. You know what? I always tip 15 percent.

▲ 7. The FBI and CIA don't share information all that often, at least that's what I've heard.

8. You might find the parking less expensive on the street.

9. Help him! If the situation were reversed, he would help you.

▲ 10. Hip hop is better than country, any day.

11. Rodin was a master sculptor.

12. Whatever happened to Susan Boyle? You don't hear about her anymore.

▲ 13. If we want to stop the decline in enrollments here at Chaffee, we need to give students skills they can use.

## Exercise 1-16

This exercise will give you another opportunity to identify when someone is offering an argument, as distinct from doing something else.

Decide which of the lettered options serves the same kind of purpose as the original remark. Then think critically about your conclusion. Do you have a reason for it? Be ready to state your reasoning in class if called on.

**Example**

Be careful! This plate is hot.

a.  Watch out. The roads are icy.
b.  Say—why don't you get lost?

Conclusion: The purpose of (a) is most like the purpose of the original remark. Reason: Both are arguments.

1.  I'd expect that zipper to last about a week; it's made of cheap plastic.

    a.  The wrinkles on that dog make me think of an old man.
    b.  Given Sydney's spending habits, I doubt Adolphus will stick with her for long.

2.  If you recharge your battery, sir, it will be almost as good as new.

    a.  Purchasing one CD at the regular price would entitle you to buy an unlimited number of CDs at only $4.99.
    b.  I will now serve dinner, after which you can play if you want.

3.  To put out a really creative newsletter, you should get in touch with our technology people.

    a.  Do unto others as you would have them do unto you.
    b.  To put an end to this discussion, I'll concede your point.
    c.  You'd better cut down on your smoking if you want to live longer.

4.  GE's profits during the first quarter were short of GE's projections. Therefore, we can expect GE's stock to fall sharply in the next day or so.

    a.  The senator thought what he did in private was nobody's business but his own.
    b.  The dog is very hot. Probably he would appreciate a drink of water.
    c.  The dog's coat is unusually thick. No wonder he is hot.

5.  How was my date with your brother? Well . . . he has a great personality.

    a.  How do I like my steak? Not dripping blood like this thing you just served me.
    b.  How do I like your dress? Say, did you know that black is more slimming than white?

6.  The wind is coming up. We'd better head for shore.

    a.  They finally arrived. I guess they will order soon.
    b.  We shouldn't leave yet. We just got here.

7.  Good ties are made out of silk. That's why they cost so much.

    a.  Belts are like suspenders. They both keep your pants up.
    b.  Rugby has lots of injuries because rugby players don't wear pads.

8.  Daphne owns an expensive car. She must be rich.

    a.  This dog has fleas. I'll bet it itches a lot.
    b.  This dog has fleas. That explains why it scratches a lot.

9.  Dennis's salary is going up. He just got a promotion.

    a.  Dennis's salary went up after he got a promotion.
    b.  Dennis's salary won't be going up; he didn't get a promotion.

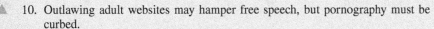

10. Outlawing adult websites may hamper free speech, but pornography must be curbed.

    a. The grass must be mowed even though it is hot.
    b. The grass is getting long; time to mow.

## Writing Exercises

1. Do people choose the sex they are attracted to? Write a one-page answer to this question, defending your answer with at least one supporting reason. Take about ten minutes to do this. Do not put your name on your essay. When everyone is finished, your instructor will collect the essays and redistribute them to the class. In groups of four or five, read the essays that have been given to your group. Divide the drafts into two batches, those that contain an argument and those that do not. Your instructor will ask each group to read to the class an essay that contains an argument and an essay that does not contain an argument (assuming that each group has at least one of each). The group should be prepared to explain why they feel each essay contains or fails to contain an argument.

2. Is it ever okay to tell a lie? Take a position on this issue and write a short essay supporting it.

# Two Kinds of Reasoning

## Students will learn to . . .

1. **Recognize general features of arguments**

2. **Distinguish between deductive and inductive arguments and evaluate them for validity, soundness, strength, and weakness**

3. **Identify unstated premises**

4. **Identify a balance of considerations argument and an inference to the best explanation (IBE)**

5. **Distinguish between ethos, pathos, and logos as means of persuasion**

6. **Use techniques for understanding and evaluating the structure and content of arguments**

Time to look more closely at arguments—the kind that actually show something (unlike the red herrings and emotional appeals and other fallacies we are going to be talking about later).

## ARGUMENTS: GENERAL FEATURES

To repeat, an argument consists of two parts. One part, the premise, is intended to provide a reason for accepting the second part, the conclusion. This statement is *not* an argument:

> God exists.

It's just a statement.
   Likewise, *this* is not an argument:

> God exists. That's as plain as the nose on your face.

It's just a slightly more emphatic statement.
   Nor is this an argument:

> God exists, and if you don't believe it, you will go to hell.

It just tries to scare us into believing God exists.

Also not an argument:

> I think God exists, because I was raised a Baptist.

Yes, it looks a bit like an argument, but it isn't. It merely explains why I believe in God.

On the other hand, this *is* an argument:

> God exists because something had to cause the universe.

The difference between this and the earlier examples? This example has a premise ("something had to cause the universe") and a conclusion ("God exists").

As we explained in Chapter 1 (see page 8), an argument always has two parts: a premise part and a conclusion part. The premise part is intended to give a reason for accepting the conclusion part.

This probably seems fairly straightforward, but one or two complications are worth noting.

## Conclusions Used as Premises

The same statement can be the conclusion of one argument and a premise in another argument:

> **Premise:** The brakes aren't working, the engine burns oil, the transmission needs work, and the car is hard to start.
> **Conclusion 1:** The car has outlived its usefulness.
> **Conclusion 2:** We should get a new car.

In this example, the statement "The car has outlived its usefulness" is the conclusion of one argument, and it is also a premise in the argument that we should get a new car.

Clearly, if a premise in an argument is uncertain or controversial or has been challenged, you might want to defend it—that is, argue that it is true. When you do, the premise becomes the conclusion of a new argument. However, every chain of reasoning must begin somewhere. If we ask a speaker to defend each premise with a further argument, and each premise in that argument with a further argument, and so on and so on, we eventually find ourselves being unreasonable, much like four-year-olds who keep asking "Why?" until they become exasperating. If we ask a speaker why he thinks the car has outlived its usefulness, he may mention that the car is hard to start. If we ask him why he thinks the car is hard to start, he probably won't know what to say.

## Unstated Premises and Conclusions

Another complication is that arguments can contain unstated premises. For example:

> **Premise:** You can't check out books from the library without an ID.
> **Conclusion:** Bill won't be able to check out any books.

The unstated premise must be that Bill has no ID.

An argument can even have an unstated conclusion. Here is an example:

## Conclusion Indicators

When the words in the following list are used in arguments, they usually indicate that a premise has just been offered and that a conclusion is about to be presented. (The three dots represent the claim that is the conclusion.)

| | |
|---|---|
| Thus . . . | Consequently . . . |
| Therefore . . . | So . . . |
| Hence . . . | Accordingly . . . |
| This shows that . . . | This implies that . . . |
| This suggests that . . . | This proves that . . . |

Example:

Stacy drives a Porsche. This suggests that either she is rich or her parents are.

The conclusion is

Either she is rich or her parents are.

The premise is

Stacy drives a Porsche.

---

The political party that best reflects mainstream opinion will win the presidency in 2020 and the Republican Party best reflects mainstream opinion.

If a person said this, he or she would be implying that the Republican Party will win the presidency in 2020; that would be the unstated conclusion of the argument.

Unstated premises are common in real life because sometimes they seem too obvious to need mentioning. The argument "the car is beyond fixing, so we should get rid of it" actually has an unstated premise to the effect that we should get rid of any car that is beyond fixing; but this may seem so obvious to us that we don't bother stating it.

Unstated conclusions also are not uncommon, though they are less common than unstated premises.

We'll return to this subject in a moment.

## TWO KINDS OF ARGUMENTS

Good arguments come in two varieties: deductive demonstrations and inductive supporting arguments.

### Deductive Arguments

The premise (or premises) of a good *deductive* argument, if true, *proves or demonstrates* (these being the same thing for our purposes) its conclusion. However, there is more to this than meets the eye, and we must begin with the fundamental concept

## Premise Indicators

When the words in the following list are used in arguments, they generally introduce premises. They often occur just *after* a conclusion has been given. A premise would replace the three dots in an actual argument.

> Since . . .
> For . . .
> In view of . . .
> This is implied by . . .

Example:

> Either Stacy is rich or her parents are, since she drives a Porsche.

The premise is the claim that Stacy drives a Porsche; the conclusion is the claim that either Stacy is rich or her parents are.

of deductive logic, *validity.* An argument is **valid** *if it isn't possible for the premise (or premises) to be true and the conclusion false.* This may sound complicated, but it really isn't. An example of a valid argument will help:

> **Premises:** Jimmy Carter was president immediately before Bill Clinton, and George W. Bush was president immediately after Bill Clinton.
> **Conclusion:** Jimmy Carter was president before George W. Bush.

As you can see, it's impossible for these premises to be true and this conclusion to be false. So the argument is valid.

However, you may have noticed that the premises contain a mistake. Jimmy Carter was not president immediately before Bill Clinton. George H. W. Bush was president immediately before Bill Clinton. Nevertheless, even though a premise of the preceding argument is not true, the argument is still valid, because it isn't possible for the premises to be true and the conclusion false. Another way to say this: If the premises *were* true, the conclusion *could not* be false—and that's what "valid" means.

Now, when the premises of a valid argument *are* true, there is a word for it. In that case, the argument is said to be **sound.** Here is an example of a sound argument:

> **Premises:** Bill Clinton is taller than George W. Bush, and Jimmy Carter is shorter than George W. Bush.
> **Conclusion:** Therefore, Bill Clinton is taller than Jimmy Carter.

This argument is sound because it is valid and the premises are true. As you can see, if an argument is sound, then its conclusion has been demonstrated.

### Inductive Arguments

Again, the premise of a good deductive argument, if true, demonstrates that the conclusion is true. This brings us to the second kind of argument, the *inductive* argument. The premise of a good *inductive* argument doesn't demonstrate its conclusion; it *supports* it. For example:

> After 2 P.M. the traffic slows to a crawl on the Bay Bridge.
> Therefore, it probably does the same thing on the Golden Gate Bridge.

The fact that traffic slows to a crawl after 2 P.M. on the Bay Bridge does not demonstrate or prove that it does that on the Golden Gate Bridge; it *supports* that conclusion. It makes it somewhat more likely that traffic on the Golden Gate Bridge slows to a crawl after 2 P.M.

Here is another example of an inductive argument:

> Nobody has ever run a mile in less than three minutes.
> Therefore, nobody will ever run a mile in less than three minutes.

Like the first argument, the premise supports the conclusion but does not demonstrate or prove it.

If you are thinking that support is a matter of degree and that it can vary from just a little to a whole lot, you are right. Thus, inductive arguments are better or worse on a scale, depending on how much support their premises provide for the conclusion. Logicians have a technical word to describe this situation. The more support the premise of an inductive argument provides for the conclusion, the **stronger** the argument; the less support it provides, the **weaker** the argument. Put another way, one argument for a conclusion is weaker than another if it fails to raise the probability of the conclusion by as much. Thus, the first argument given above is weaker than the following argument:

> After 2 P.M. the traffic slows to a crawl on the Bay Bridge, the San Mateo Bridge, the San Rafael Bridge, and the Dumbarton Bridge.
> Therefore, it probably does the same thing on the Golden Gate Bridge.

This argument is stronger than the first argument because its premise makes the conclusion more likely. The more bridges in a region on which traffic slows at a given time, the more likely it is that that phenomenon is universal on the bridges in the region.

One more example of an inductive argument:

> Alexandra rarely returns texts.
> Therefore, she probably rarely returns emails.

Once again, the premise supports but does not demonstrate or prove the conclusion. The differences between texting and emailing are sufficiently significant that the premise does not offer a great deal of support for the conclusion, but it does offer some. If Alexandra rarely returned telephone calls or letters as well as texts, that would make the argument stronger.

In Chapter 11 we will explain the criteria for evaluating inductive arguments.

## BEYOND A REASONABLE DOUBT

In common law, the highest standard of proof is proof "beyond a reasonable doubt." If you are a juror in a criminal trial, evidence will be presented to the court—facts that the interested parties consider relevant to the crime. Additionally, the prosecutor and counsel for the defense will offer arguments connecting the evidence to (or disconnecting it from) the guilt or innocence of the defendant. When the jury is asked to return a verdict, the judge will tell the jury that the defendant must be found not guilty unless the evidence proves guilt *beyond a reasonable doubt.*

Proof beyond a reasonable doubt actually is a lower standard than deductive demonstration. Deductive demonstration corresponds more to what, in ordinary English, might be expressed by the phrase "beyond any *possible* doubt." Recall that in logic, a proposition has been demonstrated when it has been shown to be the conclusion of a sound argument—an argument in which (1) all premises are true and (2) it is impossible for the premises to be true and for the conclusion to be false. In this sense, many propositions people describe as having been demonstrated or proved, such as that smoking causes lung cancer or that the DNA found at a crime scene was the defendant's, have not actually been proved in the logician's sense of the word. So, in real life, when people say something has been demonstrated, they may well be speaking informally. They may not mean that something is the conclusion of a sound deductive argument. However, when we—the authors—say that something has been demonstrated, that is *exactly* what we mean.

## TELLING THE DIFFERENCE BETWEEN DEDUCTIVE AND INDUCTIVE ARGUMENTS

A useful strategy for telling the difference between deductive and inductive arguments is to memorize a good example of each kind. Here are good examples of each:

> **Valid Deductive Argument:** Juan lives on the equator. Therefore, Juan lives midway between the North and South poles.

> **Relatively Strong Inductive Argument:** Juan lives on the equator. Therefore, Juan lives in a humid climate.

Study the two examples so that you understand the difference between them. In the left example, if you know the definition of "equator," you already know it is midway between the poles. The right example is radically different. The definition of "equator" does not contain the information that it is humid. So:

> If the conclusion of an argument is true *by definition* given the premise or premises, it is a valid deductive argument.

Often it is said that a valid deductive argument is valid due to its "form." Thus, consider this argument:

> If Juan is a fragglemop, then Juan is a snipette. Juan is not a snipette. Therefore, Juan is not a fragglemop.

What makes this argument valid is its form:

> If P then Q.
> Not-Q.
> Therefore not-P.

You can see, however, that ultimately what makes the argument valid, and makes its form a valid form, is the way the words "If . . . then" and "not" work. If you know the way those words work, then you already know that the conclusion must be true given the two premises.

Another way of telling the difference between a deductive argument and an inductive argument is this: You generally would not say of a deductive argument that it supports or provides evidence for its conclusion. It would be odd to say that Juan's living on the equator is *evidence* that he lives midway between the poles, or that it *supports* that claim. Thus:

> If it sounds odd to speak of the argument as providing evidence or support for a contention, that's an indication it is a deductive argument.

It would sound very odd to say, "The fact that Fido is a dog is evidence Fido is a mammal." Fido's being a dog isn't *evidence* Fido is a mammal: it's *proof*. "Fido is a dog; therefore Fido is a mammal" is a valid deductive argument.

## DEDUCTION, INDUCTION, AND UNSTATED PREMISES

Somebody announces, "Rain is on its way." Somebody else asks how he knows. He says, "There's a south wind." Is the speaker trying to *demonstrate* rain is coming? Probably not. His thinking, spelled out, is probably something like this:

> **Stated premise:** The wind is from the south.
> **Unstated premise:** Around here, south winds are usually followed by rain.
> **Conclusion:** There will be rain.

In other words, the speaker was merely trying to show that rain was a good possibility.

Notice, though, that the unstated premise in the argument could have been a universal statement to the effect that a south wind *always* is followed by rain at this particular location, in which case the argument would be deductive:

> **Stated premise:** The wind is from the south.
> **Unstated premise:** Around here, a south wind is always followed by rain.
> **Conclusion:** There will be rain.

Spelled out this way, the speaker's thinking is deductive: It isn't possible for the premises to be true and the conclusion to be false. So one might wonder abstractly what the speaker intended—an inductive argument that supports the belief that rain is coming, or a deductive demonstration.

There is, perhaps, no way to be certain short of asking the speaker something like, "Are you 100 percent positive?" But experience ("background knowledge") tells us that wind from a particular direction is not a surefire indicator of rain. So probably the speaker did have in mind merely the first argument. He wasn't trying to present a 100 percent certain, knock-down demonstration that it would rain; he was merely trying to establish there was a good chance of rain.

You can always turn an inductive argument with an unstated premise into a deductively valid argument by supplying the right universal premise—a statement that something holds without exception or is true everywhere or in all cases. Is that what the speaker really has in mind, though? You have to use background knowledge and common sense to answer the question.

For example, you overhear someone saying,

> Stacy and Justin are on the brink of divorce. They're always fighting.

One could turn this into a valid deductive argument by adding to it the universal statement "Every couple fighting is on the brink of divorce." But such an unqualified universal statement seems unlikely. Probably the speaker wasn't trying to demonstrate that Stacy and Justin are on the brink of divorce. He or she was merely trying to raise its likelihood. He or she was presenting evidence that Stacy and Justin are on the brink of divorce.

Often it is clear that the speaker does have a *deductive* argument in mind and has left some appropriate premise unstated. You overhear Professor Greene saying to Professor Brown,

> "Flunk her! This is the second time you've caught her cheating."

It would be strange to think that Professor Greene is merely trying to make it more likely that Professor Brown should flunk the student. Indeed, it is hard even to make sense of that suggestion. Professor Greene's argument, spelled out, must be this:

> **Stated premise:** This is the second time you've caught her cheating.
> **Unstated premise:** Anyone who has been caught cheating two times should be flunked.
> **Conclusion:** She should be flunked.

So context and content often make it clear what unstated premise a speaker has in mind and whether the argument is deductive or inductive.

Unfortunately, though, this isn't always the case. We might hear someone say,

> The bars are closed; therefore it is later than 2 A.M.

If the unstated premise in the speaker's mind is something like "In this city, the bars all close at 2 A.M.," then presumably he or she is thinking deductively and is evidently proffering proof that it's after 2. But if the speaker's unstated premise is something like "Most bars in this city close at 2 A.M." or "Bars in this city usually close at 2 A.M.," then we have an inductive argument that merely supports the conclusion. So which is the unstated premise? We really can't say without knowing more about the situation or the speaker.

## Is an Ad Photo an Argument?

The short answer: No. The longer version: Still no. An advertising photograph can "give you a reason" for buying something only in the sense that it can *cause* you to think of a reason. A photo is not an argument.

The bottom line is this. Real-life arguments often leave a premise unstated. One such unstated premise might make the argument inductive; another might make it deductive. Usually, context or content make reasonably clear what is intended; other times they may not. When they don't, the best practice is to attribute to a speaker an unstated premise that at least is believable, everything considered. We'll talk about believability in Chapter 4.

### BALANCE OF CONSIDERATIONS

Should I get a dog? Miss class to attend my cousin's wedding? Get chemo? Much everyday reasoning requires weighing considerations for and against thinking or doing something. Such reasoning, called **balance of considerations reasoning,** often contains both deductive and inductive elements. Here is an example:

> Should assault weapons be banned? On the one hand, doing that would violate the Second Amendment to the U.S. Constitution. But on the other hand, when guns were outlawed in Australia the number of accidental gun deaths fell dramatically; that would probably happen here, too. It is a tough call.

The first consideration mentioned in this passage—that banning assault weapons would violate the Second Amendment and therefore should not be done—is a deductive argument. The second consideration mentioned—that banning assault weapons would reduce the number of accidental gun deaths—is an inductive argument.

Inductive arguments can be compared as to strength and weakness; deductive arguments can be compared as to validity and soundness. Assigning weight to considerations can be difficult, of course, but it is not hopelessly arbitrary. In Chapter 12 of this book, we discuss the perspectives within which moral evaluations are made; you will see there that weighing considerations of the sort presented in the example above depend to a certain extent on the moral perspective one adheres to.

## INFERENCE TO THE BEST EXPLANATION (IBE)

An **Inference to the Best Explanation (IBE)** concludes that something exists or holds true or is a fact because that supposition best explains something we have observed or otherwise know. An example:

> Neither the dog nor my husband is home, and the dog's leash is gone. The best explanation of this is that my husband is out walking the dog. Therefore, my husband is out walking the dog.

Here is another example:

> Sometimes my back really aches. Let's see. Could it be due to gardening? Or lifting weights perhaps? No—it hurts all the time. Plus it seems to hurt more in the morning. And it started right after I bought that expensive mattress. Therefore, it's the mattress that is hurting my back.

The conclusion of the argument is that the mattress is hurting my back; that supposition best explains the fact that my back hurts. Notice that the argument explicitly compares alternative explanations. It thus qualifies as a balance of considerations argument as well as an IBE, the "considerations" in this instance being alternative explanations.

Two more examples:

> Sarah and another candidate were finalists for the teaching position. Sarah had better qualifications, but she had tattoos. The candidate who got the position didn't have tattoos. Therefore, the fact she had tattoos caused Sarah to lose out on the position.

> There is water on the floor. Neither the bathtub nor the sink has been used and the ceiling isn't leaking. The only source of water in the room is the toilet. Therefore, the toilet is leaking.

In the first example, the best explanation of Sarah's not getting the position is thought to be the fact that she has tattoos. Since no other explanation was considered, you might say the tattoo explanation wins by default. In the second example, the leaking-toilet explanation was explicitly compared to other possible explanations and declared the winner.

Sometimes IBE is referred to as "abduction." We treat it as a type of inductive reasoning, reasoning used to support rather than demonstrate a conclusion. In Chapter 11, we explore factors in terms of which one type of explanation might be said to be better than another.

## WHAT ARE NOT PREMISES, CONCLUSIONS, OR ARGUMENTS

We hope you've noticed, when we use the word "argument," we are not talking about two people having a feud or fuss about something. That use of the word has nothing much to do with critical thinking, though many a heated exchange could use some critical thinking. Arguments in our sense do not even need two people; we make arguments for our own use all the time. And when we evaluate them, we think critically.

Speaking of what arguments are not, it's important to realize that not everything that might look like an argument, or like a premise or a conclusion, is one.

### Pictures

Pictures are not premises, conclusions, or arguments. Neither are movies. Your iPhone can do lots of things, but it isn't an argument. Sorry. Arguments have two parts, a premise part and a conclusion part, and both parts are propositional entities, which means (to repeat) that both parts must be expressible in declarative, true-or-false sentences. Movies and pictures can be moving, compelling, beautiful, complex, realistic, and so forth—but they cannot be either true or false. You can ask if what is depicted in a movie actually happened, or if the story upon which it is based is a true story, but you can't really ask if a movie itself is true or false—or valid or invalid or relatively strong or weak. Such questions don't make literal sense. If it doesn't make sense to think of a thing as true or false, it cannot be a premise or a conclusion. If it doesn't make sense to think of it as valid or invalid, or as being relatively strong or weak, it cannot be an argument.

The list of things that aren't premises or conclusions or arguments therefore also includes emotions, feelings, landscapes, faces, gestures, grunts, groans, bribes, threats, amusement parks, and hip-hop. Since they may *cause* you to have an opinion or to form a judgment about something or produce an argument, you might be tempted to think of them as premises, but causes are not premises. A cause isn't a propositional entity: it is neither true nor false. So it cannot be a premise.

### If . . . then . . . Sentences

Sometimes sentences like the following are taken to state arguments:

> If you wash your car now, then it will get spots.

This statement might be the premise of an argument whose conclusion is "Therefore you shouldn't wash your car now." It might also be the conclusion of an argument whose premise is "It is raining." But though it *could* be a premise or a conclusion, it is not *itself* an argument. An argument has a premise and a conclusion, and, though the preceding statement has two parts, neither part by itself is either a premise or a conclusion. "If you wash your car now" is not a statement, and neither is "Then it will get spots." Neither of these phrases qualifies as either a premise or a conclusion. Bottom line: "If . . . then . . ." sentences are not arguments.

### Lists of Facts

Though the following might look like an argument, it is nothing more than a list of facts:

> Identity theft is up at least tenfold over last year. More people have learned how easy it is to get hold of another's Social Security number, bank account numbers, and such. The local police department reminds everyone to keep close watch on who has access to such information.

Although they are related by being about the same subject, none of these claims is offered as a reason for believing another, and thus there is no argument here. But the following passage is different. See if you can spot why it makes an argument:

> The number of people who have learned how to steal identities has doubled in the past year. So you are now more likely to become a victim of identity theft than you were a year ago.

Here, the first claim offers a reason for accepting the second claim; we now have an argument.

## "A because B"

Sometimes the word "because" refers to the cause of something. But other times it refers to a premise of an argument. Mike walks into the motel lobby, wearing a swimsuit and dripping wet. Consider these two statements:

> "Mike is in his swimsuit because he was swimming."

> "Mike was swimming because he's in his swimsuit."

These two sentences have the same form, "X because Y." But the sentence on the left *explains why* Mike is wearing a swimsuit. The sentence on the right offers an argument *that* Mike was swimming. Only the sentence on the right is an argument. Put it this way: What follows "because" in the sentence on the left is the *cause*. What follows "because" in the right-hand sentence is *evidence*.

Be sure you understand the difference between these two sentences. Arguments and cause-and-effect statements can both employ the phrase *"X because Y."* But there the similarity ends. When what follows "because" is a *reason* for accepting a contention, or evidence for it, we have an argument; when what follows "because" states the *cause* of something, we have a cause-and-effect explanation. These are entirely different enterprises. Arguing *that* a dog has fleas is different from explaining what *gave* it fleas. Arguing *that* violent crime has increased is different from explaining what *caused* it to increase.

## ETHOS, PATHOS, AND LOGOS

When he was a young man, Alexander the Great conquered the world. Alexander was enormously proud of his accomplishment, and named several cities after himself. Alexander's teacher, the Greek philosopher Aristotle, had no cities named after him (there is no indication that this disappointed Aristotle). Nevertheless, Aristotle's imprint on civilization turned out to be even more profound than Alexander's.

First known pic of Aristotle taking a selfie.

Aristotle, who now is regarded as the father of logic, biology, and psychology, made enduring contributions to virtually every subject. These include (in addition to those just mentioned) physics, astronomy, meteorology, zoology, metaphysics, political science, economics, ethics, and rhetoric.

Among Aristotle's contributions in the last field (rhetoric) was a theory of persuasion, which famously contained the idea that there are three modes by which a speaker may persuade an audience. Paraphrasing very loosely, Aristotle's idea was that we can be persuaded, first of all, by a speaker's personal attributes, including such things as his or her background, reputation, accomplishments, expertise, and similar things. Aristotle referred to this mode of persuasion as *ethos*. Second, a speaker can persuade us by connecting with us on a personal level, and by arousing and appealing to our emotions by a skillful use of rhetoric. This mode of persuasion Aristotle termed *pathos*. And third, the speaker may persuade us by using information and arguments—what he called *logos*.

Unfortunately, logos—rational argumentation—is one of the least effective ways of winning someone to your point of view. That's why advertisers rarely bother with it. When the sellers of the first home automatic breadmaker found that its new kitchen device didn't interest people, they advertised the availability of a second model of the same machine, which was only slightly larger but much more expensive. When consumers saw that the first model was a great buy, they suddenly discovered they wanted one, and began snapping it up. Why try to persuade people by rational argument that they need a breadmaker when you can get them to think they do simply by making them believe they have sniffed out a bargain?*

Still, despite the general inefficacy of logos as a tool of persuasion, people do frequently use arguments when they try to persuade others. This might lead you to *define* an argument as an attempt to persuade. But that won't do. Remember, there are two kinds of argument. Deductive arguments are either sound or unsound, and whether a deductive argument is one or the other doesn't depend in the least on whether anyone is persuaded by it. Likewise, inductive arguments are in varying degrees strong or weak; their strength depends on the degree to which their premises elevate the probability of the conclusion, and that, too, is independent of whether anyone finds them persuasive. The very same argument might be persuasive to Parker but not to Moore, which shows that the persuasiveness of an argument is a subjective question of psychology, not of logic. Indeed, the individual who does *not* think critically is precisely the person who is persuaded by specious reasoning. People notoriously are unfazed by good arguments while finding even the worst arguments compelling. If you want to persuade people of something, try propaganda. Flattery has been known to work, too.

We will be looking at alternative modes of persuasion—what Aristotle called ethos and pathos—in considerable detail in Chapters 4, 5, 6, 7, and 8. However, we do this not so you can persuade people, but so you can be alert to the influence of ethos and pathos on your own thinking.

Now, we aren't suggesting it is a bad thing to be a persuasive writer or speaker. Obviously it isn't; that's what rhetoric courses are for—to teach you to write persuasively. Let's just put it this way: Whenever you find yourself being persuaded by what someone says, find the "logos" in the "pathos," and be persuaded by it alone.

---

*Dan Ariely, *Irrational Predictability* (New York: HarperCollins, 2008), 14, 15.

The following exercises will give you practice (1) identifying premises and conclusions as well as words that indicate premises and conclusions, (2) telling the difference between deductive demonstrations and inductive supporting arguments, and (3) identifying balance of considerations arguments and inferences to the best explanation.

Exercise 2-1

▲—See the answers section at the back of the book.

Indicate which blanks would ordinarily contain premises and which would ordinarily contain conclusions.

▲  1. ___a___, and ___b___. Therefore, ___c___.

▲  2. ___a___. So, since ___b___, ___c___.

▲  3. ___a___, clearly. After all, ___b___.

▲  4. Since ___a___ and ___b___, ___c___.

▲  5. ___a___. Consequently, ___b___, since ___c___ and ___d___.

Identify the premise(s) and conclusion in each of the following arguments.

Exercise 2-2

▲  1. Since all Communists are Marxists, all Marxists are Communists.

  2. The Lakers almost didn't beat the Kings. They'll never get past Dallas.

  3. If the butler had done it, he could not have locked the screen door. Therefore, since the door was locked, we know the butler is in the clear.

▲  4. That cat loves dogs. Probably she won't be upset if you bring home a new dog for a pet.

  5. Hey, he can't be older than his mother's daughter's brother. His mother's daughter has only one brother.

  6. Mr. Hoover will never make it into the state police. They have a weight limit, and he's over it.

▲  7. Presbyterians are not fundamentalists, but all born-again Christians are. So, no born-again Christians are Presbyterians.

  8. I guess Thork doesn't have a thing to do. Why else would he waste his time watching daytime TV?

  9. "There are more injuries in professional football today than there were twenty years ago," he reasoned. "And if there are more injuries, then today's players suffer higher risks. And if they suffer higher risks, then they should be paid more. Consequently, I think today's players should be paid more," he concluded.

▲ 10. Let's see . . . since the clunk comes only when I pedal, the problem must be in the chain, the crank, or the pedals.

Identify the premises and the conclusions in the following arguments.

Exercise 2-3

▲  1. The darned engine pings every time we use the regular unleaded gasoline, but it doesn't do it with super. I'd bet that there is a difference in the octane ratings between the two in spite of what my mechanic says.

  2. Chances are I'll be carded at JJ's, since Kera, Sherry, and Bobby were all carded there, and they all look as though they're about thirty.

3. Seventy percent of first-year students at Cal Poly San Luis Obispo come from wealthy families; therefore, probably about the same percentage of all Cal Poly San Luis Obispo students come from wealthy families.

▲ 4. When blue jays are breeding, they become aggressive. Consequently, scrub jays, which are very similar to blue jays, can also be expected to be aggressive when they're breeding.

5. I am sure Marietta comes from a wealthy family. She told me her parents benefited from the cut in the capital gains tax.

6. According to *Nature*, today's thoroughbred racehorses do not run any faster than their grandparents did. But human Olympic runners are at least 20 percent faster than their counterparts of fifty years ago. Most likely, racehorses have reached their physical limits but humans have not.

▲ 7. Dogs are smarter than cats, since it is easier to train them.

8. "Let me demonstrate the principle by means of logic," the teacher said, holding up a bucket. "If this bucket has a hole in it, then it will leak. But it doesn't leak. Therefore, obviously, it doesn't have a hole in it."

9. We shouldn't take a chance on this new candidate. She's from Alamo Polytech, and the last person we hired from there was incompetent.

▲ 10. If she was still interested in me, she would have called, but she didn't.

**Exercise 2-4**    Five of these items are best viewed as deductive arguments and five as inductive arguments. Which are which?

▲ 1. No mayten tree is deciduous, and all nondeciduous trees are evergreens. It follows that all mayten trees are evergreens.

2. Mike must belong to the Bartenders and Beverage Union Local 165, since almost every Las Vegas bartender does.

3. Either Colonel Mustard or Reverend Green killed Professor Plum. But whoever ran off with Mrs. White did not kill the professor. Since Reverend Green ran off with Mrs. White, Colonel Mustard killed Professor Plum.

▲ 4. I've never met a golden retriever with a nasty disposition. I bet there aren't any.

5. Since some grapes are purple, and all grapes are fruit, some fruit is purple.

6. Why is Shrilla so mean to Timeeda? The only thing I can think of is that she's jealous. Jealousy is what's making her mean.

▲ 7. Biden would have made a fine president. After all, he made a fine vice president.

8. The figure he drew has only three sides, so it isn't a square.

9. It was the pizza that made my stomach churn. What else could it be? I was fine until I ate it.

▲ 10. It's wrong to hurt someone's feelings, and that is exactly what you are doing when you speak to me like that.

**Exercise 2-5**    Which of the following items are intended to be deductive arguments?

▲ 1. Miss Scarlet's fingerprints were on the knife used to kill Colonel Mustard. Furthermore, he was killed in the pantry, and she was the only person who had a key to the pantry. Clearly she killed the colonel.

2. Outlawing guns would be a violation of the U.S. Constitution. Therefore, they should not be outlawed.

3. There are sunfish in the water behind this dam, but none in the water released from it. Ordinarily this kind of thing happens only when the released water comes from the bottom of the dam, because then the released water is too cold for sunfish. Therefore the water released from this dam comes from the bottom.

▲ 4. Sparky is scratching again. He must either have a skin infection or flea bites.

5. Outlawing guns reduced gun deaths in Australia; therefore it would do the same here.

6. I'm sleepy again. I guess I didn't get enough sleep last night.

▲ 7. I didn't get enough sleep last night; therefore I should get to bed earlier tonight.

8. The victims' blood was on a glove found behind Simpson's house. This shows that Simpson committed the murders, because he alone had access to that area.

9. The indentation on the west coast of Africa is about the same size as the bulge on the east coast of South America, indicating that the two continents were once connected.

▲ 10. I can hear you lots better now! You must be holding the phone in a different position.

Identify each of the following as either　　　　　　　　　　Exercise 2-6
    a. IBE
    b. balance of considerations reasoning
    c. neither of the above

▲ 1. Let's go now. I know you wanted to work in the yard, but if we wait longer, we won't make the movie. Plus, it's gonna get cold if we don't make tracks.

2. He said he was for the bill when it was proposed, and now he vetoes it? The only thing I can see is, he must be trying to get the teachers' vote.

3. Yes, a card laid is a card played, but I kept my hand on it, so I didn't actually lay it.

▲ 4. All things considered, we'd be better off taking the Suburban. Plus, let's get AAA to help us make reservations.

5. Jackson will get an A in the course, since he aced the final.

6. "A gentleman goes forth on a showery and miry day. He returns immaculate in the evening with the gloss still on his hat and his boots. He has been a fixture therefore all day. He is not a man with intimate friends. Where, then, could he have been? Is it not obvious?"

    —*Arthur Conan Doyle,* The Hound of the Baskervilles, Chapter 3

▲ 7. It's longer taking the 405, but you can drive faster—though who knows what the traffic's like at this hour. I would say if you want to play it safe, stay on the 5.

8. He made threats, plus he had the motive. Not only that, but who else had access to a gun? If Mitchell didn't do it, I don't know who did.

9. The question is, are you running a temperature? Because if you are, it can't be a cold. The runny nose and the sore throat could be a cold, but not the temperature. Only the flu would give you a temperature.

▲ 10. Sherry seems right for the job to me. She speaks French, knows biology, has people skills, and makes a great impression. The only down side is, she can't start until October. That pretty much eliminates her, unfortunately.

**Exercise 2-7**    Identify each of the following as either

    a. IBE
    b. balance of considerations reasoning
    c. neither of the above

▲   1. These tomatoes got plenty of sunlight and water. The only thing that could account for their being rotten is the soil.

    2. Should we outlaw assault weapons? No. That would be a violation of the Second Amendment.

    3. Should we outlaw assault weapons? Well, that depends. The Second Amendment gives us the right to bear arms, but outlawing them might make the country a safer place.

▲   4. Priglet messed on the carpet again! Is he sick do you suppose? Or is he trying to tell us something? It seems like he does that only when we leave him alone for a long time. I bet he just has a weak bladder.

    5. Either God exists or He does not. By believing that He exists, you lose nothing if you are wrong; but if you are right, He will reward you with happiness and eternal life. By believing He does not exist, you lose nothing if you are right; but if you are wrong, you may suffer eternal damnation. It is therefore prudent to believe that He exists.

                               —*A paraphrase of Blaise Pascal (1623–1662)*

    6. Professor Stooler has been teaching here thirty years and he still hasn't unpacked his boxes from graduate school. It seems likely he won't ever unpack them.

▲   7. "The man I found in the room was definitely a fighter and a smart one too. He hid his gun, chest rack, and hand grenades just out of reach and well enough for us not to see them on our initial entry into the room."

                                   —*Mark Owen*, No Easy Way

    8. I don't like Mr. Biden's personality, but I think he may be better than Mrs. Clinton at working with people. Plus he has been around longer than she. That's why I support him.

    9. Susan doesn't laugh at my jokes anymore. Maybe I'm not as funny as I think I am.

▲  10. I am reading this sentence; therefore I am alive.

## TECHNIQUES FOR UNDERSTANDING ARGUMENTS

If an argument has been offered to us, before we can evaluate it we must understand it. Many arguments are difficult to understand because they are spoken and go by so quickly we cannot be sure of the conclusion or the premises. Others are difficult to understand because they have a complicated structure. Still others are difficult to understand because they are embedded in nonargumentative material consisting of background information, prejudicial coloring, illustrations, parenthetical remarks, digressions, subsidiary points, and other window dressing. And some arguments are difficult to understand because they are confused or because the reasons they contain are so poor that we are not sure whether to regard them as reasons.

In understanding an argument that has been given to us, the first task is to find the conclusion—the main point or thesis of the passage. The next step is to locate the reasons that have been offered for accepting the conclusion—that is, to find the premises. Next, we look for the reasons, if any, offered for accepting these premises. To proceed through these steps, you have to learn both to spot premises and conclusions when they occur in spoken and written passages and to understand the interrelationships among these claims—that is, the structure of the argument.

### Clarifying an Argument's Structure

Let's begin with how to understand the relationships among the argumentative claims, because this problem is sometimes easiest to solve. If you are dealing with written material that you can mark up, one useful technique is to number the premises and conclusions and then use the numbers to lay bare the structure of the argument. Let's start with this argument as an example:

> I don't think we should get Carlos his own car. He is not responsible in view of the fact that he doesn't care for his things. And anyway, we don't have enough money for a car for him, since we even have trouble making our own car payments. Last week you yourself complained about our financial situation, and you never complain without really good reason.

We want to display the structure of this argument clearly. First, circle all premise and conclusion indicators, and then bracket each premise and conclusion, numbering them consecutively, like this:

> ① [I don't think we should get Carlos his own car.] ② [He is not responsible] in view of the fact that ③ [he doesn't care for his things.] And anyway, ④ [we don't have enough money for a car for him], since ⑤ [we even have trouble making our own car payments.] ⑥ [Last week you yourself complained about our financial situation], and ⑦ [you never complain without really good reason.]

Then we diagram the argument. Using an arrow to mean therefore, we diagram the first three claims in the argument as follows:

Now, ⑥ and ⑦ together support ④; that is, they are part of the same argument for ④. To show that ⑥ and ⑦ go together, we simply draw a line under them, put a plus sign between them, and draw the "therefore" arrow from the line to ④, like this:

Because ⑤ and ⑥ + ⑦ are separate arguments for ④, we can represent the relationship between them and ④ as follows:

Finally, because ④ and ② are separate arguments for ①, the diagram of the entire passage is this:

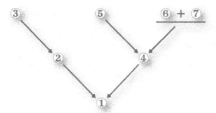

So the conventions governing this approach to revealing argument structure are very simple: First, circle all premise- and conclusion-indicating words. Then, assuming you can identify the claims that function in the argument (a big assumption, as you will see before long), number them consecutively. Then display the structure of the argument, using arrows for "therefore" and plus signs over a line to connect two or more premises that depend on one another.

Some claims, incidentally, may constitute reasons for more than one conclusion. For example:

> ① [Carlos continues to be irresponsible.] ② [He certainly should not have his own car], and, as far as I am concerned, ③ [he can forget about that trip to Hawaii this winter, too.]

Structure:

Frequently, too, a passage may entertain counterarguments to its ultimate conclusion. For example, this passage contains a counterargument:

① We really should have more African Americans on the faculty. ② That is why the new diversity program ought to be approved. True, ③ it may involve an element of unfairness to whites, but ④ the benefits to society of having more black faculty outweigh the disadvantages.

As you can see, claim ③ introduces a consideration that runs counter to the conclusion of the passage, which is stated in ②. We can indicate counterclaims by crossing the "therefore" arrow with lines, thus:

This diagram indicates that item ③ has been introduced by the writer as a consideration that runs counter to ②.

Of course, one might adopt other conventions for clarifying argument structure—for example, circling the main conclusion and drawing solid lines under supporting premises and wavy lines under the premises of subarguments. The technique we have described is simply one way of doing it; any of several others might work as well for you. However, *no* technique for revealing argument structure will work if you cannot spot the argumentative claims in the midst of a lot of background material.

### Distinguishing Arguments from Window Dressing

It is not always easy to isolate the argument in a speech or a written piece. Often, speakers and writers think that because their main points are more or less clear to them, they will be equally apparent to listeners and readers. But it doesn't always work that way.

If you have trouble identifying a conclusion in what you hear or read, it *could* be the passage is not an argument at all. Make sure the passage in question is not a report, a description, an explanation, or something else altogether, rather than an argument. The key here is determining whether the speaker or writer is offering reasons intended to support or demonstrate one or more claims.

The problem could also be that the conclusion is left unstated. Sometimes it helps simply to put the argument aside and ask yourself, "What is this person trying to prove?" In any case, the first and essential step in understanding an argument is to spot the conclusion.

If you are having difficulty identifying the *premises,* consider the possibility that you have before you a case of rhetoric (see Chapter 5). (You can't find premises in a piece of pure rhetoric because there *are* no premises.) You will have an advantage over many students in having learned about rhetorical devices in Chapters 5, 6, 7, and 8. By that time, you should be getting pretty good at recognizing them.

As you apply what you learn in this book to arguments you encounter in real life, you are apt to encounter arguments and argumentative essays whose organization is difficult to comprehend. When you do, you may find diagramming a useful technique. Also, as is obvious, what we have said in this section applies to arguments that others give us or that we otherwise encounter. You don't diagram what's in your head, though you need to be clear on your own conclusions, tentative or otherwise, and the reasons you have for accepting them. However, the diagramming technique does apply to material you write for others. If you find you have difficulty diagramming your arguments, you should reorganize your essay and make the structure of your reasoning clearer.

## EVALUATING ARGUMENTS

Thinking critically requires us to evaluate arguments, and evaluating arguments has two parts. First, there is the *logic* part: Does the argument either demonstrate or support its conclusion? Is this argument either deductively valid or inductively relatively strong? You know now what these questions mean theoretically; over the course of this book, you will see what they involve in fact.

The other part, of course, is the *truth* part. Are the premises actually true? As we explain in Chapter 4, it is best to be suspicious of a premise that conflicts with our background information or other credible claims, as well as a premise that comes from a source that lacks credibility. And, as we develop at length in Chapters 5, 6, and 7, we want to avoid being tricked into accepting a claim by rhetoric or other psychological gimmickry. It also almost goes without saying that premises that are unclear require clarification before one accepts them—as we explain in Chapter 3. In general, determining the truth of premises requires knowledge, experience, a level head, and the inclination to look into things.

## Recap

The main ideas of the chapter are these:

- Arguments always have two parts, a premise (or premises) and a conclusion.
- The same statement can be a premise in one argument and a conclusion in a second argument.
- The two fundamental types of reasoning are deductive demonstration and inductive support.
- A deductive argument is used to demonstrate or prove a conclusion, which it does if it is sound.
- An argument is sound if it is valid and its premise (or premises) is true.
- An argument is valid if it isn't possible for its premise or premises to be true and its conclusion to be false.
- An inductive argument is used to support rather than to demonstrate a conclusion.
- An argument supports a conclusion if it increases the likelihood that the conclusion is true.
- Support is a matter of degrees: An argument supports a conclusion to the extent its premise (or premises) makes the conclusion likely.
- An argument that offers more support for a conclusion is said to be stronger than one that offers less support; the latter is said to be weaker than the former.

&#9642; Some instructors use the word "strong" in an absolute sense to denote inductive arguments whose premise (or premises) makes the conclusion more likely than not.

&#9642; If it doesn't make sense to think of an argument as providing evidence or support for a contention, it is probably because it is a deductive argument.

&#9642; Inductive arguments and deductive arguments can have unstated premises.

&#9642; Whether an argument is deductive or inductive may depend on what the unstated premise is said to be.

&#9642; If an argument is written, diagramming it may help you understand it.

&#9642; Balance of considerations reasoning often involves deductive and inductive elements.

&#9642; Inference to best explanation is a common type of inductive reasoning in which a supposition is said to be true because it states the best explanation of something we have observed or otherwise know.

These exercises will test your comprehension of the chapter. They will also give you additional practice (1) distinguishing between deductive demonstrations and inductive supporting arguments, (2) recognizing when a passage contains more than a single argument, (3) recognizing the difference between arguments and explanations, (4) identifying unstated assumptions, and (5) diagramming arguments.

**Additional Exercises**

## Exercise 2-8

Fill in the blanks where called for, and answer true or false where appropriate.

1. Arguments that are relatively strong or weak are called _____ arguments.
2. All valid arguments are sound arguments.
3. All sound arguments are valid arguments.
4. If a valid argument has a false conclusion, then not all its premises can be true.
5. A sound argument cannot have a false conclusion.
6. "Strong" and "weak" are absolute terms.
7. If you try to demonstrate a conclusion, you are using _____ reasoning.
8. When a conclusion has been proved beyond a reasonable doubt, it has always been demonstrated.
9. An argument can never have an unstated conclusion.
10. When you try to support a conclusion, you are using _____ reasoning.
11. The most effective way to convince someone is through argument.
12. "If . . . then . . ." sentences may be arguments.
13. "If . . . then . . ." sentences may be premises.
14. Logic should be defined as the art of persuasion.
15. "A because B" is always an argument.

16. "A because B" is never an argument.

▲ 17. "IBE" refers to a type of deductive argument.

18. Inductive and deductive arguments both may occur in balance of considerations reasoning.

## Exercise 2-9

Some of these passages are best viewed as attempted deductive demonstrations, and others are best viewed as offering inductive support. Which are which?

▲ 1. All mammals are warm-blooded creatures, and all whales are mammals. Therefore, all whales are warm-blooded creatures.

▲ 2. The brains of rats raised in enriched environments with a variety of toys and puzzles weigh more than the brains of rats raised in more barren environments. Therefore, the brains of humans will weigh more if humans are placed in intellectually stimulating environments.

3. Jones won't plead guilty to a misdemeanor, and if he won't plead guilty, then he will be tried on a felony charge. Therefore, he will be tried on a felony charge.

▲ 4. We've interviewed 200 professional football players, and 60 percent of them favor expanding the season to twenty games. Therefore, 60 percent of all professional football players favor expanding the season to twenty games.

5. Jose is taller than Bill, and Bill is taller than Margaret. Therefore, Jose is taller than Margaret.

6. Exercise may help chronic male smokers kick the habit, says a study published today. The researchers, based at McDuff University, put thirty young male smokers on a three-month program of vigorous exercise. One year later, only 14 percent of them still smoked, according to the report. An equivalent number of young male smokers who did not go through the exercise program were also checked after a year, and it was found that 60 percent still smoked.

▲ 7. Believe in God? Yes, of course I do. The universe couldn't have arisen by chance, could it? Besides, I read the other day that more and more physicists believe in God, based on what they're finding out about the big bang and all that stuff.

▲ 8. From an office memo: "I've got a good person for your opening in Accounting. Jesse Brown is his name, and he's as sharp as they come. Jesse has a solid background in bookkeeping, and he's good with computers. He's also reliable, and he'll project the right image. He will do a fine job for you."

## Exercise 2-10

Diagram the arguments contained in the following passages.

▲ 1. North Korea is a great threat to its neighbors. It has a million-person army ready to be unleashed at a moment's notice, and it also has nuclear weapons.

2. Shaun is going to the party with Mary, so she won't be going alone.

3. Michael should just go ahead and get a new car. The one he's driving is junk; also, he has a new job and can afford a new car.

4. If Karper goes to Las Vegas, he'll wind up in a casino; and if he winds up in a casino, it's a sure thing he'll spend half the night at a craps table. So you can be sure: If Karper goes to Las Vegas, he'll spend half the night at a craps table.

5. It's going to be rainy tomorrow, and Serj doesn't like to play golf in the rain. It's going to be cold as well, and he *really* doesn't like to play when it's cold. So you can be sure Serj will be someplace other than the golf course tomorrow.

▲ 6. Hey, you're overwatering your lawn. See? There are mushrooms growing around the base of that tree—a sure sign of overwatering. Also, look at all the worms on the ground. They come up when the earth is oversaturated.

7. "Will you drive me to the airport?" she asked. "Why should I do that?" he wanted to know. "Because I'll pay you twice what it takes for gas. Besides, didn't you say you were my friend?"

8. If you drive too fast, you're more likely to get a ticket, and the more likely you are to get a ticket, the more likely you are to have your insurance premiums raised. So, if you drive too fast, you are more likely to have your insurance premiums raised.

▲ 9. If you drive too fast, you're more likely to get a ticket. You're also more likely to get into an accident. So you shouldn't drive too fast.

▲ 10. There are several reasons why you should consider installing a solarium. First, you can still get a tax credit. Second, you can reduce your heating bill. Third, if you build it right, you can actually cool your house with it in the summer.

11. From a letter to the editor: "By trying to eliminate Charles Darwin from the curriculum, creationists are doing themselves a great disservice. When read carefully, Darwin's discoveries only support the thesis that species change, not that they evolve into new species. This is a thesis that most creationists can live with. When read carefully, Darwin actually supports the creationist point of view."

12. Editorial comment: "The Supreme Court's ruling, that schools may have a moment of silence but not if it's designated for prayer, is sound. Nothing stops someone from saying a silent prayer at school or anywhere else. Also, even though a moment of silence will encourage prayer, it will not favor any particular religion over any other. The ruling makes sense."

▲ 13. We must paint the house now! Here are three good reasons: (a) If we don't, then we'll have to paint it next summer; (b) if we have to paint it next summer, we'll have to cancel our trip; and (c) it's too late to cancel the trip.

## Exercise 2-11

Which of the following instances of "because" are followed by a cause, and which are followed by a premise?

▲ 1. We've had so much hot weather recently because the jet stream is unusually far north.

2. Ms. Mossbarger looks so tired because she hasn't been able to sleep for three nights.

    3. It's a bad idea to mow the lawn in your bare feet because you could be seriously injured.

▲     4. Ken mows the lawn in his bare feet because he doesn't realize how dangerous it is.

    5. Ryan will marry Beth because he told me he would.

    6. I'd change before going into town because your clothes look like you slept in them.

▲     7. You have high blood pressure because you overeat.

    8. You'd better cut back on the salt because you could become hypertensive.

▲     9. It's a good bet Iran wants to build nuclear weapons because the UN inspectors found devices for the enrichment of plutonium.

    10. Iran wants to build nuclear weapons because it wants to gain control over neighboring Middle Eastern countries.

## Exercise 2-12

Which of the following statements could not possibly be false?

▲     1. Squares have four sides.

    2. You will not live to be 130 years old.

    3. A cow cannot yodel.

▲     4. A six-foot person is taller than a five-foot person.

    5. If the sign on the parking meter says "Out of Order" the meter won't work.

    6. Nobody can be her own mother.

▲     7. God exists or does not exist.

    8. They will never get rid of all disease.

    9. The ice caps couldn't melt entirely.

▲     10. The day two days after the day before yesterday is today.

## Exercise 2-13

For each of the following, supply a universal principle (a statement that says that something holds without exception) that turns it into a valid deductive argument.

**Example**

    Tay is opinionated. She should be more open-minded.

**One universal principle that makes it valid**

    Opinionated people should all be more open-minded. (*Note:* There are alternative ways of phrasing this.)

▲     1. Jamal keeps his word, so he is a man of good character.

    2. Betty got an A in the course, so she must have received an A on the final.

    3. Iraq posed a threat to us, so we had a right to invade it.

▲     4. Colonel Mustard could not have murdered Professor Plum, because the two men were in separate rooms when the professor was killed.

5. Avril is no liberal, since she voted against gun control.

6. Jimmi has a gentle soul; if there is a heaven, he should go there when he dies.

▲ 7. Of course that guy should be executed; he committed murder, didn't he?

8. I don't think you could call the party a success; only eight people showed up.

9. Mzbrynski proved Goldbach's conjecture; that makes him the greatest mathematician ever.

▲ 10. The fan needs oil; after all, it's squeaking.

## Exercise 2-14

For each of the following arguments, supply a principle that makes it inductive rather than deductive.

**Example**

Ryder is sharp, so he will get a good grade in this course.

**One claim that makes it inductive**

Most sharp people get good grades in this course.

▲ 1. There are puddles everywhere; it must have rained recently.

2. The lights are dim; therefore, the battery is weak.

3. Simpson's blood matched the blood on the glove found at the victim's condo: He killed her.

▲ 4. Of course it will be cold tomorrow! It's been cold all week, hasn't it?

5. Ambramoff isn't very good with animals. I doubt he'd make a great parent.

6. The dog has either fleas or dry skin; it's scratching a lot.

▲ 7. Why do I say their party wasn't a success? Remember all the leftovers?

8. Cheston owns a rifle; he's sure to belong to the NRA.

9. The dessert contained caffeine, so you might have trouble sleeping tonight.

▲ 10. I took Zicam, and my cold disappeared like magic. Obviously, it works.

## Exercise 2-15

Diagram the following "arguments."

▲ 1. ①, in light of the fact that ② and ③. [Assume ② and ③ are part of the same argument for ①.]

2. ① and ②; therefore ③. [Assume ① and ② are separate arguments for ③.]

3. Since ①, ②; and since ③, ④. And since ② and ④, ⑤. [Assume ② and ④ are separate arguments for ⑤.]

▲ 4. ①; therefore ② and ③. And in light of the fact that ② and ③, ④. Consequently, ⑤. Therefore, ⑥. [Assume ② and ③ are separate arguments for ④.]

5. ①, ②, ③; therefore ④. ⑤, in view of ①. And ⑥, since ②. Therefore ⑦. [Assume ①, ②, and ③ are part of the same argument for ④.]

## Exercise 2-16

What does each diagram display—a or b?

1.

   a. 1 supports 3, as does 2.
   b. 1 in combination with 2 demonstrates 3.

2.

   a. 1 demonstrates 3, as does 2,
   b. 1 in combination with 2 demonstrates 3.

3.

   a. 3, which is supported by 1, supports two things, 2 and 4.
   b. 3, which is supported by 1, supports 2, which in turn supports 4.

4.

   a. In view of 5, 3 must be true, and it must also be true because of 2, which follows from 1 combined with 4.
   b. 2 must be true because of 1 in combination with 4; and 2 and 5 combined demonstrate 3.

5.

   a. 1 in combination with 2 support 5. In addition, 3 supports 5, as does 4. So despite the fact that 6 indicates that 5 is false, 5.
   b. 6 follows from 3, and it follows from 4 as well. It is also supported by 5, which follows from 1 in combination with 2.

## Exercise 2-17

Diagram the arguments contained in the following passages.

1. Dear Jim,

    Your distributor is the problem. Here's why. There's no current at the spark plugs. And if there's no current at the plugs, then either your alternator is shot or your distributor is defective. But if the problem were in the alternator, then your dash warning light would be on. So, since the light isn't on, the problem must be in the distributor. Hope this helps.

> Yours,
> Benita Autocraft

2. The slide in the dollar must be stopped. It contributes to inflation and increases the cost of imports. True, it helps exports, but on balance it is bad for the economy.

3. It's high time professional boxing was outlawed. Boxing almost always leads to brain damage, and anything that does that ought to be done away with. Besides, it supports organized crime.

4. They really ought to build a new airport. It would attract more business to the area, not to mention the fact that the old airport is overcrowded and dangerous.

5. Vote for Cuomo? No way. He's too radical, and he's too inexperienced, and those two things make him dangerous. I do like his stand on trade, but I still don't think you should vote for him.

## Exercise 2-18

Diagram the arguments contained in the following passages.

1. Cottage cheese will help you be slender, youthful, and more beautiful. Enjoy it often.

2. If you want to listen to loud music, do it when we are not at home. It bothers us, and we're your parents.

3. If you want to see the best version of *The Three Musketeers*, try the 1948 version. Lana Turner is luscious; Vincent Price is dastardly; Angela Lansbury is exquisitely regal; and nobody ever has or ever will portray D'Artagnan with the grace, athleticism, or skill of Gene Kelly. Download it. It's a must.

4. From a letter to the editor: "The idea of a free press in America today is a joke. A small group of people, the nation's advertisers, control the media more effectively than if they owned it outright. Through fear of an advertising boycott, they can dictate everything from programming to news report content. Politicians as well as editors shiver in their boots at the thought of such a boycott. This situation is intolerable and ought to be changed. I suggest we all listen to National Public Radio and public television."

5. Too many older Americans, veterans with disabilities, and families with children are paying far too much of their incomes for housing. Proposition 168 will help clear the way for affordable housing construction for these groups. Proposition 168 reforms the outdated requirement for an election before affordable housing can even be approved. Requiring elections for every publicly assisted housing venture, even when there is no local opposition, is a waste of taxpayers' money. No other state constitution puts such a roadblock in front of efforts to house senior citizens and others in need. Please support Proposition 168.

6. Decades after President John F. Kennedy's assassination, it's no easier to accept the idea that a loser like Lee Harvey Oswald committed the crime of the century all by himself with a $12.78 mail-order rifle and a $7.17 scope.

Yet even though 2,000+ books and films about the episode have been made, there is no credible evidence to contradict the Warren Commission finding that "the shots which killed President Kennedy and wounded Governor Connally were fired by Lee Harvey Oswald" and that "Oswald acted alone."

After all these years, it's time to accept the conclusion. The nation pays a heavy price for chronic doubts and mistrust. Confidence in the government has declined. Participation in the voting process has steadily slid downward. The national appetite for wild theories encourages peddlers to persist. Evil is never easy to accept. In the case of JFK, the sooner we let it go, the better.

▲ 7. Most schools should offer single-sex classes. Single-sex classes promote learning. Girls do better in math and science courses when they are alone with other girls. Gender offers distractions that interfere with learning. Research also shows that in mixed classrooms most instructors will spend more time answering questions from boys. Schools that offer single-sex classes always report learning gains for students of both sexes.

8. "And we thought we'd heard it all. Now the National Rifle Association wants the U.S. Supreme Court to throw out the ban on private ownership of fully automatic machine guns.

"As the nation's cities reel under staggering murder totals, as kids use guns simply to get even after feuds, as children are gunned down by random bullets, the NRA thinks it is everybody's constitutional right to have their own personal machine gun.

"This is not exactly the weapon of choice for deer hunting or for a homeowner seeking protection. It is an ideal weapon for street gangs and drug thugs in their wars with each other and the police.

"To legalize fully automatic machine guns is to increase the mayhem that is turning this nation—particularly its large cities—into a continual war zone. Doesn't the NRA have something better to do?"

—Capital Times, *Madison, Wisconsin*

9. From a letter to the editor: "Recently the California Highway Patrol stopped me at a drunk-drive checkpoint. Now, I don't like drunk drivers any more than anyone else. I certainly see why the police find the checkpoint system effective. But I think our right to move about freely is much more important. If the checkpoint system continues, then next there will be checkpoints for drugs, seat belts, infant car seats, drivers' licenses. We will regret it later if we allow the system to continue."

▲ 10. "Well located, sound real estate is the safest investment in the world. It is not going to disappear, as can the value of dollars put into savings accounts. Neither will real estate values be lost because of inflation. In fact, property values tend to increase at a pace at least equal to the rate of inflation. Most homes have appreciated at a rate greater than the inflation rate (due mainly to strong buyer demand and insufficient supply of newly constructed homes)."

—*Robert Bruss,* The Smart Investor's Guide to Real Estate

11. "The constitutional guarantee of a speedy trial protects citizens from arbitrary government abuse, but it has at least one other benefit, too. It prevents crime.

"A recent Justice Department study found that more than a third of those with serious criminal records—meaning three or more felony convictions—are arrested for new offenses while free on bond awaiting federal court trial. You don't have to be a social scientist to suspect that the longer the delay, the greater the likelihood of further violations. In short, overburdened courts mean much more than justice delayed; they quite literally amount to the infliction of further injustice."

—*Scripps Howard* News Service

▲ 12. As we enter a new decade, about 200 million Americans are producing data on the Internet as rapidly as they consume it. Each of these users is tracked by technologies ever more able to collate essential facts about them—age, address, credit rating, marital status, etc.—in electronic form for use in commerce. One website, for example, promises, for the meager sum of seven dollars, to scan "over two billion records to create a single comprehensive report on an individual." It is not unreasonable, then, to believe that the combination of capitalism and technology poses a looming threat to what remains of our privacy.

—*Loosely adapted from* Harper's

13. Having your car washed at the car wash may be the best way to go, but there are some possible drawbacks. The International Carwashing Association (ICA) has fought back against charges that automatic car washes, in recycling wash water, actually dump the salt and dirt from one car onto the next. And that brushes and drag cloths hurt the finish. Perhaps there is some truth to these charges.

The ICA sponsored tests that supposedly demonstrated that the average home car wash is harder on a car than an automatic wash. Maybe. But what's "the average" home car wash? And you can bet that the automatic car washes in the test were in perfect working order.

There is no way you or I can tell for certain if the filtration system and washing equipment at the automatic car wash are properly maintained. And even if they are, what happens if you follow some mud-caked pickup through the wash? Road dirt might still be caught in the bristles of the brushes or strips of fabric that are dragged over your car.

Here's my recommendation: Wash your own car.

▲ 14. **Argument in Favor of Measure A**

"Measure A is consistent with the City's General Plan and City policies directing growth to the City's non-agricultural lands. A 'yes' vote on Measure A will affirm the wisdom of well-planned, orderly growth in the City of Chico by approving an amendment to the 1982 Rancho Arroyo Specific Plan. Measure A substantially reduces the amount of housing previously approved for Rancho Arroyo, increases the number of parks and amount of open space, and significantly enlarges and enhances Bidwell Park.

"A 'yes' vote will accomplish the following: • Require the development to dedicate 130.8 acres of land to Bidwell Park • Require the developer to dedicate seven park sites • Create 53 acres of landscaped corridors and greenways • Preserve existing arroyos and protect sensitive plant habitats and other environmental features • Create junior high school and church sites • Plan a series of villages within which, eventually, a total of 2,927 residential dwelling units will be developed • Plan area which will provide onsite job opportunities and retail services."

—*County of Butte sample ballot*

15.                         **Rebuttal to Argument in Favor of Measure A**

"Villages? Can a project with 3,000 houses and 7,000 new residents really be regarded as a 'village'? The Sacramento developers pushing the Rancho Arroyo project certainly have a way with words. We urge citizens of Chico to ignore their flowery language and vote no on Measure A.

"These out-of-town developers will have you believe that their project protects agricultural land. Hogwash! Chico's Greenline protects valuable farmland. With the Greenline, there is enough land in the Chico area available for development to build 62,000 new homes. . . .

"They claim that their park dedications will reduce use of our overcrowded Bidwell Park. Don't you believe it! They want to attract 7,000 new residents to Chico by using Rancho Arroyo's proximity to Bidwell Park to outsell other local housing projects.

"The developers imply that the Rancho Arroyo project will provide a much needed school site. In fact, the developers intend to sell the site to the school district, which will pay for the site with taxpayers' money.

"Chico doesn't need the Rancho Arroyo project. Vote no on Measure A."

*—County of Butte sample ballot*

16. Letter to the editor: "I recently read about a man who killed another man several years ago, then he made a plea-bargain with the District Attorney's office and thus got a reduced charge and a shorter sentence. He didn't even serve all of that sentence, because he got some time off for good behavior. After being out of prison for only a few months, he killed somebody else!

"I cannot understand how our so-called system of 'justice' allows this sort of thing to happen. According to FBI statistics, not a half-hour goes by without there being a murder somewhere in this country. How many of these murders are committed by people who have been released from prison? I can answer that: too many!

"The main reason there are so many people released from prisons is that there are not enough prisons to hold them all. If, on average, there is a murder every half hour, then, on average, there should be an execution every half hour. That would open up some more room in prisons and allow the authorities to keep both killers and non-killers off the streets. We'd all be safer as a result.

"It isn't like the people I'm saying should be executed don't deserve to die. They gave up their right to live the minute they pulled the trigger or wielded the knife or whatever means they used in their crime. We have to get tough about this or none of us will be safe."

*—Corning News & Review*

17. Letter to the editor: "In regard to your editorial, 'Crime bill wastes billions,' let me set you straight. Your paper opposes mandatory life sentences for criminals convicted of three violent crimes, and you whine about how criminals' rights might be violated. Yet you also want to infringe on a citizen's right to keep and bear arms. You say you oppose life sentences for three-time losers because judges couldn't show any leniency toward the criminals no matter how trivial the crime. What is your definition of trivial, busting an innocent child's skull with a hammer?"

*—North State Record*

18. Freedom means choice. This is a truth antiporn activists always forget when they argue for censorship. In their fervor to impose their morality, groups like

Enough Is Enough cite extreme examples of pornography, such as child porn, suggesting that they are easily available in video stores.

This is not the way it is. Most of this material portrays not actions such as this but consensual sex between adults.

The logic used by Enough Is Enough is that, if something can somehow hurt someone, it must be banned. They don't apply this logic to more harmful substances, such as alcohol or tobacco. Women and children are more adversely affected by drunken driving and secondhand smoke than by pornography. Few Americans would want to ban alcohol or tobacco, even though these substances kill hundreds of thousands of people each year.

## Writing Exercises

1. Write a one-page essay in which you determine whether and why it is better (you get to define "better") to look younger than your age, older than your age, or just your age. Then number the premises and conclusions in your essay and diagram it.

2. Should there be a death penalty for first-degree murder? On the top half of a sheet of paper, list considerations supporting the death penalty, and on the bottom half, list considerations opposing it. Take about ten minutes to compile your two lists.

   After everyone is finished, your instructor will call on people to read their lists. He or she will then give everyone about twenty minutes to write a draft of an essay that addresses the issue "Should there be a death penalty for first-degree murder?" Put your name on the back of your essay. After everyone is finished, your instructor will collect the essays and redistribute them to the class. In groups of four or five, read the essays that have been given to your group. Do not look at the names of the authors. Select the best essay in each group. Your instructor will ask each group to read the essay it has selected as best.

   As an alternative, your instructor may have each group rank-order their essays and ask a neighboring group which of their top-ranked essays is best. The instructor will read the top-ranking essays to the class, for discussion.

3. Is it possible to tell just by looking at someone whether he or she is telling the truth? Do a little Internet research and then take a position on the issue and defend it in a two-page essay. This assignment will help prepare you for Chapter 4.

# Clear Thinking, Critical Thinking, and Clear Writing

## Students will learn to . . .

1. Determine acceptable and unacceptable degrees of vagueness

2. Understand and identify types of ambiguity

3. Identify the problems generality causes in language

4. Understand the uses and types of definitions

5. Acquire skills for writing an effective argumentative essay

**T**his appeared as part of an agreement one of your authors was required to sign for a credit card:

> All transactions effected pursuant to this instrument shall be effected for the account and risk and in the name of the undersigned; and the undersigned hereby agrees to indemnify and hold harmless from, and to pay promptly on demand, any and all losses arising therefrom or any debit balance due thereon.

This turns out to mean simply that the cardholder is responsible for anything owed on the account. It is an example of gobbledygook, which is pretentious or unintelligible jargon designed as much to bewilder as to inform.*

This chapter is about dealing with this and other obstacles to clear thinking, speaking, and especially writing. Here's another example of bewildering prose, from former Canadian

---

*The word "gobbledygook" was first used by Texas representative Maury Maverick in 1944 to apply to language often used by government officials.

## Let Obscurity Bloom

Allan Bloom, the famous American educator who authored *The Closing of the American Mind*, which was read (or at least purchased) by millions, wrote in that book:

> If openness means to "go with the flow," it is necessarily an accommodation to the present. That present is so closed to doubt about so many things impeding the progress of its principles that unqualified openness to it would mean forgetting the despised alternative to it, knowledge of which makes us aware of what is doubtful in it.

Is this true? Well, that's hard to say. The problem is that we don't know exactly what Professor Bloom is asserting. It may look profound, but it may be that it simply makes no sense. Whatever he has in mind, he has asked us to work too hard to understand it.

prime minister Jean Chrétien, when asked in Parliament about old versus new money in the health care program:

> They say that the money we had promised three years ago to be new money this year is not new money. We have not paid it yet and it is old money versus new money. For me new money is new money if paying in $5 or $10, it's the same money.*

Those who survived the San Francisco earthquake said, "Thank God, I'm still alive." But, of course, those who died—their lives will never be the same again.

—U.S. SENATOR BARBARA BOXER (D), California

We have no clue what he had in mind.

One of the authors noticed this tease on the front page of a newspaper: "49ers upset." This probably means that somebody who was not supposed to beat the San Francisco football team managed to beat them. On the other hand, it *could* mean that the team is dismayed about something.

Although obscurity can issue from various causes, four are paramount: excessive vagueness, ambiguity, excessive generality, and undefined terms. In this chapter, we will consider vagueness, ambiguity, and generality in some detail and then talk about definitions. We will also provide pointers about writing an argumentative essay, an essay in which one takes a position, supports it, and rebuts contrary positions.

## VAGUENESS

A word or phrase is **vague** if we cannot say with certainty what it includes and excludes. Consider the word "bald." It's clear that Kim Kardashian is *not* bald. It's equally clear that Pitbull *is* bald. (See box on next page.) But there are lots of people in between (including both your authors). Many are borderline cases: It is not clear whether the word "bald" should apply to them—it's the sort of thing about which reasonable people could disagree. Baldness is a vague concept.

■ That we might find Einstein's essay "Foundation of General Relativity" difficult to understand does not mean it is obscure to a trained physicist.

*Reported in the *Globe and Mail*, February 7, 2003.

## Vagueness at the Border

Vagueness results when the scope of a concept is not clear—that is, when there are borderline cases. "Bald" is a typical example. Kim Kardashian is clearly *not* bald and Pitbull clearly *is* bald. But whether Bruce Willis is bald or not is a good question. He has hair—although it seems to be on the wane—but much of the time he keeps his head shaved and thus appears bald. How much hair would he have to lose to be bald whether or not he shaved his head? There is no correct answer. Vague words like "bald," "blond," and "wealthy" clearly apply in some cases, but they all have borderline cases to which it isn't clear whether they apply.

Kim Kardashian

Willis, with . . .

. . . and without

Pitbull

> If I said anything which implies that I think that we didn't do what we should have done given the choices we faced at the time, I shouldn't have said that.
>
> —BILL CLINTON (reported by Larry Engelmann)

> Has anyone put anything in your baggage without your knowledge?
>
> **This question was asked of our colleague Becky White by an airport security employee.**

> Man is ready to die for an idea, provided that idea is not quite clear to him.
>
> —PAUL ELDRIDGE

> Everything is vague to a degree you do not realize until you have tried to make it precise.
>
> —BERTRAND RUSSELL

Vagueness plays an important role in much that we do. In the law, for example, how we deal with vagueness is crucial. Whether the word "torture" applies to various types of interrogation techniques, especially including "waterboarding," for example, has been a serious issue for several years. Whether your driving is "reckless" or not may determine whether you pay a small fine or a large one—or even go to jail. Because "driving too fast for the conditions" is vague, speed limits are clearly spelled out.

Sometimes vagueness is annoying. Suppose it's late and you're looking for someone's house and you're instructed, "go down this street a ways until you get to the first major intersection, make a sharp right, then, when the street starts to curve to the left, you'll be there." The vagueness in these directions is more likely to get your blood pressure up than to help you find your destination. How do you decide that a particular intersection is "major," for example?

Vagueness is often intentionally used to avoid giving a clear, precise answer. Politicians often resort to vague statements if they don't want their audience to know exactly where they stand. A vague answer to the question "Do you love me?" may mean there's trouble ahead in the relationship.

Vagueness occurs in varying degrees, and it is impossible to get rid of it entirely. Fortunately, there is no need to do this. We live comfortably with vagueness in much of what we say. "Butte City is a small town" presents no problems under ordinary circumstances, despite the vagueness of "small town." "Darren has no school loans because his parents are rich" doesn't tell us how much money his parents have, but it tells us enough to be useful. "Rich" and "small," like "bald," are vague words; there is no accepted clear line between the things to which they apply and those to which they don't. Nonetheless, they have their uses. Problems arise with vagueness when there is too much of it, as in our previous direction-giving example.

So, when is a level of vagueness acceptable and when is it not? It's difficult to give a general rule, aside from urging due care and common sense, but we might say this:

> When a claim is too vague to convey appropriately useful information, its level of vagueness is not acceptable.

For example, if you tell your mechanic you have an engine problem, he or she will ask you to be more specific. If we tell you that missing too many classes will have consequences, you will ask us for more details. If the rental car agent tells you there will be refueling charges if you return the car with less than a full tank, you would do well to ask if these include costs other than for gasoline.

## AMBIGUITY

A word, phrase, or sentence is said to be **ambiguous** when it has more than one meaning. Does "Paul cashed a check" mean that Paul gave somebody cash, or that somebody gave cash to him? It could mean either. "Jessica is renting her house" could mean that she's renting it *to* someone or *from* someone. Jennifer gets up from her desk on Friday afternoon and says, "My work here is finished." She might mean that she has finished the account she was working on, or that her whole week's work is done and she's leaving for the weekend, or that she's fed up with her job and is leaving the company. If you look online, you can find several collections of amusing headlines that are funny because of their ambiguity: "Kids make nutritious snacks," for example, or "Miners refuse to work after death."

Most of the time the interpretation that a speaker or writer intends for a claim is obvious, as in the case of these headlines. But ambiguity can have consequences beyond making us smile.

In discussions of gay rights, we've seen an ambiguity in the term "rights" that often stymies rational debate. The issue is whether laws should be passed to prevent discrimination against gays in housing, in the workplace, and so forth. One side claims that such laws would themselves be discriminatory because they would specifically grant to gay people rights that are not specifically guaranteed to others—they would be "special" rights. The other side claims that the laws are only to guarantee for gays the right to be treated the same as others under the law. When the two sides fail to sort out just what

Ask a man which way he is going to vote, and he will probably tell you. Ask him, however, why, and vagueness is all.

—BARNARD LEVIN

Asked why the desertion rate in the army had risen so much, director of plans and resources for Army personnel Roy Wallace replied, "We're asking a lot of soldiers these days."

**You might at first want to know what they're asking the soldiers, until you see the ambiguity in Wallace's remark.**

Marco Rubio is not pleased with this book. Of course, he is not displeased, either, since it's almost certain he's never heard of it. Note the ambiguity in the original statement.

they mean by their key terms, the result is at best a great waste of breath and at worst angry misunderstanding.

## Semantic Ambiguity

A claim can be ambiguous in more than one way. The most obvious way is by containing an ambiguous word or phrase, which produces a case of **semantic ambiguity.** See if you can explain the ambiguity in each of the following claims:

> Collins, the running back, always lines up on the right side.
>
> Jessica is cold.
>
> Aunt Delia never used glasses.

In the first case, it may be that it's the right and not the left side where Collins lines up, *or* it may be that he always lines up on the correct side. The second example may be saying something about Jessica's temperature or something about her personality. In the third case, it may be that Aunt Delia always had good eyes, but it also might mean that she drank her beer directly from the bottle (which was true of one of your authors' Aunt Delia). Semantically ambiguous claims can be made unambiguous ("disambiguated") by substituting a word or phrase that is not ambiguous for the one making the trouble. "Correct" for "right," for example, in #1; "eyeglasses" for "glasses" in #3.

## Grouping Ambiguity

There is a special kind of semantic ambiguity, called **grouping ambiguity,** that results when it is not clear whether a word is being used to refer to a group collectively or to members of the group individually. Consider:

> Secretaries make more money than physicians do.

The example is true if the speaker refers to secretaries and physicians collectively, since there are many more secretaries than there are physicians. But it is obviously false if the two words refer to individual secretaries and physicians.

"Lawn mowers create more air pollution than dirt bikes do" is something a dirt biker might say in defense of his hobby. And, because it is ambiguous, there is an interpretation under which his claim is probably true as well as one under which it is probably false. Taken collectively, lawn mowers doubtlessly create more pollution because there are many more of them. Individually, we'd bet it's the dirt bike that does more damage.

Like other types of ambiguity, grouping ambiguity can be used intentionally to interfere with clear thinking. When taxes are increased, opponents can smear it as "the biggest tax increase in history" if the total revenue brought in by the increase is very large, even if individual taxes have not gone up much.

## Syntactic Ambiguity

**Syntactic ambiguity** occurs when a claim is open to two or more interpretations because of its *structure*—that is, its syntax. Not long ago, one of us received information from the American Automobile Association prior to driving to British

---

What day is the day after three days before the day after tomorrow?

**Complicated, but neither vague nor ambiguous.**

---

The story goes that a burglar and his 16-year-old accomplice tripped a silent alarm while breaking into a building. The accomplice was carrying a pistol, and when police arrived and tried to talk him out of the weapon, the older burglar said, "Give it to him!" whereupon the youngster shot the policeman.

—Courtesy of COLLEN JOHNSON, currently of the California State Prison, Tehachapi

**Ambiguity can be dangerous!**

Columbia. "To travel in Canada," the brochure stated, "you will need a birth certificate or a driver's license and other photo ID." What does this mean? There are two possibilities:

> [You will need a birth certificate or a driver's license] *and* [other photo ID].
> [You will need a birth certificate] *or* [a driver's license and other photo ID].

Depending on the intended interpretation, the original should have been written as either:

> You will need either a birth certificate or a driver's license *and you will also need* an additional photo ID.
> Or
> You will need either a birth certificate or *both* a driver's license and an additional photo ID.

Neither of these is ambiguous.

Here are some other examples of syntactic ambiguity, along with various possible interpretations, to help you get the idea.

> Players with beginners' skills only may use Court 1.

In this case, we don't know what the word "only" applies to. This word, as we'll see in later chapters, is both useful and easy to use incorrectly. Here, it might mean that beginners may use *only Court 1*. Or it might mean that players with *only beginners' skills* may use Court 1. Finally, it might mean that *only players with beginners' skills* may use Court 1. Obviously, whoever puts up such a sign needs to be more careful. (And so does the person who put up a sign in our university's student union that said, "Cash only this line." Do you see the ambiguity?)

> Susan saw the farmer with binoculars.

This ambiguity results from a modifying phrase ("with binoculars") that is not clear in its application. Who had the binoculars in this case? Presumably Susan, but it looks as though it was the farmer. "Looking through her binoculars, Susan saw the farmer" clears it up.

> People who protest often get arrested.

This is similar to the previous example: Does "often" apply to protesting or to getting arrested?

> There's somebody in the bed next to me.

Does "next to me" apply to a person or to a bed? One might rewrite this either as "There's somebody next to me in the bed" or as "There's somebody in the bed next to mine."

**Ambiguous pronoun references** occur when it is not clear to what or whom a pronoun is supposed to refer. "The boys chased the girls and they giggled a lot"

Neurosis is the inability to tolerate ambiguity.

—SIGMUND FREUD

**Okay. But it's still true that we should not have to live with too much of it!**

It's hard enough just to keep track of the things that are really happening, without having to worry about all the things that aren't really happening.

—Former secretary of defense Donald Rumsfeld, at a Department of Defense news briefing

**We suspect the problem is that there are just so many things that are not happening.**

70     CHAPTER 3: CLEAR THINKING, CRITICAL THINKING, AND CLEAR WRITING

## Making Ambiguity Work for You

Have you ever been asked to write a letter of recommendation for a friend who was, well, incompetent? To avoid either hurting your friend's feelings or lying, Robert Thornton of Lehigh University has some ambiguous statements you can use. Here are some examples:

I most enthusiastically recommend this candidate with no qualifications whatsoever.

I am pleased to say that this candidate is a former colleague of mine.

I can assure you that no person would be better for the job.

I would urge you to waste no time in making this candidate an offer of employment.

All in all, I cannot say enough good things about this candidate or recommend the candidate too highly.

In my opinion, you will be very fortunate to get this person to work for you.

does not make clear who did the giggling. "They" could be either the boys or the girls. A similar example: "After their father removed the trash from the pool, the kids played in it." A less amusing and possibly more trouble-making example: "Paul agreed that, once Gary removed the motor from the car, he could have it." What does Gary have permission to take, the motor or the car? We'd predict a lawsuit.

Sometimes examples of ambiguity are difficult to classify. Imagine telling a server, "You can bring the sauce separately, and I'll put it on myself." The ambiguity, obviously, is in *how* the speaker will put the sauce on versus *where* he or she will put it. This could be called either semantic ambiguity or syntactic ambiguity. However, it's more important to see *that* a claim is ambiguous than to be able to classify the type of ambiguity.

### GENERALITY

We turn now to the notion of generality, which is closely related to both vagueness and ambiguity and which can cause trouble in the same way they do.

From what we learned of vagueness, we realize that the word "child" is vague, since it is not clear where the line is drawn between being a child and no longer being a child. It can also be ambiguous, because it can refer not only to a person of immature years but also to a person's offspring. As if this weren't enough, it is also general because it applies to both boys and girls. **Generality** is lack of specificity. A term that refers to all the members of a group is more general than a term that refers to fewer than all members of that group. "Dog" is more general than "otterhound." "Otterhound" is more general than "blue-eyed otterhound." "Clarence was arrested" is more general than "Clarence was arrested for trespassing."

If you learn that Clarence was arrested, it may well lower your estimate of him and may prevent you from hiring him to do work around your house, for example. But if some more detail were supplied—for instance, that he had been arrested during a protest against a company that was polluting the local river—it might well make a difference in your opinion of him. The difference between a very general description and one with more specificity can be crucial to nearly any decision.

Widely discussed these days is whether the War on Terror should really be called a "war" at all. The phrase has continued to be used because "war" is both

The traveler must, of course, always be cautious of the overly broad generalization. But I am an American, and a paucity of data does not stop me from making sweeping, vague, conceptual statements, and, if necessary, following these statements up with troops.

—GEORGE SAUNDERS, *The Guardian,* July 22, 2006

vague and general. Some believe that the word as traditionally used requires an enemy that is organized and identifiable, such as a country or province, and those are difficult to identify in the War on Terror. Still less clearly a war is the so-called War on Drugs. This seems to be a purely metaphorical use of the word "war," meant to show only that somebody is serious about the issue and to justify the expense of prosecuting drug cases.

We don't mean to confuse you with these closely related and overlapping pitfalls—vagueness, ambiguity, and generality. In practical fact, it is less important that you classify the problem that infects a claim or idea than that you see what's going on and can explain it. For example, "Just what do you mean by 'war'?" is a good response to someone who is using the word too loosely. In some of the exercises that follow, we'll ask you to identify problems in different passages in order to help you become familiar with the ideas. In others, we'll simply ask you to explain what is needed for clarification.

Anyhow, with all these potential pitfalls to clear thinking and clear communication, what is a critically thinking person to do? To start, we can do the best we can to be clear in what our words mean. So after the following exercises we will turn our attention to the definition of terms.

Here are several exercises to give you practice identifying precision (or lack thereof) in sentences.

The lettered words and phrases that follow each of the following fragments vary in their precision. In each instance, determine which is the most precise and which is the least precise; then rank the remainder in order of precision, to the extent possible. If these exercises are discussed in class, you'll discover that many leave room for disagreement. Discussion with input from your instructor will help you and your classmates reach closer agreement about items that prove especially difficult to rank.

▲ —See the answers section at the back of the book.

**Exercise 3-1**

**Example**

Over the past ten years, the median income of wage earners in St. Paul
a. nearly doubled
b. increased substantially
c. increased by 85.5 percent
d. increased by more than 85 percent

**Answer**

Choice (b) is the least precise because it provides the least information; (c) is the most precise because it provides the most detailed figure. In between, (d) is the second most precise, followed by (a).

▲ 1. Eli and Sarah
   a. decided to sell their house and move
   b. made plans for the future
   c. considered moving
   d. talked
   e. discussed their future
   f. discussed selling their house

2. Manuel

   a. worked in the yard all afternoon
   b. spent the afternoon planting flowers in the yard
   c. was outside all afternoon
   d. spent the afternoon planting salvia alongside his front sidewalk
   e. spent the afternoon in the yard

3. The American Civil War

   a. was the bloodiest in American history
   b. resulted in the highest percentage of deaths of U.S. males of any war
   c. saw 10 percent of young Northern males and 30 percent of young Southern males lose their lives
   d. resulted in the deaths of approximately 750,000 soldiers, North and South

4. The recent changes in the tax code

   a. will substantially increase taxes paid by those making more than $200,000 per year
   b. will increase by 4 percent the tax rate for those making more than $200,000 per year; will leave unchanged the tax rate for people making between $40,000 and $200,000; and will decrease by 2 percent the tax rate for those making less than $40,000
   c. will make some important changes in who pays what in taxes
   d. are tougher on the rich than the provisions in the previous tax law
   e. raise rates for the wealthy and reduce them for those in the lowest brackets

5. Smedley is absent because

   a. he's not feeling well
   b. he's under the weather
   c. he has an upset stomach and a fever
   d. he's nauseated and has a fever of more than 103°
   e. he has flulike symptoms

6. Candice

   a. had a nice trip to her home town
   b. took a vacation
   c. visited her mother back in Wichita Falls
   d. was out of town for a while
   e. visited her mother

7. Hurricane Sandy

   a. was the second most costly storm to hit the United States
   b. took over 200 lives in seven countries along its path
   c. killed people in several countries
   d. killed 253 people from Jamaica to Canada and did $65 million worth of damage
   e. was the most lethal storm to hit the United States since Katrina

8. The Miami Heat

   a. beat the Atlanta Hawks last night
   b. 104, the Atlanta Hawks 101
   c. squeaked by the Atlanta Hawks last night
   d. beat the Atlanta Hawks by three points in a playoff game last night
   e. won last night

9. Roy and Jaydee are
   a. driving less because they want to reduce auto emissions
   b. trying to reduce their carbon footprint
   c. concerned about the effects of carbon emissions on the world's climate
   d. carpooling with neighbors to keep down the amount of carbon they cause to be emitted
   e. worried about global climate change

10. The Tea Party
    a. was unsuccessful in at least one Senate race
    b. has supported candidates who failed to win in the general election
    c. has caused a shift in the policies adopted by the Republican Party
    d. supported a candidate for the Senate in Missouri who lost the election

You do not always have to classify problematic sentences as too vague, ambiguous, or too general, but practice in doing so can help you learn to spot problems quicker.

Exercise 3-2

For each of the following, determine if it is too vague or too ambiguous, or simply not useful because of either of these faults. Explain your answer.

**Example**

Full implementation of the Affordable Care Act ("Obamacare") will cause a serious increase in health care costs.

**Answer**

This claim is too vague to be very useful. The problem is the phrase "serious increase," which could mean anything within a wide range of cost increases. What is a serious increase to one person may not be serious at all to another.

 1. Full implementation of the Affordable Care Act ("Obamacare") will cause a noticeable decrease in health care costs.

2. I would not advise going to Raymond's party; he invites all kinds of people to those things.

3. Sign in store window: Help Wanted.

4. He chased the girl in his car.

5. Remember, you have an appointment tomorrow afternoon.

6. The new tax plan will only affect rich people.

7. He gave her cat food.

8. Professional football needs new rules about excessive violence in the game.

9. She had her daughter's family over and served them a very nice meal.

10. Headline: Killer sentenced to die for the second time in ten years.

11. You only need modest exercise to stay healthy.

12. Yes, I saw the robber; he looked perfectly ordinary.

13. Prostitutes appeal to the mayor.

14. Athletes have to stay in training year round.

15. They're looking for teachers of Spanish, French, and German.

Source: Hi and Lois: © 1986 King Features Syndicate, Inc., World Rights Reserved.

Exercise 3-3

Which of each set of claims suffers least from excessive vagueness, ambiguity, or excessive generality?

**Example**

    a. The trees served to make shade for the patio.
    b. He served his country proudly.

**Answer**

The use of "served" in (b) is more vague than that in (a). We know exactly what the trees did; we don't know what he did.

    1.  a. Rooney served the church his entire life.
        b. Rooney's tennis serve is impossible to return.

    2.  a. The window served its purpose.
        b. The window served as an escape hatch.

    3.  a. Throughout their marriage, Alfredo served her dinner.
        b. Throughout their marriage, Alfredo served her well.

    4.  a. Minta turned her ankle.
        b. Minta turned to religion.

    5.  a. These scales will turn on the weight of a hair.
        b. This car will turn on a dime.

    6.  a. Fenner's boss turned vicious.
        b. Fenner's boss turned out to be forty-seven.

    7.  a. Time to turn the garden.
        b. Time to turn off the sprinkler.

    8.  a. The wine turned to vinegar.
        b. The wine turned out to be vinegar.

    9.  a. Harper flew around the world.
        b. Harper departed around 3:00 A.M.

    10.  a. Clifton turned out the light.
        b. Clifton turned out the vote.

    11.  a. The glass is full to the brim.
        b. Mrs. Couch has a rather full figure.

12. a. Kathy gave him a full report.
    b. "Oh, no, thank you! I am full."
13. a. Oswald was dealt a full house.
    b. Oswald is not playing with a full deck.
14. a. Money is not the key to happiness.
    b. This is not the key to the garage.
▲ 15. a. Porker set a good example.
    b. Porker set the world record for the 100-meter dash.

## DEFINING TERMS

When today's typical student hears the word "definition," we wouldn't be surprised if the first thing to come to mind is television. "Ultra-high definition" is now the standard of clarity in what we see on the home screen. This is directly analogous to the clarity and distinctness we're looking for as critical thinkers, and the careful definition of terms is one of our most useful tools in pursuing this goal. While the business of definitions may seem straightforward ("'carrot' refers to a tapering, orange-colored root eaten as a vegetable"), you'll soon see that there's more to it than you might have thought. For example, a multitude of attempts have been made to construct a definition of "person" (or, if you like, "human being"). Everything from "rational animal" to "featherless biped" has been suggested. But such important issues as whether abortion is morally permissible, whether fetuses have rights, whether a fetus is correctly referred to as an "unborn child," and doubtless many others—all turn on how we define "person" and some of these other basic concepts. Indeed, if we define "abortion" as "the murder of an unborn child," the debate on abortion is over before it begins.

Some arguments against the acceptance of rights for gay men and lesbians depend on the claim that their orientation is "unnatural."* But to arrive at a definition of "natural" (or "unnatural") is no easy task. If you spend a few minutes thinking about this difficulty—even better, if you discuss it with others—we think you'll see what we mean. What is "natural," depending on who is defining the term, can mean anything from "occurs in nature" to "correct in the eyes of God."

As you will see in Chapter 12, the definition of the word "use" by the U.S. Supreme Court made a difference of thirty years in the sentence of John Angus Smith in a recent criminal case.** Definitions matter. Now, let's have a look at how to deal with them.

### Purposes of Definitions

Definitions can serve several purposes, but we want to call your attention to three:

1. **Lexical definitions** are definitions like those we find in dictionaries; they tell us what a word ordinarily means. (An example from the dictionary: "*Tamarin. noun:* a small, forest-dwelling south American monkey of the marmoset family,

> A definition is the start of an argument, not the end of one.
>
> —NEIL POSTMAN, author of *Amusing Ourselves to Death: Public Discourse in the Age of Show Business*

---

*Here is an example: "[W]e're talking about a particular behavior that most American's [*sic*] consider strange and unnatural, and many Americans consider deeply immoral." "Equal Rights for Homosexuals," by Gregory Kouki, www.str.org/site/News2?page=NewsArticle&id=5226.
**See Exercise 12–13, p. 89, for details.

typically brightly colored and with tufts and crests of hair around the face and neck.") You might ask, Isn't this what all definitions do? A good question, and the answer is *no*. Check the following.

2. **Precising or stipulative definitions** are designed to make a term more precise (i.e. less vague or general) or to stipulate a new or different meaning from the ordinary one. For example, the word "dollars" is too general to be used in its normal sense in an international sales contract, because it could apply to U.S. dollars, Canadian dollars, Australian dollars, etc. So we make the meaning precise by *stipulating* that, *In this contract, the term 'dollars' will refer exclusively to Canadian dollars.*

We can also stipulate that a word will have a new meaning in a given context. For example, *In this environment, 'desktop' means the basic opening screen of the operating system—the one with the trash can.*

3. **Persuasive** or **rhetorical definitions** are used *to persuade or slant* someone's attitude or point of view toward whatever the "defined" term refers to. This kind of definition can be troublesome, because it often distorts the real meaning of a term in order to cause the listener or reader to favor or disfavor a person, policy, object, or event.

If a liberal friend tries to "define" a conservative as *a hidebound, narrow-minded hypocrite who thinks the point to life is making money and ripping off poor people,* you know the point here is not the clarification of the meaning of the word "conservative." It is a way of trashing conservatives. Such rhetorical uses of definitions frequently make use of the *emotive meaning* or the *rhetorical force* of words. By this we mean the positive or negative associations of a word. Consider the difference between *government guaranteed health care* and *a government takeover of health care.* These terms might reasonably be used to refer to the same thing, but they clearly have different emotional associations—one positive and one negative. The word "connotation" is the traditional term for these associations.* Our definition of "abortion" as "the murder of an unborn child" at the beginning of this section is another much-quoted example of this use of definition.

### Kinds of Definitions

The purpose of a definition and the kind of definition it is are different things. (Compare: The *purpose* of food is to nourish our bodies and please our palettes, whereas *kinds* of food are vegetables, meat, Pringles, etc.) Regardless of what purpose is served by defining a term, most definitions are of one of the three following kinds:

1. **Definition by example** (also called **ostensive definition**): Pointing to, naming, or otherwise identifying one or more examples of the sort of thing to which the term applies: *"By 'scripture,' I mean writings like the Bible and the Koran." "A mouse is this thing here, the one with the buttons."*

2. **Definition by synonym:** Giving another word or phrase that means the same as the term being defined. *"'Fastidious' means the same as 'fussy.'" "'Pulsatile' means 'throbbing.'" "To be 'lubricious' is the same as to be 'slippery.'"*

---

*Much more will be said about rhetorical force (emotive meaning, connotation) in Chapter 5.

3. **Analytical definition:** Specifying the features a thing must possess in order for the term being defined to apply to it. These definitions often take the form of a genus-and-species classification. For example, *"A samovar is an urn that has a spigot and is used especially in Russia to boil water for tea." "A mongoose is a ferret-sized mammal native to India that eats snakes and is related to civets."*

Almost all dictionary definitions, often said to be **lexical definitions,** are of the analytical variety.

## Tips on Definitions

So far, we've seen that definitions serve a variety of purposes and take several forms. Combinations can be of many sorts: a definition by synonym that is precising *("minor" means under eighteen)*; an analytical definition designed just to persuade *(a liberal is somebody who wants the able and willing to take care of both the unable and the unwilling).* But what makes a definition a good one?

First, definitions should not prejudice the case against one side of a debate or the other. This is one form of *begging the question,* which will be discussed in detail in Chapter 6. For now, just recall that one cannot usually win a debate simply by insisting on one's own favored definition of key terms, since those who disagree with your position will also disagree with your definitions. Definitions are instances in which people have to try to achieve a kind of neutral ground.

Second, definitions should be clear. They are designed to clear the air, not muddy the water. This means they should be expressed in language that is as clear and simple as the subject will allow. If we define a word in language that is more obscure than the original word, we accomplish nothing. This includes avoiding emotionally charged language.

Third, realize that sometimes you must get along with incomplete definitions. In real life, we sometimes have to deal with claims that include such big-league abstractions as friendship, loyalty, fair play, freedom, rights, and so forth. If you have to give a *complete* definition of "freedom" or "fair play," you'd best not plan on getting home early. Such concepts have subtle and complex parameters that

## Arguments and Tainted Definitions

Definitions, or the lack of them, can cause great confusion in argumentation. Consider the following "argument"

> Whenever you can, you act so as to satisfy your desires.
>
> Acting to satisfy your desires is acting selfishly.
>
> Therefore, whenever you can, you act selfishly.

We hope you're not persuaded by this. If you look carefully at this argument you should notice that hidden in it is an odd "definition" of acting selfishly—acting so as to satisfy your desires. Indeed, given this definition, you act selfishly whenever you can. But the ordinary understanding of acting selfishly is putting your own interests above those of others. Given the ordinary definition of the phrase, you do not necessarily always act selfishly.

If an argument leads to a surprising result, the first thing to do is check definitions!

might take a lifetime to pin down. (Plato, generally recognized as a smart cookie, wrote an entire book in an attempt to define "justice.") For practical purposes, what is usually needed for words like these is not a complete definition but a precise definition that focuses on one aspect of the concept and provides sufficient guidance for the purposes at hand something like, *"To me, the word 'justice' does not include referring to a person's private life when evaluating his or her work performance."*

The following exercise will give you practice with definitions:

**Exercise 3-4**

In groups (or individually if your instructor prefers), determine what term in each of the following is being defined and whether the definition is by example or by synonym or an analytical definition. If it is difficult to tell which kind of definition is present, describe the difficulty.

 1. A piano is a stringed instrument in which felt hammers are made to strike the strings by an arrangement of keys and levers.

2. "Decaffeinated" means without caffeine.

3. Carly Fiorina is my idea of a successful philosophy major.

4. The red planet is Mars.

5. "UV" refers to ultraviolet light.

6. The Cheyenne perfectly illustrate the sort of Native Americans who were Plains Indians.

7. Data, in our case, is raw information collected from survey forms, which is then put in tabular form and analyzed.

8. "Chiaroscuro" is just a fancy word for shading.

9. Bifocals are glasses with two different prescriptions ground into each lens, making it possible to focus at two different distances from the wearer.

10. Red is the color that we perceive when our eyes are struck by light waves of approximately seven angstroms.

11. A significant other can be taken to be a person's spouse, lover, long-term companion, or just girlfriend or boyfriend.

12. "Assessment" means evaluation.

13. A blackout is "a period of total memory loss, as one induced by an accident or prolonged alcoholic drinking." When your buddies tell you they loved your rendition of the Lambada on Madison's pool table the other night and you don't even remember being at Madison's, that is a blackout.

*—Adapted from the CalPoly, San Luis Obispo,* Mustang Daily

14. A pearl, which is the only animal-produced gem, begins as an irritant inside an oyster. The oyster then secretes a coating of nacre around the irritating object. The result is a pearl, the size of which is determined by the number of layers with which the oyster coats the object.

15. According to my cousin, who lives in Tulsa, the phrase "bored person" refers to anybody who is between the ages of sixteen and twenty-five and lives in Eastern Oklahoma.

**79**

## WRITING ARGUMENTATIVE ESSAYS

In an argumentative essay you state an issue, take a position on it, support or defend it, and rebut contrary arguments. This isn't a book on writing, but writing an argumentative essay is so closely related to thinking critically that we would like to take the opportunity to offer our recommendations. We know professors who have retired because they could not bear to read another student essay. As a result, we offer our two bits' worth here in hopes of continuing to see familiar faces.

As we just said, an argumentative essay generally has four components:

> **A statement of the issue**
> **A statement of one's position on that issue**
> **Arguments that support one's position**
> **Rebuttals of arguments** that **support contrary positions**

Ideally, your essay should begin with an introduction to the issue that demonstrates that the issue is important or interesting. This is not always easy, but even when you are not excited about the subject yourself, it is still good practice to try to make your reader interested. Your statement of the issue should be fair; that is, don't try to state the issue in such a way that your position on it is obviously the only correct one. This can make your reader suspicious; the burden of convincing him or her will come later, when you give your arguments.

Your position on the issue should be clear. Try to be brief. If you have stated the issue clearly, it should be a simple matter to identify your position.

Your arguments in support of your position also should be as succinct as you can make them, but it is much more important to be clear than to be brief. After all, this is the heart of your essay. The reasons you cite should be clearly relevant, and they should be either clearly reliable or backed up by further arguments. Much of the rest of this book is devoted to how this is done; hang in there.

If there are well-known arguments for the other side of the issue, you should acknowledge them and offer some reason to believe that they are unconvincing. You can do this either by attacking the premises that are commonly given or by trying to show that those premises do not actually support the opposing conclusion. More on these topics later too.

Following are some more detailed hints that might be helpful in planning and writing an argumentative essay:

1. *Focus.* Make clear at the outset what issue you intend to address and what your position on the issue will be. However, nothing is quite so boring as starting off with the words "In this essay, I will argue that X, Y, and Z," and then going on to itemize everything you are about to say, and at the end concluding with the words "In this essay, I argued that X, Y, and Z." As a matter of style, you should let the reader know what to expect without using trite phrases and without going on at length. However, you should try to find an engaging way to state your position. For example, instead of "In this essay, I will discuss the rights of animals to inherit property from their masters," you might begin, "Could your inheritance wind up belonging to your mother's cat?"

2. *Stick to the issue.* All points you make in an essay should be connected to the issue under discussion and should always either (a) support, illustrate, explain, clarify, elaborate on, or emphasize your position on the issue or (b) serve as responses to anticipated objections. Rid the essay of irrelevancies and dangling thoughts.

3. *Arrange the components of the essay in a logical sequence.* This is just common sense. Make a point before you clarify it, for example, not the other way around.

When supporting your points, bring in examples, clarification, and the like in such a way that a reader knows what in the world you are doing. A reader should be able to discern the relationship between any given sentence and your ultimate objective, and he or she should be able to move from sentence to sentence and from paragraph to paragraph without getting lost or confused. If a reader cannot outline your essay with ease, you have not properly sequenced your material. Your essay might be as fine as a piece of French philosophy, but it would not pass as an argumentative essay.

4. *Be complete.* Accomplish what you set out to accomplish, support your position adequately, and anticipate and respond to possible objections. Keep in mind that many issues are too large to be treated exhaustively in a single essay. The key to being complete is to define the issue sharply enough that you can be complete. Thus, the more limited your topic, the easier it is to be complete in covering it.

Also, be sure there is closure at every level. Sentences should be complete, paragraphs should be unified as wholes (and usually each should stick to a single point), and the essay should reach a conclusion. Incidentally, reaching a conclusion and summarizing are not the same thing. Short essays do not require summaries.

### Good Writing Practices

Understanding the four principles just mentioned is one thing, but actually employing them may be more difficult. Fortunately, there are five practices that a writer can follow to improve the organization of an essay and to help avoid other problems. We offer the following merely as a set of recommendations within the broader scope of thinking critically in writing.

I'm for abolishing and doing away with redundancy.

—J. Curtis McKay, of the Wisconsin State Elections Board (reported by Ross and Petras)

**We ourselves are also for that too.**

1. At some stage *after* the first draft, outline what you have written. Then, make certain the outline is logical and that every sentence in the essay fits into the outline as it should. Some writers create an informal outline before they begin, but many do not. Our advice: Just identify the issue and your position on it, and start writing by stating them both.

   Incidentally, for most people, the hardest sentence to write is the first one. H. L. Mencken once said, "Writing is easy. All you do is stare at a blank piece of paper until drops of blood form on your forehead." We have better advice: Just begin using your keyboard. Say anything. You can always throw away what you write at first, but just the act of writing will help you get started. Eventually, you'll say something relevant to your topic and then you're off and running.

2. Revise your work. Revising is the secret to good writing. Even major-league writers revise what they write, and they revise continuously. Unless you are more gifted than the very best professional writers, revise, revise, revise. Don't think in terms of two or three drafts. Think in terms of *innumerable* drafts.

3. Have someone else read your essay and offer criticisms of it. Revise as required.

4. If you have trouble with grammar or punctuation, reading your essay out loud may help you detect problems your eyes have missed.

5. After you are completely satisfied with the essay, put it aside. Then, come back to it later for still further revisions.

### Essay Types to Avoid

Seasoned instructors know that the first batch of essays they get from a class will include samples of each of the following types. We recommend avoiding these mistakes:

- **The Windy Preamble.** Writers of this type of essay avoid getting to the issue and instead go on at length with introductory remarks, often about how important the issue is, how it has troubled thinkers for centuries, how opinions on the issue are many and various, and so on, and so on. Anything you write that smacks of "When in the course of human events . . . " should go into the trash can immediately.

- **The Stream-of-Consciousness Ramble.** This type of essay results when writers make no attempt to organize their thoughts and simply spew them out in the order in which they come to mind.

- **The Knee-Jerk Reaction.** In this type of essay, writers record their first reaction to an issue without considering the issue in any depth or detail. It always shows.

- **The Glancing Blow.** In this type of essay, writers address an issue obliquely. If they are supposed to evaluate the health benefits of bicycling, they will bury the topic in an essay on the history of cycling; if they are supposed to address the history of cycling, they will talk about the benefits of riding bicycles throughout history.

- **Let the Reader Do the Work.** Writers of this type of essay expect the reader to follow them through *non sequiturs,* abrupt shifts in direction, and irrelevant sidetracks.

## And While We're on the Subject of Writing

Don't forget these rules of good style:

1. Avoid clichés like the plague.
2. Be more or less specific.
3. NEVER generalize.
4. The passive voice is to be ignored.
5. Never, ever be redundant.
6. Exaggeration is a billion times worse than understatement.
7. Make sure verbs agree with their subjects.
8. Why use rhetorical questions?
9. Parenthetical remarks (however relevant) are (usually) unnecessary.
10. Proofread carefully to see if you any words out.
11. And it's usually a bad idea to start a sentence with a conjunction.

This list has been making the rounds on the Internet.

## Persuasive Writing

The primary aim of argumentation and the argumentative essay is to support or demonstrate a position on an issue. Good writers, however, write for an audience and hope their audience will find what they write persuasive. If you are writing for an audience of people who think critically, it is helpful to adhere to these principles:

> Confine your discussion of an opponent's point of view to issues rather than personal considerations.
>
> When rebutting an opposing viewpoint, avoid being strident or insulting. Don't call opposing arguments absurd or ridiculous.
>
> If an opponent's argument is good, concede that it is good.
>
> If space or time is limited, be sure to concentrate on the most important considerations. Don't become obsessive about refuting every last criticism of your position.
>
> Present your strongest arguments first.

There is nothing wrong with trying to make a persuasive case for your position. However, in this book we place more emphasis on making and recognizing good arguments than on simply devising effective techniques of persuasion. Some people can be persuaded by poor arguments and doubtful claims, and an argumentative essay can be effective as a piece of propaganda even when it is a rational and critical failure. One of the most difficult things you are called upon to do as a critical thinker is to construct and evaluate claims and arguments independently of their power to win a following. The remainder of this book—after a section on writing and diversity—is devoted to this task.

## Writing in a Diverse Society

In closing, it seems appropriate to mention how important it is to avoid writing in a manner that reinforces questionable assumptions and attitudes about people's gender, ethnic background, religion, sexual orientation, physical ability or disability, or other characteristics. This isn't just a matter of ethics; it is a matter of clarity and good sense. Careless word choices relative to such characteristics not only are imprecise and inaccurate but also may be viewed as biased even if they were not intended to be, and thus they may diminish the writer's credibility. Worse, using sexist or racist language may distort the writer's own perspective and keep him or her from viewing social issues clearly and objectively.

"Always" and "never" are two words you should always remember never to use.

—WENDELL JOHNSON

Another tip on writing.

But language isn't entirely *not* a matter of ethics, either. We are a society that aspires to be just, a society that strives not to withhold its benefits from individuals on the basis of their ethnic or racial background, skin color, religion, gender, or disability. As a people, we try to end practices and change or remove institutions that are unjustly discriminatory. Some of these unfair practices and institutions are, unfortunately, embedded in our language.

Some common ways of speaking and writing, for example, assume that "normal" people are all white males. It is still not uncommon, for instance, to mention a person's race, gender, or ethnic background if the person is *not* a white male, and *not* to do so if the person *is*. Of course, it may be relevant to whatever you are writing about to state that this particular individual is a male of Irish descent, or whatever; if so, there is absolutely nothing wrong with saying so.

Some language practices are particularly unfair to women. Imagine a conversation among three people, you being one of them. Imagine that the other two talk only to each other. When you speak, they listen politely; but when you are finished, they continue as though you had never spoken. Even though what you say is true and relevant to the discussion, the other two proceed as though you were invisible. Because you are not being taken seriously, you are at a considerable disadvantage. You have reason to be unhappy.

In an analogous way, women have been far less visible in language than men and have thus been at a disadvantage. Another word for the human race is not "woman," but "man" or "mankind." The generic human has often been referred to as "he." How do you run a project? You *man* it. Who supervises the department or runs the meeting? The chair*man*. Who heads the crew? The fore*man*. Picture a research scientist to yourself. Got the picture? Is it a picture of a *woman?* No? That's because the standard picture, or stereotype, of a research scientist is a picture of a man. Or, read this sentence: "Research scientists often put their work before their personal lives and neglect their husbands." Were you surprised by the last word? Again, the stereotypical picture of a research scientist is a picture of a man.

A careful and precise writer finds little need to converse in the lazy language of stereotypes, especially those that perpetuate prejudice. As long as the idea prevails that the "normal" research scientist is a man, women who are or who wish to become research scientists will tend to be thought of as out of place. So they must carry an *extra* burden, the burden of showing that they are *not* out of place. That's unfair. If you unthinkingly always write, "The research scientist . . . he," you are perpetuating an image that places women at a disadvantage. Some research scientists are men, and some are women. If you wish to make a claim about male research scientists, do so. But if you wish to make a claim about research scientists in general, don't write as though they were all males.

The rule to follow in all cases is this: Keep your writing free of *irrelevant implied evaluation* of gender, race, ethnic background, religion, or any other human attribute.

**Recap**

This list summarizes the topics covered in this chapter:

- Clarity of language is extremely important to the ability to think critically.
- Clarity of language can often be lost as a result of multiple causes, including, importantly, vagueness, ambiguity, and generality.
- Vagueness is a matter of degree; what matters is not being too vague for the purposes at hand.
- A statement is ambiguous when it is subject to more than one interpretation and it isn't clear which interpretation is the correct one.
- Some main types of ambiguity are semantic ambiguity, syntactic ambiguity, grouping ambiguity, and ambiguous pronoun reference.
- A claim is overly general when it lacks sufficient detail to restrict its application to the immediate subject.
- To reduce vagueness or eliminate ambiguity, or when new or unfamiliar words are brought into play, or familiar words are used in an unusual way, definitions are our best tool.

- The most common types of definitions are definition by synonym, definition by example, and analytical definition.
- Some "definitions" are used not to clarify meaning but to express or influence attitude. This is known as the rhetorical use of definition.
- The rhetorical use of definitions accomplishes its ends by means of the rhetorical force (emotive meaning) of terms.
- Critical thinking done on paper is known as an argumentative essay, a type of writing worth mastering, perhaps by following our suggestions.

## Additional Exercises

### Exercise 3-5

Are the italicized words or phrases in each of the following too imprecise given the implied context? Explain.

1. Please cook this steak *longer*. It's too rare.
2. If you get ready for bed quickly, Mommy has a *surprise* for you.
3. This program contains language that some viewers may find offensive. It is recommended for *mature* audiences only.
4. *Turn down the damned noise!* Some people around here want to sleep!
5. Based on our analysis of your eating habits, we recommend that you *lower* your consumption of sugar and refined carbohydrates.
6. NOTICE: Hazard Zone. *Small* children not permitted beyond this sign.
7. SOFAS CLEANED: $150 & *up*. MUST SEE TO GIVE *EXACT* PRICES.
8. And remember, all our mufflers come with a *lifetime guarantee*.
9. CAUTION: *To avoid* unsafe levels of carbon monoxide, do not set the wick on your kerosene stove *too high*.
10. Uncooked Frosting: Combine 1 unbeaten egg white, ½ cup corn syrup, ½ teaspoon vanilla, and dash salt. Beat with electric mixer until of fluffy spreading consistency. Frost cake. Serve *within a few hours* or refrigerate.

### Exercise 3-6

Read the following passage, paying particular attention to the italicized words and phrases. Determine whether any of these expressions are too vague in the context in which you find them here.

Term paper assignment: Your paper *should be* typed, *between eight and twelve pages in length,* and double-spaced. You should *make use of* at least three *sources*. Grading will be based on *organization, use of sources, clarity of expression, quality of reasoning,* and *grammar*.

A *rough draft* is due *before Thanksgiving*. The final version is due *at the end of the semester*.

## Exercise 3-7

Read the following passage, paying particular attention to the italicized words and phrases. All of these expressions would be too imprecise for use in *some* contexts; determine which are and which are not too imprecise in *this* context.

> In view of what can happen in twelve months to the fertilizer you apply at any one time, you can see why just one annual application may not be adequate. Here is a guide to timing the *feeding* of some of the more common types of garden flowers.
>
> Feed begonias and fuchsias *frequently* with label-recommended amounts or less frequently with *no more than half* the recommended amount. Feed roses with *label-recommended amounts* as a *new year's growth begins* and as *each bloom period ends.* Feed azaleas, camellias, rhododendrons, and *similar* plants *immediately after bloom* and again *when the nights begin cooling off.* Following these simple instructions can help your flower garden be as attractive as it can be.

## Exercise 3-8

Rewrite the following claims to remedy problems of ambiguity. Do *not* assume that common sense by itself solves the problem. If the ambiguity is intentional, note this fact, and do not rewrite.

**Example**

> Former professional football player Jim Brown was accused of assaulting a thirty-three-year-old woman with a female accomplice.

**Answer**

> This claim is syntactically ambiguous because grammatically it isn't clear what the phrase "with a female accomplice" modifies—Brown, the woman who was attacked, or, however bizarre it might be, the attack itself (he might have thrown the accomplice at the woman). To make it clear that Brown had the accomplice, the phrase "with a female accomplice" should have come right after the word "Brown" in the original claim.

1. The Raider tackle threw a block at the Giants linebacker.
2. Please close the door behind you.
3. We heard that he informed you of what he said in his letter.
4. "How Therapy Can Help Torture Victims"

   —*Headline in newspaper*

5. Charles drew his gun.
6. They were both exposed to someone who was ill a week ago.
7. Chelsea has Hillary's nose.
8. I flush the cooling system regularly and just put in new thermostats.
9. "Tuxedos Cut Ridiculously!"

   —*An ad for formal wear, quoted by Herb Caen*

10. "Police Kill 6 Coyotes After Mauling of Girl."

    —*Headline in newspaper*

11. "We promise nothing."

*—Aquafina advertisement*

12. A former governor of California, Pat Brown, viewing an area struck by a flood, is said to have remarked, "This is the greatest disaster since I was elected governor."

*—Quoted by Lou Cannon in the* Washington Post

13. "Besides Lyme disease, two other tick-borne diseases, babesiosis and HGE, are infecting Americans in 30 states, according to recent studies. A single tick can infect people with more than one disease."

*—Self magazine*

14. "Don't freeze your can at the game."

*—Commercial for Miller beer*

15. Volunteer help requested: Come prepared to lift heavy equipment with construction helmet and work overalls.

16. "GE: We bring good things to life."

*—Television commercial*

17. "Tropicana 100% Pure Florida Squeezed Orange Juice. You can't pick a better juice."

*—Magazine advertisement*

18. "It's biodegradable! So remember, Arm and Hammer laundry detergent gets your wash as clean as can be [pause] without polluting our waters."

*—Television commercial*

19. If you crave the taste of a real German beer, nothing is better than Dunkelbrau.

20. Independent laboratory tests prove that Houndstooth cleanser gets your bathroom cleaner than any other product.

21. We're going to look at lots this afternoon.

22. Jordan could write more profound essays.

23. "Two million times a day Americans love to eat, Rice-a-Roni—the San Francisco treat."

*—Advertisement*

24. "New York's first commercial human sperm-bank opened Friday with semen samples from 18 men frozen in a stainless steel tank."

*—Strunk and White,* The Elements of Style

25. She was disturbed when she lay down to nap by a noisy cow.

26. "More than half of expectant mothers suffer heartburn. To minimize symptoms, suggests Donald O. Castell, M.D., of the Graduate Hospital in Philadelphia, avoid big, high-fat meals and don't lie down for three hours after eating."

*—Self magazine*

27. "Abraham Lincoln wrote the Gettysburg address while traveling from Washington to Gettysburg on the back of an envelope."

*—Richard Lederer*

▲ 28. "When Queen Elizabeth exposed herself before her troops, they all shouted 'harrah.'"

*—Richard Lederer*

29. "In one of Shakespeare's famous plays, Hamlet relieves himself in a long soliloquy."

*—Richard Lederer*

30. The two suspects fled the area before the officers' arrival in a white Ford Mustang, being driven by a third male.

▲ 31. "AT&T, for the life of your business."

▲ 32. The teacher of this class might have been a member of the opposite sex.

▲ 33. "Woman gets 9 years for killing 11th husband."

*—Supposedly, a Headline in newspaper*

34. "Average hospital costs are now an unprecedented $3,146 per day in California. Many primary plans don't pay 20% of that amount."

*—AARP Group Health Insurance Program advertisement*

35. "I am a huge Mustang fan."

*—Ford Mustang advertisement*

36. "Visitors are expected to complain at the office between the hours of 9:00 and 11:00 A.M. daily."

*—Supposedly, a sign in an Athens, Greece, hotel*

37. "Order your summers suit. Because is big rush we will execute customers in strict rotation."

*—Supposedly, a sign in a Rhodes tailor shop*

38. "Please do not feed the animals. If you have any suitable food, give it to the guard on duty."

*—Supposedly, a sign at a Budapest zoo*

39. "Our wines leave you with nothing to hope for."

*—Supposedly, from a Swiss menu*

40. "Our Promise—Good for life."

*—Cheerios*

41. Thinking clearly involves hard work.

42. "Cadillac—Break Through"

## Exercise 3-9

Determine which of the italicized expressions are ambiguous, which are more likely to refer to the members of the class taken as a group, and which are more likely to refer to the members of the class taken individually.

**Example**

*Narcotics* are habit forming.

**Answer**

In this claim, *narcotics* refers to individual members of the class because it is specific narcotics that are habit forming. (One does not ordinarily become addicted to the entire class of narcotics.)

1. *Swedes* eat millions of quarts of yogurt every day.
2. *Professors at the university* make millions of dollars a year.
3. *Our amplifiers* can be heard all across the country.
4. *Students at Pleasant Valley High School* enroll in hundreds of courses each year.
5. *Cowboys* die with their boots on.
6. The *angles of a triangle* add up to 180 degrees.
7. *The New York Giants* played mediocre football last year.
8. On our airline, *passengers* have their choice of three different meals.
9. On our airline, *passengers* flew fourteen million miles last month without incident.
10. *Hundreds of people* have ridden in that taxi.
11. *All our cars* are on sale for two hundred dollars over factory invoice.
12. *Chicagoans* drink more beer than *New Yorkers*.
13. *Power lawn mowers* produce more pollution than *motorcycles*.
14. *The Baltimore Orioles* may make it to the World Series in another six or seven years.
15. *People* are getting older.

## Exercise 3-10

Determine which of the following definitions are more likely designed to persuade and which are not.

1. "Punk is musical freedom. It's saying, doing and playing what you want. In Webster's terms, 'nirvana' means freedom from pain, suffering and the external world, and that's pretty close to my definition of Punk Rock."

   —*Kurt Cobain*

2. "Congress's definition of torture . . . [is] the infliction of severe mental or physical pain."

   —*John Yoo*

3. "'Democrats' definition of 'rich'—always seems to be set just above whatever the salary happens to be for a member of Congress. Perhaps that says it all."

   —*Steve Steckler*

4. "That is the definition of faith—acceptance of that which we imagine to be true, that which we cannot prove."

   —*Dan Brown*

5. "Sin: That's anything that's so much fun it's difficult not to do it."

*—Dave Kilbourne*

## Exercise 3-11

Make up six definitions, two of which are designed to make the thing defined look good, two of which are designed to make it look bad, and two of which are neutral.

## Exercise 3-12

The sentences in this Associated Press health report have been scrambled. Rearrange them so that the report makes sense.

1. The men, usually strong with no known vices or ailments, die suddenly, uttering an agonizing groan, writhing and gasping before succumbing to the mysterious affliction.
2. Scores of cases have been reported in the United States during the past decade.
3. In the United States, health authorities call it "Sudden Unexplained Death Syndrome," or "SUDS."
4. Hundreds of similar deaths have been noted worldwide.
5. The phenomenon is known as "lai tai," or "nightmare death," in Thailand.
6. In the Philippines, it is called "bangungut," meaning "to rise and moan in sleep."
7. Health officials are baffled by a syndrome that typically strikes Asian men in their thirties while they sleep.
8. Researchers cannot say what is killing SUDS victims.

## Exercise 3-13

 The sentences in the following passage have been scrambled. Rearrange them so that the passage makes sense. You'll find an answer in the answers section.

1. Weintraub's findings were based on a computer test of 1,101 doctors twenty-eight to ninety-two years old.
2. She and her colleagues found that the top ten scorers aged seventy-five to ninety-two did as well as the average of men under thirty-five.
3. "The test measures memory, attention, visual perception, calculation, and reasoning," she said.
4. "The studies also provide intriguing clues to how that happens," said Sandra Weintraub, a neuropsychologist at Harvard Medical School in Boston.
5. "The ability of some men to retain mental function might be related to their ability to produce a certain type of brain cell not present at birth," she said.
6. The studies show that some men manage to escape the trend of declining mental ability with age.
7. Many elderly men are at least as mentally able as the average young adult, according to recent studies.

## Exercise 3-14

This billboard, one of many put up across the country in recent times, was sponsored by the local (Butte County, California) Coalition of Reason and the national United Coalition of Reason. The billboards created controversy in many towns, and as happened in many other parts of the country, at least one local billboard was vandalized. (The word "Don't" was painted over.)

In a brief essay of no more than two pages, present a case on one side or the other of this issue: Should an organization be allowed to put up billboards that many members of a community will find offensive?

## Exercise 3-15

Rewrite each of the following claims in gender-neutral language.

**Example**

We have insufficient manpower to complete the task.

**Answer**

We have insufficient personnel to complete the task.

1. A student should choose his major with considerable care.
2. When a student chooses his major, he must do so carefully.
3. The true citizen understands his debt to his country.
4. If a nurse can find nothing wrong with you in her preliminary examination, she will recommend a physician to you. However, in this city the physician will wish to protect himself by having you sign a waiver.
5. You should expect to be interviewed by a personnel director. You should be cautious when talking to him.
6. The entrant must indicate that he has read the rules, that he understands them, and that he is willing to abide by them. If he has questions, then he should bring them to the attention of an official, and he will answer them.
7. A soldier should be prepared to sacrifice his life for his comrades.
8. If anyone wants a refund, he should apply at the main office and have his identification with him.

9. The person who has tried our tea knows that it will neither keep him awake nor make him jittery.

▲ 10. If any petitioner is over sixty, he (she) should have completed form E-7.

11. Not everyone has the same beliefs. One person may not wish to put himself on the line, whereas another may welcome the chance to make his view known to his friends.

12. God created man in his own image.

▲ 13. Language is nature's greatest gift to mankind.

14. Of all the animals, the most intelligent is man.

15. The common man prefers peace to war.

▲ 16. The proof must be acceptable to the rational man.

▲ 17. The Founding Fathers believed that all men are created equal.

18. Man's pursuit of happiness has led him to prefer leisure to work.

19. When the individual reaches manhood, he is able to make such decisions for himself.

▲ 20. If an athlete wants to play for the National Football League, he should have a good work ethic.

21. The new city bus service has hired several women drivers.

22. The city is also hiring firemen, policemen, and mailmen; and the city council is planning to elect a new chairman.

23. Harold Vasquez worked for City Hospital as a male nurse.

▲ 24. Most U.S. senators are men.

25. Mr. and Mrs. Macleod joined a club for men and their wives.

26. Mr. Macleod lets his wife work for the city.

▲ 27. Macleod doesn't know it, but Mrs. Macleod is a women's libber.

28. Several coeds have signed up for the seminar.

29. A judge must be sensitive to the atmosphere in his courtroom.

▲ 30. To be a good politician, you have to be a good salesman.

## Classroom/Writing Exercise

This exercise is designed for use in the classroom, although your instructor may make a different kind of assignment. Consider the claim, "genetically modified food is unnatural." Many people agree or disagree with this statement even though they have only the most rudimentary idea of what it might mean. Discuss what you think might be meant by the claim, taking note of any vagueness or ambiguity that might be involved.

## More Writing Exercises

Everyone, no matter how well he or she writes, can improve. And the best way to improve is to practice. Since finding a topic to write about is often the hardest part of a writing assignment, we're supplying three subjects for you to write about. For each—or whichever your instructor might assign—write a one- to two-page essay in which you clearly identify the issue (or issues), state your position on the issue (a hypothetical position if you don't have one), and give at least one good reason in support of your position. Try also to give at least one reason why the opposing position is wrong.

1. The exchange of dirty hypodermic needles for clean ones, or the sale of clean ones, is legal in many states. In such states, the transmission of HIV and hepatitis from dirty needles is down dramatically. But bills [in the California legislature] to legalize clean-needle exchanges have been stymied by the last two governors, who earnestly but incorrectly believed that the availability of clean needles would increase drug abuse. Our state, like every other state that has not yet done it, should immediately approve legislation to make clean needles available.

> *—Adapted from an editorial by Marsha N. Cohen,*
> *professor of law at Hastings College of Law*

2. On February 11, 2003, the Eighth Circuit Court of Appeals ruled that the state of Arkansas could force death-row prisoner Charles Laverne Singleton to take antipsychotic drugs to make him sane enough to execute. Singleton was to be executed for felony capital murder but became insane while in prison. "Medicine is supposed to heal people, not prepare them for execution. A law that asks doctors to make people well so that the government can kill them is an absurd law," said David Kaczynski, the executive director of New Yorkers Against the Death Penalty.

3. Some politicians make a lot of noise about how Canadians and others pay much less for prescription drugs than Americans do. Those who are constantly pointing to the prices and the practices of other nations when it comes to pharmaceutical drugs ignore the fact that those other nations lag far behind the United States when it comes to creating new medicines. Canada, Germany, and other countries get the benefits of American research but contribute much less than the United States does to the creation of drugs. On the surface, these countries have a good deal, but in reality everyone is worse off, because the development of new medicines is slower than it would be if worldwide prices were high enough to cover research costs.

> *—Adapted from an editorial by Thomas Sowell,*
> *senior fellow at the Hoover Institution*

4. If a law is unjust, but the lawmaking process can't overturn the law in a timely way, then justice demands that the law be broken.

> *—Paraphrase of Henry David Thoreau*

# 4

# Credibility

Raymond James Merrill was in a funk. He had broken up with his girlfriend, and he did not want to be alone. Then a website that featured "Latin singles" led him to Regina Rachid, an attractive woman with a seductive smile who lived in southern Brazil, and suddenly Merrill was in love. Desperately so, it seems. He believed everything Rachid told him and was credulous enough to make three trips to Brazil to be with her, to give her thousands of dollars in cash, and to buy her a $20,000 automobile. He even refused to blame her when thousands of dollars in unexplained charges turned up on his credit card account. Sadly, Rachid was more interested in Merrill's money than in his affection, and when he went to Brazil the third time, to get married and begin a new life, he disappeared. The story ended tragically: Merrill's strangled and burned body was found in an isolated spot several miles out of town. Rachid and two accomplices were put in jail for the crime.* The moral of the story: It can be a horrible mistake to let our needs and desires overwhelm our critical abilities when we are not sure with whom or with what we're dealing. Our focus in this chapter is on how to determine when a claim or a source of a claim is credible enough to warrant belief.

A second story, less dramatic but much more common, is about a friend of ours named Dave, who not long ago received

## Students will learn to . . .

1. Evaluate the sources of claims
2. Evaluate the content of claims
3. Evaluate the credibility of sources
4. Understand the influences and biases behind media messages
5. Understand the impact of advertising on consumer behavior

*The whole story can be found at www.justice4raymond.org.

"All I know is what's on the internet."

—Donald J. Trump

an email from Citibank. It notified him that there might be a problem with his credit card account and asked him to visit the bank's website to straighten things out. A link was provided to the website. When he visited the site, he was asked to confirm details of his personal information, including account numbers, Social Security number, and his mother's maiden name. The website looked exactly like the Citibank website he had visited before, with the bank's logo and other authentic-appearing details. But very shortly after this episode, he discovered that his card had paid for a new smart phone, a home theater set, and a couple of expensive car stereos, none of which he had ordered or received.

Dave was a victim of "phishing," a ploy to identify victims for identity theft and credit card fraud. The number of phishing scams continues to rise, with millions of people receiving phony emails alleging to be from eBay, PayPal, and other Internet companies as well as an assortment of banks and credit card companies. Some of these phishing expeditions threaten to suspend or close the individual's account if no response is made. Needless to say, a person should give *no credibility* to an email that purports to be from a bank or other company and asks for personal identifying information via email or a website.

There are two grounds for suspicion in cases where credibility is the issue. The first ground is the claim itself. Dave should have asked himself just how likely it is that Citibank would notify him of a problem with his account by email and would ask him for his personal identifying information. (Once again, *no* bank will approach its customers for such information by email or telephone.) The second ground for suspicion is the source of the claim. In this case, Dave believed the source was legitimate. But here's the point, one that critical thinkers are well aware of these days: *On the Internet, whether by website or email, the average person has no idea where the stuff on the computer screen comes from.* Computer experts have methods that can sometimes identify the source of an email, but most of us are very easy to mislead.

## The Nigerian Advance Fee 4-1-9 Fraud: The Internet's Longest-Running Scam Is Still Running Strong

If you have an email account, chances are you've received an offer from someone in Nigeria, probably claiming to be a Nigerian civil servant, who is looking for someone just like you who has a bank account to which several millions of dollars can be sent—money that results from "overinvoicing" or "double invoicing" oil purchases or otherwise needs laundering outside the country. You will receive a generous percentage of the money for your assistance, but you will have to help a bit at the outset by sending some amount of money to facilitate the transactions, or to show *your* good faith!

This scam, sometimes called "4-1-9 Fraud," after the relevant section of Nigeria's criminal code, is now celebrating more than forty years of existence. (It operated by letter, telephone and fax before the web was up and running.) Its variations are creative and numerous. Critical thinkers immediately recognize the failure of credibility such offers have, but thousands of people have not, and from a lack of critical thinking skills or from simple greed, hundreds of millions of dollars have been lost to the perpetrators of this fraud.

To read more about this scam, google "419 scam."

Dave is no dummy; being fooled by such scams is not a sign of a lack of intelligence. His concern that his account might be suspended caused him to overlook the ominous possibility that the original request might be a fake. In other cases, such as the one described in the "4-1-9 Fraud" box, it may be wishful thinking or a touch of simple greed that causes a person to lower his or her credibility guard.

Every time we revise and update this book, we feel obliged to make our warnings about Internet fraud more severe.* And every time we seem to be borne out by events. The level of theft, fraud, duplicity, and plain old vandalism seems to rise like a constant tide. We'll have some suggestions for keeping yourself, your records, and your money safe later in the chapter. For now, just remember that you need your critical thinking lights on whenever you open your browser.

## THE CLAIM AND ITS SOURCE

As indicated in the phishing story, there are two arenas in which we assess credibility: the first is that of *claims* themselves; the second is the claims' *sources*. If we're told that ducks can communicate by quacking in Morse code, we dismiss the claim immediately. Such claims lack credibility no matter where they come from. (They have no initial plausibility, a notion that will be explained later.) But the claim that ducks mate for life is not at all outrageous; it might be true: it's a credible claim.** Whether we should believe it depends on its source; if we read it in a bird book or hear it from a bird expert, we are much more likely to believe it than if we hear it from our editor, for example.

There are degrees of credibility and incredibility; they are not all-or-nothing kinds of things, whether we're talking about claims or sources. Consider the claim that a month from now everyone in the world will die in an epidemic caused by a mysterious form of bacteria. This is highly unlikely, of course, but it is not as unlikely as the claim that everyone in the world will die a month from now due to an invasion of aliens from outer space. Sources (i.e., people) vary in their credibility just as do the claims they offer. If the next-door neighbor you've always liked is arrested for bank robbery, his denials will probably seem credible to you. But he loses credibility if it turns out he owns a silencer and a .45 automatic with the serial numbers removed. Similarly, a knowledgeable friend who tells us about an investment opportunity has a bit more credibility if we learn he has invested his own money in the idea. (At least we could be assured he believed the information himself.) On the other hand, he has less credibility if we learn he will make a substantial commission from our investment in it.

So, there are always two questions to be asked about a claim with which we're presented. First, when does a *claim itself* lack credibility—that is, when does its *content* present a credibility problem? Second, when does the *source* of a claim lack credibility?

We'll turn next to the first of these questions, which deals with what a claim actually says. The general answer is

> A claim lacks inherent credibility to the extent that it conflicts with what we have observed or what we think we know—our background information—or with other credible claims.

---

*Recently, one of the authors had his bank account raided and four phony payments totaling almost $2,000 were made to his utility company. The money actually went to some private source. Both the author and his credit union were reimbursed for the loss. Moral: check accounts frequently!

**Bank vultures, swans, albatrosses, and several other species reportedly mate for life.

Just what this answer means will be explained in the section that follows. After that, we'll turn our attention to the second question we asked earlier, about the credibility of sources.

## ASSESSING THE CONTENT OF THE CLAIM

So, some claims stand up on their own; they tend to be acceptable regardless of from whom we hear them. But when they fail on their own, as we've said, it's because they come into conflict either with our own observations or with what we call our "background knowledge." We'll discuss each of these in turn.

### Does the Claim Conflict with Our Personal Observations?

Our own observations provide our most reliable source of information about the world. It is therefore only reasonable to be suspicious of any claim that comes into conflict with what we've observed. Imagine that Moore has just come from the home of Mr. Marquis, a mutual friend of his and Parker's, and has seen his new red Mini Cooper automobile. He meets Parker, who tells him, "I heard that Marquis has

## Incredible Claims!

Lunatic headlines from the supermarket tabloids (as well as from "straight" newspapers) provide more fun than information. Most of the following are from the *Weekly World News.*

**Statistics show that teen pregnancy drops off significantly after age 25.**
[Amazing what you can prove with statistics.]

**Homicide victims rarely talk to police.**
[Or to anybody else.]

**Starvation can lead to health hazards.**
[Dr. Donohue's health column breaking new dietary ground.]

**End of World Confirmed (December 20, 2012)**
[Mayan archaeologists met in Guatemala and confirmed the end date of December 20, 2012.]

**End of the World Postponed (December 21, 2012)**
[Make up your mind.]

**China Buys Grand Canyon**
[They're trying to figure out how to move it nearer to Beijing.]

**Aliens Abduct Cheerleaders**
[They say they want to learn how to make those pyramids.]

## When Personal Observation Fails . . .

According to the Innocence Project, a group in New York that investigates wrongful convictions, eyewitness misidentification is the single greatest cause of conviction of innocent persons. Of all the convictions overturned by DNA analysis, witness misidentification played a role in over 75 percent. Of the first 239 DNA exonerations, 62 percent of the defendants were misidentified by one witness; in 25 percent of the cases, the defendant was misidentified by two witnesses; and *in 13 percent of the cases the same innocent defendant was misidentified by three or more separate eyewitnesses.* Even though eyewitness testimony can be persuasive before a judge and jury, it may be *much* more unreliable than we generally give it credit for being.

From http://www.innocenceproject.org/causes-wrongful-conviction/the-science-behind-eyewitness-identification-reform.

bought a new Mini Cooper, a bright blue one." Moore does not need critical thinking training to reject Parker's claim about the color of the car, because of the obvious conflict with his earlier observation.

But observations and short-term memory are far from infallible. Stories abound of recalled observations that turned out to be mistaken, from cases of surgeons operating on the wrong limb of a patient to, most notoriously, cases in which witnesses misidentified the perpetrators of a crime. The box above, "When Personal Observation Fails . . ." gives startling statistics about innocent persons being wrongly convicted as a result of faulty eyewitness identifications.

Our observations and our recollections of them can go wrong for all manner of reasons. An observer might be tired, distracted, worried about an unrelated matter, emotionally upset, feeling ill, and so on. (A crime victim would be an extreme example of such a person!) Further, such physical conditions as bad lighting, noise, and speed of events can affect our observations.

It's also important to remember that people are not all created equal when it comes to making observations. We hate to say it, dear reader, but there are lots of people who see better, hear better, and remember better than you. Of course, that goes for us as well.

Our beliefs, hopes, fears, and expectations affect our observations. Tell us that a house is infested with fleas, we are apt to see every little black bug as a flea. Inform someone who believes in ghosts that a house is haunted, and she may well believe she sees evidence of ghosts.* At séances staged by the Society for Psychical Research to test the observational powers of people under séance conditions, some observers insist that they see numerous phenomena that simply do not exist.** Teachers who are told that the students in a particular class are brighter than usual may be apt to believe that the work those students produce is better than average, even when it is not.

In Chapter 6, we discuss a very common error called *wishful thinking,* which occurs when we allow hopes and desires to influence our judgment and color our beliefs. Most of the people who fall for the 4-1-9 Fraud Internet scam (see the box on page 94) are almost surely victims of wishful thinking. It is unlikely that somebody, somewhere, wants to send you millions of dollars just because you have a bank account and that the money the person asks for really is just to facilitate the transaction. The most gullible victim, with no stake in the matter, would probably realize this. But the idea of getting one's hands on a great pile of money can blind a person to even the most obvious facts.

Our personal interests and biases affect our perceptions and the judgments we base on them. We overlook many of the mean and selfish actions of the people we like or love—and when we are infatuated with someone, everything that person does seems wonderful. By contrast, people we detest can hardly do anything that we don't perceive

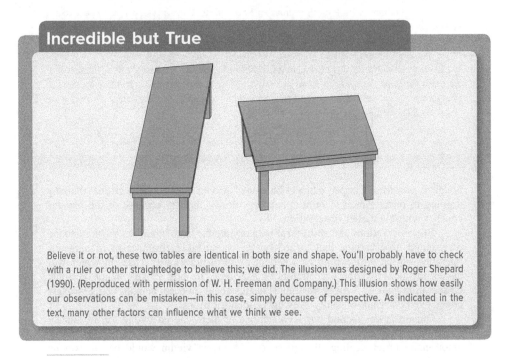

**Incredible but True**

Believe it or not, these two tables are identical in both size and shape. You'll probably have to check with a ruler or other straightedge to believe this; we did. The illusion was designed by Roger Shepard (1990). (Reproduced with permission of W. H. Freeman and Company.) This illusion shows how easily our observations can be mistaken—in this case, simply because of perspective. As indicated in the text, many other factors can influence what we think we see.

---

*C. E. M. Hansel, *Parapsychology, A Scientific Evaluation.*
**Ibid.

as mean and selfish. If we desperately wish for the success of a project, we are likely to see more evidence for that success than is actually present. On the other hand, if we wish for a project to fail, we may exaggerate flaws that we see in it or imagine flaws that are not there at all. If a job, chore, or decision is one that we wish to avoid, we tend to draw worst-case implications from it and thus come up with reasons for not doing it. However, if we are predisposed to want to do the job or make the decision, we are more likely to focus on whatever positive consequences it might have.

Finally, as we hinted earlier, above, the reliability of our observations is no better than the reliability of our memories, except in those cases where we have the means at our disposal to record our observations. And memory, as most of us know, can be deceptive. Critical thinkers are always alert to the possibility that what they remember having observed may not be what they did observe.

But even though firsthand observations are not infallible, they are still the best source of information we have. Any report that conflicts with our own direct observations is subject to serious doubt.

## Does the Claim Conflict with Our Background Information?

Reports must always be evaluated against our **background information**—that immense body of justified beliefs that consists of facts we learn from our own direct observations and facts we learn from others. Such information is "background" because we may not be able to specify where we learned it, unlike something we know because we witnessed it this morning. Much of our background information is well confirmed by a variety of sources. Reports that conflict with this store of information are usually quite properly dismissed, even if we cannot disprove them through direct observation. We immediately reject the claim "Palm trees grow in abundance near the North Pole," even though we are not in a position to confirm or disprove the statement by direct observation.

Indeed, this is an example of how we usually treat claims when we first encounter them: We begin by assigning them a certain **initial plausibility,** a rough assessment of how credible a claim seems to us. This assessment depends on how consistent the claim is with our background information—how well it "fits" with that information. If it fits very well, we give the claim some reasonable degree of initial plausibility—there is a reasonable expectation of its being true. If, however, the claim conflicts with our background information, we give it low initial plausibility and lean toward rejecting it unless very strong evidence can be produced on its behalf. The claim "More guitars were sold in the United States last year than saxophones" fits very well with the background information most of us share, and we would hardly require detailed evidence before accepting it. However, the claim "Charlie's eighty-seven-year-old grandmother swam across Lake Michigan in the middle of winter" cannot command much initial plausibility because of the obvious way it conflicts with our background information about eighty-seven-year-old people, about Lake Michigan, about swimming in cold water, and so on. In fact, short of observing the swim ourselves, it isn't clear just what *could* persuade us to accept such a claim. And even then, we should consider the likelihood that we're being tricked or fooled by an illusion.

Obviously, not every oddball claim is as outrageous as the one about Charlie's grandmother. Several years ago, we read a report about a house being stolen in Lindale, Texas—a brick house. This certainly is implausible—how could anyone steal a home? Yet there is credible documentation that it happened,* and even stranger things

There are three types of men in the world. One type learns from books. One type learns from observation. And one type just has to urinate on the electric fence.

—Dr. Laura Schlessinger
(reported by Larry Englemann)

The authority of experience.

---

*Associated Press report, March 25, 2005.

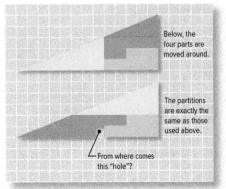

Below, the four parts are moved around.

The partitions are exactly the same as those used above.

From where comes this "hole"?

■ This optical illusion has made the rounds on the web. It takes a very close look to identify how the illusion works, although it's *certain* that *something* sneaky is going on here. The problem is solved in the answers section at the back of the book.

occasionally turn out to be true. That, of course, means that it can be worthwhile to check out implausible claims if their being true might be of consequence to you.

Unfortunately, there are no neat formulas that can resolve conflicts between what you already believe and new information. Your job as a critical thinker is to trust your background information when considering claims that conflict with that information—that is, claims with low initial plausibility—but at the same time to keep an open mind and realize that further information may cause you to give up a claim you had thought was true. It's a difficult balance, but it's worth getting right. For example, let's say you've been suffering from headaches and have tried all the usual methods of relief: aspirin, antihistamines, whatever your physician has recommended, and so on. Finally, a friend tells you that she had headaches that were very similar to yours, and nothing worked for her, either, until she had an aromatherapy treatment. Then, just a few minutes into her aromatherapy session, her headaches went away. Now, we (Moore and Parker) are not much inclined to believe that smelling oils will make your headache disappear, but we think there is little to lose and at least a small possibility of something substantial to be gained by giving the treatment a try. It may be, for example, that the treatment relaxes a person and relieves tension, which can cause headaches. We wouldn't go into it with great expectations, however.

The point is that there is a scale of initial plausibility ranging from quite plausible to only slightly so. Our aromatherapy example would fall somewhere between the plausible (and in fact true) claim that Parker went to high school with Bill Clinton and the rather implausible claim that Kim Kardashian has a PhD in physics.

As mentioned, background information is essential to adequately assess a claim. It is difficult to evaluate a report if you lack background information relating

## Fib Wizards

In *The Sleeping Doll*, novelist Jeffery Deaver invents a character who is incredibly adept at reading what people are thinking from watching and listening to them. This is fiction, but there seems to be at least a bit of substance to the claim that such talents exist.

After testing 13,000 people for their ability to detect deception, Professor Maureen O'Sullivan of the University of San Francisco identified 31 who have an unusual ability to tell when someone is lying to them. These "wizards," as she calls them, are especially sensitive to body language, facial expressions, hesitations in speech, slips of the tongue, and similar clues that a person may not be telling the truth. The wizards are much better than the average person at noticing these clues and inferring the presence of a fib from them.

Professor O'Sullivan presented her findings to the American Medical Association's 23rd Annual Science Reporters Conference.

Maybe a few people can reliably tell when someone is lying. But we'd bet there are many more who merely *think* they can do this. We want to play poker with them.

From an Associated Press report.

to the topic. This means the broader your background information, the more likely you are to be able to evaluate any given report effectively. You'd have to know a little economics to evaluate assertions about the dangers of a large federal deficit, and knowing how Social Security works can help you know what's misleading about calling it a savings account. Read widely, converse freely, and develop an inquiring attitude; there's no substitute for broad, general knowledge.

▲ —See the answers section at the back of the book.

Exercise 4-1

1. The text points out that physical conditions around us can affect our observations. List at least four such conditions.
2. Our own mental state can affect our observations as well. Describe at least three of the ways this can happen, as mentioned in the text.
3. According to the text, there are two ways credibility should enter into our evaluation of a claim. What are they?
4. A claim lacks inherent credibility, according to the text, when it conflicts with what?
5. Our most reliable source of information about the world is _____.
6. The reliability of our observations is not better than the reliability of _____.
7. True/False: Initial plausibility is an all-or-nothing characteristic; that is, a claim either has it or it doesn't.

▲ In your judgment, are any of these claims less credible than others? Discuss your opinions with others in the class to see if any interesting differences in background information emerge.

Exercise 4-2

1. They've taught crows how to play poker.
2. The center of Earth consists of water.
3. Stevie Wonder is just faking his blindness.
4. The car manufacturers already can build cars that get more than 100 miles per gallon; they just won't do it because they're in cahoots with the oil industry.
5. If you force yourself to go for five days and nights without any sleep, you'll be able to get by on less than five hours of sleep a night for the rest of your life.
6. It is possible to read other people's minds through mental telepathy.
7. A diet of mushrooms and pecans supplies all necessary nutrients and will help you lose weight. Scientists don't understand why.
8. Somewhere on the planet is a person who looks exactly like you.
9. The combined wealth of the world's 225 richest people equals the total annual income of the poorest 2.5 billion people, which is nearly half the world's total population.
10. The *Kansas City Star* has reported that the Kansas Anti-Zombie Militia is preparing for a zombie apocalypse. A spokesperson said, "If you're ready for zombies, you're ready for anything."
11. Daddy longlegs are the world's most poisonous spider, but their mouths are too small to bite.

102

12. Static electricity from your body can cause your gas tank to explode if you slide across your seat while fueling and then touch the gas nozzle.

13. Japanese scientists have created a device that measures the tone of a dog's bark to determine what the dog's mood is.

14. Barack Obama (a) is a socialist, (b) is a Muslim, (c) was not born in the United States.

15. Hugh Hefner, founder of *Playboy* magazine, was eighty-seven years old when he married Crystal Harris, who was twenty-seven at the time.

## THE CREDIBILITY OF SOURCES

We turn now from the credibility of claims themselves to the credibility of the sources from which we get them. We are automatically suspicious of certain sources of information. (If you were getting a divorce, you wouldn't ordinarily turn to your spouse's attorney for advice.) We'll look at several factors that should influence how much credence we give to a source.

### Interested Parties

Gold and silver are money,
Everything else is credit.

—J. P. MORGAN

We'll begin with a very important general rule for deciding whom to trust. Our rule makes use of two correlative concepts, interested parties and disinterested parties:

> A person who stands to gain from our belief in a claim is known as an **interested party,** and interested parties must be viewed with much more suspicion than **disinterested parties,** who have no stake in our belief one way or another.

## Not All That Glitters

When the U.S. dollar began to decline seriously in about 2004, quite a few financial "experts" claimed that gold is one of the few ways to protect one's wealth and provide a hedge against inflation. Some of their arguments make some good sense, but it's worth pointing out that many of the people advocating the purchase of gold turn out to be brokers of precious metals themselves, or are hired by such brokers to sell their product. As we emphasize in the text: Always beware of interested parties!

It would be hard to overestimate the importance of this rule—in fact, if you were to learn only one thing from this book, this would be a good candidate. Of course, not all interested parties are out to hoodwink us, and certainly not all disinterested parties have good information. But, all things considered, the rule of trusting the latter before the former is a crucially important weapon in the critical thinking armory.

We'll return to this topic later, both in the text and in some exercises.

## Physical and Other Characteristics

The feature of being an interested or disinterested party is highly relevant to whether he, she, it, or they should be trusted. Unfortunately, we often base our judgments on irrelevant considerations. Physical characteristics, for example, tell us little about a person's credibility or its lack. Does a person look you in the eye? Does he perspire a lot? Does he have a nervous laugh? Despite being generally worthless in this regard, such characteristics are widely used in sizing up a person's credibility. Simply being taller, louder, and more assertive can enhance a person's credibility, according to a Stanford study.* A practiced con artist can imitate a confident teller of the truth, just as an experienced hacker can cobble up a genuine-appearing website. ("Con," after all, is short for "confidence.")

Other irrelevant features we sometimes use to judge a person's credibility include gender, age, ethnicity, accent, and mannerisms. People also make credibility judgments

## Does Your Face Give You Away?

Some researchers, like Alan Stevens in Australia, believe that conclusions about your character and health can be drawn from your facial structures. Here are some examples:

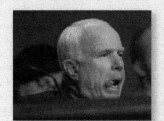

**Face width:** A man with a wide face (they say) generally has higher levels of testosterone and is more likely to be aggressive than one with a narrower face.

**Cheek size:** Fuller cheeks (they say) may indicate a person's greater likelihood of catching illnesses and infections. According to Benedict Jones at Glasgow University, larger-cheeked people are more likely to be depressed or anxious.

**Nose size and shape:** A large nose supposedly indicates a person is ambitious, confident, and self-reliant, a born leader. People who have neutral nose tips—neither round nor sharp—are said to be sweet, mild-tempered, and have endearing personalities.

We have our doubts. There may be weak associations between genetically determined facial structures and not-entirely-genetically-determined character traits, but we don't need to look at Santa's nose to know he is sweet.

From http://www.bustle.com/articles/110866-what-your-facial-features-say-about-you-according-to-science.
Also see *In Your Face: What Facial Features Reveal About People You Know and Love,* by Bill Cordingley.

---

*The study, conducted by Professor Lara Tiedens of the Stanford University Graduate School of Business, was reported in *USA Today,* July 18, 2007.

on the basis of the clothes a person wears. A friend told one of us that one's sunglasses "make a statement"; maybe so, but that statement doesn't say much about credibility. A person's occupation certainly bears a relationship to his or her knowledge or abilities, but as a guide to moral character or truthfulness, it is hardly reliable.

Which considerations are relevant to judging someone's credibility? We will get to these in a moment, but appearance isn't one of them. You may have the idea that you can size up a person just by looking into his or her eyes. This is a mistake. Just by looking at someone, we cannot ascertain that person's truthfulness, knowledge, or character. (Although this is generally true, there may be rare exceptions. See the "Fib Wizards" box on page 100.)

Of course, we sometimes get in trouble even when we accept credible claims from credible sources. Many rely, for example, on credible advice from qualified and honest professionals in preparing our tax returns. But qualified and honest professionals can make honest mistakes, and we can suffer the consequences. In general, however, trouble is much more likely if we accept either doubtful claims from credible sources or credible claims from doubtful sources (not to mention doubtful claims from doubtful sources). If a mechanic says we need a new transmission, the claim itself may not be suspicious—maybe the car we drive has many miles on it; maybe we neglected routine maintenance; maybe it isn't shifting smoothly. But remember that the mechanic is an interested party; if there's any reason to suspect he or she would exaggerate the problem to get work, we'd get a second opinion.

One of your authors has an automobile which the dealership said had an oil leak it would cost almost a thousand dollars to fix. Because he'd not seen oil on his garage floor, your cautious author decided to wait to see how serious the problem was. Well, a year after the "problem" was diagnosed, there was still no oil on the garage floor, and the car had used less than half a quart of oil, about what one would have expected over the course of a year. What to conclude? The dealership is an interested party. If its service rep convinces your author that the oil leak is serious, the dealership makes almost a thousand dollars. This makes it worth a second opinion, or, in this case, the author's own investigation. He now believes his car will never need this thousand-dollar repair.

> Remember: Interested parties are less credible than other sources of claims.

I looked the man in the eye. I found him to be very straightforward and trustworthy. We had a very good dialogue. I was able to sense his soul.

—GEORGE W. BUSH, commenting on his first meeting with Russian president Vladimir Putin

**Bush later changed his mind about Putin, seeing him as a threat to democracy. So much for the "blink" method of judging credibility.**

## War-Making Policies and Interested Parties

In the 1960s, the secretary of defense supplied carefully selected information to President Lyndon Johnson and to Congress. Would Congress have passed the Gulf of Tonkin Resolution, which authorized the beginning of the Vietnam War, if its members had known that the secretary of defense was determined to begin hostilities there? We don't know, but certainly they and the president should have been more suspicious if they had known this fact. Would President Bush and his administration have been so anxious to make war on Iraq if they had known that Ahmad Chalabi, one of their main sources of information about that country and its ruler, Saddam Hussein, was a very interested party? (He hoped to be the next ruler of Iraq if Hussein were overthrown, and much of his information turned out to be false or exaggerated.) We don't know that either, of course. But it's possible that more suspicion of interested parties may have slowed our commitment to two costly wars.

### Expertise

Much of our information comes from people about whom we have no reason to suspect prejudice, bias, or any of the other features that make interested parties bad sources. However, we might still doubt a source's actual knowledge of an issue in question. A source's knowledge depends on a number of factors, especially expertise and experience. Just as you generally cannot tell merely by looking at a source whether he or she is speaking truthfully, objectively, and accurately, you can't judge his or her knowledge or expertise by looking at surface features. A British-sounding scientist may appear more knowledgeable than a scientist who speaks, say, with a Texas drawl, but accent, height, gender, ethnicity, and clothing don't bear on a person's knowledge. In the municipal park in our town, it can be difficult to distinguish people who teach at the university from people who live in the park, based on physical appearance.

So, then, how do you judge a person's **expertise?** Education and experience are often the most important factors, followed by accomplishments, reputation, and position, in no particular order. It is not always easy to evaluate the credentials of a source, and credentials vary considerably from one field to another. Still, there are useful guidelines worth mentioning.

Education includes, but is not strictly limited to, formal education—the possession of degrees from established institutions of learning. (Some "doctors" of this and that received their diplomas from mail-order houses that advertise on matchbook covers. The title "doctor" is not automatically a qualification.)

Experience—both the kind and the amount—is an important factor in expertise. Experience is important if it is relevant to the issue at hand, but the mere fact that someone has been on the job for a long time does not automatically make him or her good at it.

Accomplishments are an important indicator of someone's expertise but, once again, only when those accomplishments are directly related to the question at hand. A Nobel Prize winner in physics is not necessarily qualified to speak publicly about toy safety, public school education (even in science), or nuclear proliferation. The last issue may involve physics, it's true, but the political issues are the crucial ones, and they are not taught in physics labs.

A person's reputation is obviously very important as a criterion of his or her expertise. But reputations must be seen in a context; how much importance we should attach to somebody's reputation depends on the people among whom the person has that reputation. You may have a strong reputation as a pool player among the denizens of your local pool hall, but that doesn't necessarily put you in the same league with Allison Fisher. Among a group of people who know nothing about investments, someone who knows the difference between a 401(k) plan and a Roth IRA may seem like quite an expert. But you certainly wouldn't want to take investment advice from somebody simply on that basis.

Most of us have met people who were recommended as experts in some field but who turned out to know little more about that field than we ourselves knew. (Presumably, in such cases those doing the recommending knew even less about the subject, or they would not have been so quickly impressed.) By and large, the kind of reputation that counts most is the one a person has among other experts in his or her field of endeavor.

The positions people hold provide an indication of how well *somebody* thinks of them. The director of an important scientific laboratory, the head of an academic department at Harvard, the author of a work consulted by other experts—in each case the position itself is substantial evidence that the individual's opinion on a relevant subject warrants serious attention.

But expertise can be bought. Our earlier discussion of interested parties applies to people who possess real expertise on a topic as well as to the rest of us. Sometimes a person's position is an indication of what his or her opinion, expert or not, is likely to be. The opinion of a lawyer retained by the National Rifle Association, offered at a hearing on firearms and urban violence, should be scrutinized much more carefully (or at least viewed with more skepticism) than that of a witness from an independent firm or agency that has no stake in the outcome of the hearings. The former can be assumed to be an interested party, the latter not. It is too easy to lose objectivity where one's interests and concerns are at stake, even if one is *trying* to be objective.

Here's a more complicated story: In the 1960s and 1970s, a national concern arose about the relationship between the consumption of sugar and several serious conditions, including diabetes and heart disease. An artificial sweetener, cyclamate, was introduced to replace sugar in sodas and other products. The sugar industry, afraid of lost sales, countered with an assault on cyclamates, and Dr. John Hickson led the charge. Later, when Hickson was research director of the Cigar Research Council, he was described in a confidential memo as "a supreme scientific politician who had been successful in condemning cyclamates, on behalf of the Sugar Research Council, on somewhat shaky evidence."* The substance was banned by the FDA in 1969. A quick web search on "cyclamate ban" will reveal the story: By 1989, FDA officials were admitting they had made a mistake in issuing the ban, which was done under pressure from the U.S. Congress, which in turn was pressured by the sugar industry.

The moral of this story is that politics, and interested parties with deep pockets, can and do influence findings that are supposed to be entirely scientific.

Experts sometimes disagree, especially when the issue is complicated and many different interests are at stake. In these cases, a critical thinker is obliged to suspend judgment about which expert to endorse, unless one expert clearly represents a majority viewpoint among experts in the field or *unless one expert can be established as more authoritative or less biased than the others.*

Of course, majority opinions sometimes turn out to be incorrect, and even the most authoritative experts occasionally make mistakes. For example, various economics experts predicted good times ahead just before the Great Depression. The same was true for many advisers right up until the 2008 financial meltdown. Jim Denny, the manager of the Grand Ole Opry, fired Elvis Presley after one performance, stating that Presley wasn't going anywhere and ought to go back to driving a truck. A claim you accept because it represents the majority viewpoint or comes from the most authoritative expert may turn out to be thoroughly wrong. Nevertheless, take heart: At the time, you were rationally justified in accepting the majority viewpoint as the most authoritative claim. The reasonable position is the one that agrees with the most authoritative opinion but allows for enough open-mindedness to change if the evidence changes.

Finally, we sometimes make the mistake of thinking that whatever qualifies someone as an expert in one field automatically qualifies that person in other areas.

---

*http://legacy.library.ucsf.edu/tid/bon57a99.

## Not Paying Attention to Experts Can Be Deadly

David Pawlik called the fire department in Cleburne, Texas, in July to ask if the "blue flames" he and his wife were seeing every time she lit a cigarette were dangerous, and an inspector said he would be right over and for Mrs. Pawlik not to light another cigarette. However, anxious about the imminent inspection, she lit up and was killed in the subsequent explosion. (The home was all electric, but there had been a natural gas leak underneath the yard.)

—*Fort Worth Star Telegram*, July 11, 2007

Sometimes it is *crucial* that you take the word of an expert.

Being a top-notch programmer, for example, might not be an indication of top-notch management skills. Indeed, many programmers get good at what they do by shying away from dealing with other people—or so the stereotype runs. Being a good campaigner may not always translate into being a good office-holder. Even if the intelligence and skill required to become an expert in one field could enable someone to become an expert in any field—which is doubtful—having the ability to become an expert is not the same as actually being an expert. Claims put forth by experts about subjects outside their fields are not automatically more acceptable than claims put forth by nonexperts.

**Exercise 4-3**

A. List as many factors as you can think of that are unreliable indicators of a source's truthfulness (e.g., the firmness of a handshake).
B. List as many factors as you can that *are* reliable.

**Exercise 4-4**

A. List as many factors as you can think of that often are mistakenly taken as reliable signs of expertise on the part of a source (e.g., appearing self-confident).
B. List as many factors as you can that are reliable indicators of a source's expertise.

**Exercise 4-5**

Expertise doesn't transfer automatically from one field to another: Being an expert in one area does not automatically qualify a person as an expert (or even as competent) in other areas. Is it the same with dishonesty? Many people think dishonesty does transfer, that being dishonest in one area automatically discredits that person in all areas. For example, when Bill Clinton lied about having sexual encounters with his intern, some said he couldn't be trusted about anything.

If someone is known to have been dishonest about one thing, should we automatically be suspicious of his or her honesty regarding other things? In a short paper of no more than two pages, defend your answer to this question.

**Exercise 4-6**

1. In a sentence, describe the crucial difference between an interested party and a disinterested party.

2. Which of the two parties mentioned in item 1 should generally be considered more trustworthy? Why?

3. Invent an issue, and then identify someone who would likely be an interested party regarding that issue; then identify someone who is likely *not* to be an interested party. Explain why in each case.

**Exercise 4-7**    ▲

Suppose you're in the market for a new television, and you're looking for advice as to what to buy. Identify which of the following persons or subjects is likely to be an interested party and which is not.

1. a flyer from a local store that sells televisions
2. the *Consumer Reports* website
3. a salesperson at a local electronics store
4. the Sony website
5. an article in a major newspaper about television, including some rankings of brands

Now let's say you've narrowed your search to two brands: LG and Panasonic. Which of the following are more likely interested parties?

6. a friend who owns an LG
7. a friend who used to own a Panasonic and now owns an LG
8. a salesperson at a store that sells both Panasonic and LG

# CREDIBILITY AND THE NEWS MEDIA

The First Amendment to the U.S. Constitution was designed to encourage a free press—freedom for journalists and publications to print (and, now, to broadcast on the airwaves or the Internet) whatever they found that would enhance public opinion. The importance of such a free press was emphasized in a famous quotation from President Thomas Jefferson: "The only security of all is in a free press. The force of public opinion cannot be resisted when permitted freely to be expressed. The agitation it produces must be submitted to. It is necessary, to keep the waters pure."*

But the waters have become less pure over the last few decades, and the press has fallen on hard times. The newspaper industry shrank to less than half of what it was at the turn of this century—and this in less than fifteen years! Consumption of news on the web and on cells seemingly increases by the hour. But it is possible people no longer believe as much of what they read or see—unless they're getting news from a source that caters to their own personal beliefs. Among other things, we'll look next at reasons why confidence in the mainstream media seems to be eroding.

## Consolidation of Media Ownership

Although it is not well known to most citizens, the media have become controlled by fewer and fewer corporations, the result of many mergers and buyouts over the past three or so decades. Since 2001, when the Federal Communications Commission loosened the regulations regarding ownership of newspapers, radio stations, and television stations, the concentration of media in fewer and fewer hands has been accelerating. From thousands of independent media outlets in the mid-twentieth century, media ownership dropped to only fifty companies by 1983. As we write this, approximately 90 percent of all media companies in the United States were controlled by just five companies: Time Warner (Warner Bros., Time, Inc., HBO, CNN, etc.), Disney (ABC, ESPN, Miramax Films, etc.), News Corp. (Fox Television, Wall Street Journal, New York Post, etc.), Comcast (NBC, Universal Studios, E! Entertainment Television, etc.), and Viacom/CBS (Paramount Pictures, MTV, Comedy Central, etc.). The subsidiaries listed in parentheses are only a tiny portion of these companies' holdings.** No matter what you see on television, the great likelihood is that one or more of these companies had a hand in producing it or getting it onto your screen. The fewer hands that control the media, the easier it is for the news we get to be "managed"—either by the owners themselves or by their commercial advertisers or even, as we'll next see, by the government.

## Government Management of the News

For a while there, our only known source of *fake* news was *The Daily Show*. But the federal government got into the fake news business as well. In recent years, a number of fake news reports, paid for by the government, have appeared on television touting the virtues of government schemes from the prescription drug program to airport safety to education programs. No criticism of the programs was included, and no mention was made that these were not legitimate independent news reports but rather were produced by the very same governmental departments that implemented the policies in question.

---

*See, among other places, http://famguardian.org/Subjects/Politics/thomasjefferson/jeff1600.htm.
**For a more thorough treatment, see www.freepress.net/ownership chart.

110 CHAPTER 4: CREDIBILITY

## "The online version just doesn't offer as much coverage as printed media."

These practices provide material for stations that cannot afford to produce a full plate of news themselves, which includes many, many stations across the country. Unfortunately, many viewers accept as news what is essentially official propaganda.

Leaving aside news reporting, problems also crop up on the op-ed page. Opinion and editorial pages and television commentaries are usually presumed to present the opinions of the writers or speakers who write or speak in them. But, as it turned out, some of those are bought and paid for as well. Our favorite example turned up in 2005: Syndicated columnist Michael McManus was paid $10,000 by the Department of Health and Human Services for writing positively about one of its programs. Ironically enough, his column is titled "Ethics and Religion."

The military has had its own methods for managing the media, from not allowing photographs to be taken of the coffins of slain American soldiers when they were being brought home from Iraq to more elaborately produced examples, such as the highly staged rescue of Private Jessica Lynch from an Iraqi hospital in 2003. Sometimes management takes the form of simple suppression of news, as when it took a whistle-blower to finally make public the video of a 2007 helicopter attack that killed a news photographer, his driver, and several others in Iraq.

## It's Up to Me and Fox News

In early 2013, as a bipartisan group of senators announced a plan for immigration reform, radio host Rush Limbaugh took to the air to denounce their proposal. "I don't know that there's any stopping this," he said. "It's up to me and Fox News."

Wait. Isn't Fox News supposed to be "fair and balanced"?

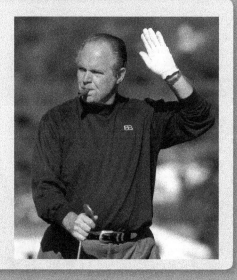

### Bias Within the Media

It is commonly said that the media are biased politically. Conservatives are convinced that they have a liberal bias and liberals are convinced the bias favors conservatives.

The usual basis for the conservative assessment is that, generally speaking, reporters and editors are more liberal than the general population. Indeed, several polls have indicated that this is the case. On the other hand, the publishers and owners of media outlets tend to be conservative—not surprisingly, since they have an orientation that places a higher value on the bottom line: They are in business to make a profit. A book by Eric Alterman* argues that the "liberal media" has always been a myth and that, at least in private, well-known conservatives like Patrick Buchanan and William Kristol are willing to admit it. On the other hand, Bernard Goldberg, formerly of CBS, argues that the liberal bias of the press is a fact.**

Making an assessment on this score is several miles beyond our scope here. But it is important to be aware that a reporter or a columnist or a broadcaster who draws conclusions without presenting sufficient evidence is no more to be believed than some guy from down the street, even if the conclusions happen to correspond nicely to your own bias—indeed, *especially* if they correspond to your own bias!

What is important to remember is that there are many forces at work in the preparation of news besides a desire to publish or broadcast the whole truth. That said, our view is that the major network news organizations are generally credible, exceptions like those noted notwithstanding. We especially prefer the Public Broadcasting System and National Public Radio; others have different preferences. Also in our view, the printed media, the *New York Times,* the *Washington Post,*

Bias in the universities? According to Lou Dobbs, former CNN news anchor (now with Fox Business News), citing a *Washington Post* survey, 72 percent of collegiate faculty across the country say they are liberal; 15 percent say they are conservative. At "elite" universities, 87 percent say they are liberal, and 3 percent say they are conservative.

*What Liberal Bias? (New York: Basic Books, 2003).
**Bias (Washington, DC: Regnery Publishing, 2001).

## Media Bias?

Mainstream media, or "lame stream" as Sarah Palin prefers it, came under increased attack during the [2012] presidential campaign, mostly among conservatives who railed against a perceived liberal tilt.

"It goes without saying that there is definitely media bias," said Paul Ryan on the stump, claiming that most people in media "want a left-of-center president." Fox News commentator Bill O'Reilly surmised that liberal bias in media gave President Obama a 3 or 4 percentage point boost, enough to have determined the outcome.

But what are today's mainstream media? The most popular news channel is Fox News; the most powerful radio talk hosts are Rush Limbaugh and Sean Hannity; and among the Internet's loudest information voices is The Drudge Report—all severely conservative. In terms of audience and influence, these outlets are about as mainstream as it gets.

Newspapers are certainly in the mainstream, but they've always been divided politically, starting with two of the nation's biggest dailies, the conservative *Wall Street Journal* and the liberal *New York Times*. In the [2012] election, the nation's 100 largest papers split almost evenly in endorsements for Obama and Romney. Romney even won more swing state newspaper endorsements, 24 to 15, according to analysis by the Poynter organization.

It seems reasonable to assume that any paper that endorsed Romney was not likely to be simultaneously biased in favor of Obama. Yet, that is what some conservatives seem to be suggesting.

Then there are legacy broadcast networks—specifically the news departments of CBS, NBC and ABC, and their principal TV news anchors. Diane Sawyer of ABC once worked for Richard Nixon; neither Brian Williams of NBC nor Scott Pelley of CBS has ever dabbled in government or politics. In my view, having worked for two of these companies, network news personnel actually bend over backwards—at times too far—trying to avoid even a hint of bias. And having written for the nation's three largest papers, I conclude that most bias is confined to the opinion pages, where it belongs.

However, the media landscape is changing in ways that do, indeed, involve bias. It's the overt posturing of Fox News Channel on the right, MSNBC on the left, and dozens of opinion-based Internet sites serving both sides. What these outlets share is an obsessive desire to protest each other's slanted reporting.

Republicans tend to distrust media more than Democrats. According to Pew polling, Republican respondents gave only two news sources high credibility ratings: Fox News and local TV news. Democrats gave high marks to a much longer list of broadcasters and newspapers.

. . .

When it comes to actual bias, there's significantly more of it in new media than in legacy media. Meanwhile, the mainstream is gradually becoming a collection of smaller streams—the most influential of which are divided politically, and even lean toward the conservative side. It's ironic that protesting by conservatives over media bias is growing in direct proportion to the emerging power of those on the right to shape media content.

. . .

Funt, Peter, "Examining Media 'Bias,'" Monterey County Herald, December 7, 2012.

the *Los Angeles Times,* and other major newspapers are generally credible, even though mistakes are sometimes made here as well. News magazines fall in the same category: usually credible but with occasional flaws.

For several years, cable news had a great influence on what became news. CNN (which stands, unsurprisingly, for "Cable News Network") began in 1980 as the first twenty-four-hours-a-day news broadcaster. Fox News and MSNBC now also compete for viewers' attention both day and night. While spreading across the hours of the day, these networks have also spread across the political spectrum. You can now find "news" that satisfies nearly any political bias. What's more, with the need to fill screens for so many hours, the notion of what actually counts as news has had to be expanded. The result has affected not just the cable networks but traditional news programs as well: "Feature stories" from prison life to restaurant kitchen tours take up more and more space that used to be devoted to so-called hard news. One of our northern California newspapers, the *Sacramento Bee,* did a story on how "silly news" was taking up more and more space in local news programs. Ben Bagdikian, author and former dean of the Graduate School of Journalism at the University of California, Berkeley, has pointed out that a commercial for Pepsi-Cola seems to connect better after a fluff piece or a sitcom than after a serious piece on, say, massacres in Rwanda or an ambush in the Middle East.*

It would be difficult to boil down our advice regarding accepting claims from the news media, but it would certainly include keeping the following points in mind:

> Like the rest of us, people in the news media sometimes make mistakes; they sometimes accept claims with insufficient evidence or without confirming the credibility of a source.
>
> The media are subject to pressure and sometimes to manipulation from government and other news sources.
>
> The media, with few exceptions, are driven in part by the necessity to make a profit, and this can bring pressure from advertisers, owners, and managers.

Finally, we might remember that the news media are to a great extent a reflection of the society at large. If we the public are willing to get by with superficial, sensationalist, or manipulated news, then we can rest assured that, eventually, that's all the news we'll get.

## Talk Radio

On the surface, talk radio seems to offer a wealth of information not available in news reports from conventional sources. And at least some talk radio hosts employ people to scour traditional legitimate news sources for information relevant to their political agenda, and to the extent that they document the source, which they often do, they provide listeners with many interesting and important facts. But radio hosts from all sides are given to distortion, misplaced emphasis, and bias with regard to selection of which facts to report. And, really, the shouting gives us a headache.

## Advocacy Television

We mentioned earlier that some cable networks have moved left while others have moved right on the political spectrum, so the news you can expect from them comes

---

*Interview on *Frontline,* http://www.pbs.org/wgbh/pages/frontline/smoke/interviews/bagdikian.html.

with a predictable slant. This is good insofar as it exposes people to opinions different from their own; it is not so good insofar as it simply reinforces what the viewer already believes, especially if there is no evidence offered in support of the opinions.

MSNBC offers *All In with Chris Hayes, The Last Word with Lawrence O'Donnell,* and *The Rachel Maddow Show,* all of which offer a liberal perspective on the news of the day, and all of which editorialize from that perspective.

Fox News features Bill O'Reilly, Sean Hannity, and Megyn Kelly, who represent various conservative constituencies and do something similar from the other side.

We could write an entire chapter on this subject, and maybe, given the influence the media have on American public opinion these days, we should. We could discuss other channels and other organizations (e.g., Accuracy in Media on the right and MoveOn.org on the left, to name just two of a thousand), but we think you get the idea: We remind you to always listen with a skeptical ear to political news and commentary. We know it's difficult, but it's important to be especially careful about accepting claims (without good evidence), and in particular, those with which you sympathize.

### The Internet, Generally

It is difficult to overestimate the importance of the Internet—that amalgamation of electronic lines and connections that allows nearly anyone with a computer or a smart phone to link up with nearly any other similarly equipped person on the planet. Although the Internet offers great benefits, the information it provides must be evaluated with even *more* caution than information from the print media, radio, or television. We presented two stories at the beginning of the chapter that show just how wrong things can go.

There are basically two kinds of information sources on the Internet. The first consists of commercial and institutional sources; the second, of individual and group sites on the World Wide Web. In the first category, we include sources like the LexisNexis facility, as well as the online services provided by newsmagazines, large electronic news organizations, and government institutions. The second category includes everything else you'll find on the web—an amazing assortment of good information, entertainment of widely varying quality, hot tips, advertisements, come-ons, fraudulent offers, and outright lies. Just as the fact that a claim appears in print or on television doesn't make it true, so it is for claims you run across online. Keep in mind that the information you get from a source is only as good as that source.

### Wikipedia

Possibly the fastest-growing source of information in terms of both its size and its influence is the online encyclopedia Wikipedia. "Wiki" refers to a collaborative voluntary association (although the word seems to have been coined by a programmer named Ward Cunningham from the Hawaiian term "wiki-wiki"—"quick-quick"). Begun in 2001 by Larry Sanger and Jimmy Wales, the encyclopedia's content and structure are determined by its users. This accounts for its major strengths as well as its major weaknesses. Because there are many thousands of contributors, the coverage is immense. There are well over four million articles in English alone, and more than two hundred other languages and dialects are also employed. Because access is available to virtually everybody who has a computer or smartphone, coverage is often very fast; articles often appear within hours of breaking events.

## Evaluating Website Credibility: A Tip from the Professionals

In a study done a few years ago,* it was determined that when it comes to evaluating the credibility of a website, experts in a field go about it much differently than do ordinary consumers. Since, as we've indicated, credibility varies hugely on the web, we must do the best job we can in assessing this feature of any website we consider important. Unfortunately, as was shown in the study just mentioned, most ordinary visitors do a much less effective job of evaluating credibility than do people knowledgeable about the field. In particular, while professionals attend most carefully to the information given at a website, most of the rest of us pay more attention to its visual appeal. Layout, typography, color schemes, and animation affect the general public's estimate of a site's credibility—54 percent of comments are about these features—whereas the professionals' interest is more in the quality of the site's references, the credentials of individuals mentioned, and so on. Only 16 percent of professional evaluators' comments had to do with a website's visual design.

What should we take from this? A general rule: Don't be taken in by how visually attractive a website might be. A flashy design with attractive colors and design features is no substitute for information that is backed up by references and put forward by people with appropriate credentials.

*Experts vs. Online Consumers, a Consumer Reports WebWatch research report, October 2009 (www.consumerwebwatch.org).

But also because of this wide access, the quality of the articles varies tremendously. You should be especially wary of recent articles; they are more likely to contain uncorrected errors that will eventually disappear as knowledgeable people visit the page and put right whatever mistakes are present. Not just factual errors, but bias and omission can affect the quality of material found on Wikipedia's pages. Occasionally, a writer will do a thorough job of reporting the side of an issue that he or she favors (or knows more about, or both), and the other side may go underreported or even unmentioned. Over time, these types of errors tend to get corrected after visits by individuals who favor the other side of the issue. But at any given moment, in any given Wikipedia entry, there is the possibility of mistakes, omissions, citation errors, and plain old vandalism.

Our advice: We think Wikipedia is an excellent starting point in a search for knowledge about a topic. We use it frequently. But you should always check the sources provided in what you find there; it should never be your sole source of information if the topic is important to you or is to become part of an assignment to be turned in for a class. That said, we add that articles dealing with technical or scientific subjects tend to be more reliable (although errors are often more difficult to spot), with an error rate (according to one study) about the same as that found in the *Encyclopedia Britannica.** (Britannica announced in March 2012 that it would no longer publish a paper version; it now exists only online.) Such articles and, as mentioned, articles that have been around for a while can be extremely helpful in whatever project you are engaged in.

*"Internet Encyclopedias Go Head to Head," by Jim Giles, *Nature,* December 12, 2005.

## Webcheckers

Along with other sites we've already mentioned, here are some other places where you can go to get to the bottom of an issue you've seen brought up on the web. We believe these to be among the most reliable sources currently available; we use them all ourselves.

*Snopes.com.* The original site for checking out rumors, stories, urban legends, and any other type of strange claim that turns up on the web. Run by Daniel and Barbara Mikkelson since 1996, it classifies as true or false a host of claims that circulate on the Internet. Analysis of the history and nature of the claims under investigation is usually provided.

*TruthorFiction.com.* A general fact-finding, debunking site. Generally up-to-date findings by owner Rich Buhler. Analyses tend to be less thorough than those found on Snopes, but a generally trustworthy site.

*Factcheck.org.* Run by Brooks Jackson, a former CNN and *Wall Street Journal* reporter out of the University of Pennsylvania's Annenberg Public Policy Center. Neutral politically, the site attacks anybody who stretches the truth concerning any topic in politics.

*PolitiFact.com.* Operated by the *St. Petersburg* (Florida) *Times* newspaper. Reporters and editors fact-check claims made by politicians, lobbyists, and interest groups. The website won a Pulitzer Prize in 2009 for its work during the presidential election of 2008.

*ConsumerReports.org.* Evaluates consumer issues (including health care and financial planning) and products. Not to be confused with other organizations with similar names, this site, like the magazine of the same name that sponsors it, accepts no advertising and bends over backward to avoid bias. Careful evaluation and analysis can be expected. The organization buys products to be evaluated from stores, just like we do, rather than being given them by manufacturers. Unbiased help in shopping for electronics can also be found at Decide.com, a recent addition to the consumer's arsenal.

For the general evaluation of websites, several checklists are available. You will find Cornell University's and the University of Maryland's checklists at www.library.cornell.edu/olinuris/ref/research/skill26.htm and www.lib.umd.edu/guides/evaluate.html.

### News from Social Media: The Echo Chamber

Until lately, the social media on the web (Facebook, Twitter, YouTube, Google Plus, and maybe a dozen more by the time you read this) have not been much thought of as sources of news. But times have changed. In 2015 alone, some of the most viewed news pieces resulted from amateur- or police-recorded video that made it onto the web and went viral.

Facebook is the number one social media source of news for the greatest number of people, with about 30 percent of U.S. adults getting news there.* YouTube and Twitter come in at 10 and 8 percent, respectively. While entertainment news is the category that garners the most interest (and that by itself is worrisome to some of us), social media has been instrumental in many breaking news events. Individual users have posted photos and videos that have sometimes made the difference in how the country understands a news event.

---

*See http://www.pewresearch.org/fact-tank/2014/09/24/how-social-media-is-reshaping-news/, on which this and much of the current section relies.

While we welcome the first-hand video of breaking events, whether recorded by private individuals or by police cameras, we have to remember that nearly every photo or video is open to interpretation in varying degrees. Furthermore, much viral video that is passed around on web is accompanied by one hysterical voice or another. We urge caution when looking at accounts—written or video—of news events, especially when presented by people who have a stake in the subject. They are, remember, the very sort of interested parties we spoke of earlier in the chapter.

A second, and maybe more serious problem, is the false impression that can be created by repeated viewings of an event or type of event. Remember from Chapter 1 how the availability heuristic affects us: The more frequently we think of an event or type of event, the greater the probability we assign to its occurrence. And seeing something happen frequently on television, on the computer, or on the smart phone is certain to cause us to think more frequently about it.

Finally, remember that social media may know more about us than we might be inclined to think. The things sent to us are frequently tailored to our interests by our website-viewing history, thus echoing and reinforcing our interests, preferences, and biases.

*To sum up:* More sources of news, everything being equal, are a good thing. But everything is not always equal, and we must proceed with caution and with our critical thinking faculties turned on when digesting news from any source, whether the *New York Times* or your cousin's videos.

### Blogs

Now we come to blogs. Blogs are simply journals, the vast majority of them put up by individuals, that are left open to the public on an Internet site. Originally more like public diaries dealing with personal matters, they now encompass specialties of almost every imaginable sort. Up to three million blogs were believed to be up and running by the end of 2004; by July 2011, there were an estimated 164 million.* We are afraid to guess how many there are now.

You can find blogs that specialize in satire, parody, and outright fabrication. They represent all sides of the political spectrum, including some sides that we wouldn't have thought existed at all. The Drudge Report is a standard on the right; the Huffington Post is equally well known on the left. On a blog site, like any other website that isn't run by a responsible organization such as most of those previously indicated, you can find *anything that a person wants to put there,* including all kinds of bad information. You can take advantage of these sources, but you should always exercise caution, and if you're looking for information, always consult another source, but be especially careful about any that are linked to your first source!

Before we leave the topic of web worthiness, we want to pass along a warning that comes from Barbara Mikkelson, co-founder of Snopes.com. (See the box, "Web-checkers," on the previous page.) She reminds us that rumors often give people a great sense of comfort; people are quick to reject nuance and facts that are contrary to their own point of view, but quickly accept them when they are agreeable to the hearer. (This is called "confirmation bias." See Chapter 1.) "When you're looking at truth versus gossip," Mikkelson says, "truth doesn't stand a chance." We hope she's being unduly pessimistic.

---

*Rightmixmarketing.com; blogging statistics.

So remember, when you take keyboard and mouse in hand, be on guard. You have about as much reason to believe the claims you find on most sites as you would if they came from any other stranger, except you can't look this one in the eye.

| Exercise 4-8 | See who in the class can find the strangest news report from a credible source. Send it to us at McGraw-Hill. If your entry is selected for printing in our next edition, Moore might send you $100. (In the next chapter you'll see why we call the word "might" a weaseler in this context.) |
|---|---|
| Exercise 4-9 | Identify at least three factors that can cause inaccuracies or a distortion of reports in the news media. |

## ADVERTISING

> Advertising [is] the science of arresting the human intelligence long enough to get money from it.
>
> —*Stephen Leacock*

It is estimated that about a half-trillion dollars are spent each year trying to get people to buy or do something. Six billion dollars were spent during the 2012 elections, most of it on advertising.

People watching a sexual program are thinking about sex, not soda pop. Violence and sex elicit very strong emotions and can interfere with memory for other things.

—BRAD BUSHMAN of Iowa State University, whose research indicated that people tend to forget the names of sponsors of violent or sexual TV shows (reported by Ellen Goodman)

"Doctor recommended."

**This ambiguous ad slogan creates an illusion that many doctors, or doctors in general, recommend the product. However, a recommendation from a single doctor is all it takes to make the statement true.**

If there is anything in modern society besides politics that truly puts our sense of what is credible to the test, it's advertising. As we hope you'll agree after reading this section, skepticism is a good policy when considering advertisements and promotions.

Ads are used to sell many products other than toasters, televisions, and toilet tissue. They can encourage us to vote for a candidate, agree with a political proposal, take a tour, give up a bad habit, or join the Tea Party or the army. They can also be used to make announcements (for instance, about job openings, lectures, concerts, or the recall of defective automobiles) or to create favorable or unfavorable climates of opinion (e.g., toward labor unions or offshore oil drilling). A "public service announcement" may even be used surreptitiously to create a climate of opinion about something or someone. To simplify this discussion, let's just refer to all these things as products.

### Three Kinds of Ads

The three modes of persuasion first written about by Aristotle and discussed in Chapter 2 of this book present a useful way of classifying ads.

1. *Logos ads:* These ads emphasize information about a product—information advertisers hope favorably influence our decision about buying their products. (Remember that "product" includes everything from balsamic vinegar to ballot initiatives.) Unfortunately, to make an informed decision on a purchase, you may need to know more than the advertiser is willing to claim, particularly because advertisers won't tell you what's wrong with their products or what's right with their competitors'. After all, they are *interested parties.* Ads are written to *sell something;* they are not designed to be informative except to help with the sales job.

   Sometimes, of course, a *logos* advertisement can provide you with information that can clinch your decision to make a purchase. Sometimes the mere existence, availability, or affordability of a product—all information an ad can convey—is all you need to make a reason-based decision to buy.

2. *Ethos ads:* These ads display a product as being used or endorsed by people we admire or identify with or feel we can trust. Potential buyers of a product are probably aware that individuals who star in advocacy ads (as they are sometimes called) are paid to be in them and are therefore interested parties. But the strategy behind such ads primarily is to create favorable associations with the product and to give the product prominent shelf space in our mind, i.e., to make us remember it when we go shopping. Obviously, neither the fact that we remember a product nor the fact that someone we like has been paid to promote it is a reason to buy it.

3. *Pathos ads:* These ads are primarily intended to arouse emotions in us. Pleasurable emotions stimulate positive memories of a product and help it stand out in a positive way when we are shopping. Negative emotions—the staple of negative political advertising—are intended to help make us think poorly of something or someone.

A common *pathos* ad technique is the narrative ad, which situates a product in an emotionally charged story. Many car ads use this technique: a good example is the 2014 ad for a Chevy Silverado which features a man, his truck, a broken fence, and a lost calf—which the man finds while driving his truck through freezing rain. Such ads often use stereotypes, in this case the positive stereotype of the tough-yet-caring cowboy, a central and iconic figure in American mythology. The ad may not make you want to rush out and buy a Silverado, but the story is compelling and may stick in your thoughts. The local Chevy dealership may be happy that, if you contemplate getting a truck, the lost-calf story comes to mind more readily than frequency of repair data you read about in *Consumer Reports.*

Of course, memories created by an advertising narrative, whether favorable or unfavorable, are not reasons to buy or avoid a product.

For people on whom good fortune has smiled, those who don't care what kind of *whatsit* they buy, or those to whom mistaken purchases simply don't matter, all that is important is knowing that a product is available. Most of us, however, need more information than ads provide to make reasoned purchasing decisions. Of course,

"Chevy runs deep."

**Meaningless but catchy slogan for Chevy trucks. Being catchy is no substitute for being relevant or being true.**

source: DILBERT © 2007 Scott Adams. Used By permission of UNIVERSAL UCLICK. All rights reserved.

we all occasionally make purchases solely on the basis of advertisements, and sometimes we don't come to regret them. In such cases, though, the happy result is due as much to good luck as to the ad.

A final suggestion on this subject. We know of only one source that maintains a fierce independence and still does a good job of testing and reporting on products in general. That's Consumers Union, the publishers of *Consumer Reports,* a magazine (mentioned in the box on page 121) that accepts no advertising and that buys all

## When Is an Ad Not an Ad? When It's a Product Placement!

When Katharine Hepburn threw Humphrey Bogart's Gordon's gin overboard in *The African Queen,* it was an early example of product placement, since the makers of Gordon's paid to have their product tossed in the drink, as it were. More recent examples of placement ads include Dodge vehicles in the Fast and Furious movies and Apple laptops just about everywhere.

These days, the paid placement of products in both movies and television (and possibly even in novels) is a serious alternative to traditional commercials, and it has the advantage of overcoming the Tivo/DVR effect: the viewer records programs and skips over the commercials when watching them.

■ We suspect the Coke can is there because Pepsi wouldn't pay enough.

## WAY Too Good to Be True!

After the country fell into a serious recession in 2008, many people found themselves unable to meet their mortgage payments, and many found themselves saddled with more credit card debt than they could manage. Easy debt-relief schemers to the rescue! Some cable TV and radio ads promised to help get your mortgage paid off, make your credit card debt shrink or disappear altogether, or make you rich by teaching you to make quick killings in real estate.

According to a *Consumer Reports Money Adviser* article (April 2010), these schemes, which are still around, tend more toward guaranteeing fees for the operators than for debt relief or riches, quick or otherwise, for the client. Many clients wind up worse off than they started after signing up for these plans. Advertising is designed to help the folks who pay for the ads. If it looks too good to be true, you can bet it *is*.

the objects it tests and reports on (rather than accepting them for free from the manufacturers, as do several other "consumer" magazines). For reliable information and fair-mindedness, we recommend them. They're also on the web at www.consumersunion.org. Also on the web, decide.com does the same for electronic gear. They're mentioned in the same box, above.

## Recap

This list summarizes the topics covered in this chapter.

- Claims lack credibility to the extent they conflict with our observations, experience, or background information, or come from sources that lack credibility.
- The less initial plausibility a claim has, the more extraordinary it seems, and the less it fits with our background information, the more suspicious we should be.
- Interested parties should be viewed with more suspicion than disinterested parties.
- Doubts about sources generally fall into two categories: doubts about the source's knowledge or expertise and doubts about the source's veracity, objectivity, and accuracy.
- We can form reasonably reliable judgments about a source's knowledge by considering his or her education, experience, accomplishments, reputation, and position.
- Claims made by experts, those with special knowledge in a subject, are the most reliable, but the claims must pertain to the area of expertise and must not conflict with claims made by other experts in the same area.
- Major metropolitan newspapers, national newsmagazines, and network news shows are generally credible sources of news, but it is necessary to keep an open mind about what we learn from them.
- Governments have been known to influence and even to manipulate the news.
- Sources like Wikipedia, institutional websites, and news organizations can be helpful, but skepticism is the order of the day when we obtain information from unknown Internet sources or advocacy TV.

- What goes for advocacy television also goes for talk radio.
- Advertising assaults us at every turn, attempting to sell us goods, services, beliefs, and attitudes. Because substantial talent and resources are employed in this effort, we need to ask ourselves constantly whether the products in question will really make the differences in our lives that their advertising claims or hints they will make. Advertisers are more concerned with selling something than with improving your life. They are concerned with improving their own lives.

## Additional Exercises

### Exercise 4-10

In groups, decide which is the best answer to each question. Compare your answers with those of other groups and your instructor.

1. "SPACE ALIEN GRAVEYARD FOUND! Scientists who found an extraterrestrial cemetery in central Africa say the graveyard is at least 500 years old! 'There must be 200 bodies buried there and not a single one of them is human,' Dr. Hugo Schild, the Swiss anthropologist, told reporters." What is the appropriate reaction to this report in the *Weekly World News?*

   a. It's probably true.
   b. It almost certainly is true.
   c. We really need more information to form any judgment at all.
   d. None of the above.

2. Is Elvis really dead? Howie thinks not. Reason: He knows three people who claim to have seen Elvis recently. They are certain that it is not a mere Elvis look-alike they have seen. Howie reasons that, since he has absolutely no reason to think the three would lie to him, they must be telling the truth. Elvis must really be alive, he concludes!

   Is Howie's reasoning sound? Explain.

3. VOICE ON TELEPHONE: Hello, Mr. Roberts, this is HSBC calling. Have you recently made a credit card purchase of $347 at Macy's in New York City?

   MR. ROBERTS: Why, no, I haven't . . .

   VOICE: We thought not, Mr. Roberts. I'm sorry to report that it is very likely that your credit card has been compromised and is being used by another party. However, we are prepared to block that card and send you another immediately, at no expense to you.

   MR. ROBERTS: Well, that's fine, I suppose.

   VOICE: Let me emphasize, you will experience very little inconvenience and no expense at all. Now, for authorization, just to make sure that we are calling the correct person, Mr. Roberts, please state the number on your credit card and the expiration date.

   Question: What should Mr. Roberts, as a critical thinker, do?

4. One Thanksgiving Day, an image said by some to resemble the Virgin Mary was observed on a wall of St. Dominic's Church in Colfax, California. A physicist asked to investigate said the image was caused by sunlight shining through a stained glass window and reflecting from a newly installed hanging

light fixture. Others said the image was a miracle. Whose explanation is more likely true?

a. the physicist's
b. the others'
c. more information is needed before we can decide which explanation is more likely

5. It is late at night around the campfire when the campers hear awful grunting noises in the woods around them. They run for their lives! Two campers, after returning the next day, tell others they found huge footprints around the campfire. They are convinced they were attacked by Bigfoot. Which explanation is more likely true?

a. The campers heard Bigfoot.
b. The campers heard some animal and are pushing the Bigfoot explanation to avoid being called chickens, or are just making the story up for unknown reasons.
c. Given this information, we can't tell which explanation is more likely.

6. Megan's aunt says she saw a flying saucer. "I don't tell people about this," Auntie says, "because they'll think I'm making it up. But this really happened. I saw this strange light, and this, well, it wasn't a saucer, exactly, but it was round and big, and it came down and hovered just over my back fence, and my two dogs began whimpering. And then it just, whoosh! It just vanished."

Megan knows her aunt, and Megan knows she doesn't make up stories.

a. She should believe her aunt saw a flying saucer.
b. She should believe her aunt was making up the story.
c. She should believe that her aunt may well have had some unusual experience, but it was probably not a visitation by extraterrestrial beings.

7. According to Dr. Edith Fiore, author of *The Unquiet Dead*, many of your personal problems are really the miseries of a dead soul who has possessed you sometime during your life. "Many people are possessed by earthbound spirits. These are people who have lived and died, but did not go into the afterworld at death. Instead they stayed on Earth and remained just like they were before death, with the fears, pains, weaknesses and other problems that they had when they were alive." She estimates that about 80 percent of her more than 1,000 patients are suffering from the problems brought on by being possessed by spirits of the dead. To tell if you are among the possessed, she advises that you look for such telltale symptoms as low energy levels, character shifts or mood swings, memory problems, poor concentration, weight gain with no obvious cause, and bouts of depression (especially after hospitalization). Which of these reactions is best?

a. Wow! I'll bet I'm possessed!
b. If these are signs of being possessed, how come she thinks that only 80 percent of her patients are?
c. Too bad there isn't more information available, so we could form a reasonable judgment.
d. Dr. Fiore doesn't know what she's talking about.

8.                        **EOC—Engine Overhaul in a Can**

Developed by skilled automotive scientists after years of research and laboratory and road tests! Simply pour one can of EOC into the oil in your crankcase. EOC contains long-chain molecules and special thermo-active metallic

alloys that bond with worn engine parts. NO tools needed! NO need to disassemble engine.

Question: Reading this ad, what should you believe?

9. ANCHORAGE, Alaska (AP)—Roped to her twin sons for safety, Joni Phelps inched her way to the top of Mount McKinley. The National Park Service says Phelps, 54, apparently is the first blind woman to scale the 20,300-foot peak.

This report is

a. probably true
b. probably false
c. too sketchy; more information is needed before we can judge

10. You read rave reviews of *The Life Plan,* a book that promises to slow aging, promote strength, enhance one's sex life, and so on through diet, exercise, and hormone therapy. Should a reader of the book expect to achieve the results described? Are there cautions you should heed before beginning such a program?

## Exercise 4-11

Within each group of observers, are some especially credible or especially not so?

1. Judging the relative performances of the fighters in a heavyweight boxing match
   a. the father of one of the fighters
   b. a sportswriter for *Sports Illustrated* magazine
   c. the coach of the American Olympic boxing team
   d. the referee of the fight
   e. a professor of physical education

2. You (or your family or your class) are trying to decide whether you should buy a Mac computer or a Windows PC. You might consult
   a. a friend who owns either a Mac or a Windows machine
   b. a friend who now owns one of the machines but used to own the other
   c. a dealer for either Mac or Windows computers
   d. a computer column in a big-city newspaper
   e. reviews in computer magazines

3. The Surgical Practices Committee of Grantville Hospital has documented an unusually high number of problems in connection with tonsillectomies performed by a Dr. Choker. The committee is reviewing her surgical practices. Those present during a tonsillectomy are
   a. Dr. Choker
   b. the surgical proctor from the Surgical Practices Committee
   c. an anesthesiologist
   d. a nurse
   e. a technician

4. The mechanical condition of the used car you are thinking of buying
   a. the used-car salesperson
   b. the former owner (who we assume is different from the salesperson)
   c. the former owner's mechanic
   d. you
   e. a mechanic from an independent garage

5. A demonstration of psychokinesis (the ability to move objects at a distance by nonphysical means)

   a. a newspaper reporter
   b. a psychologist
   c. a police detective
   d. another psychic
   e. a physicist
   f. a customs agent
   g. a magician

## Exercise 4-12

For each of the following items, discuss the credibility and authority of each source relative to the issue in question. Whom would you trust as most reliable on the subject?

▲ 1. Issue: Is Crixivan an effective HIV/AIDS medication?

   a. *Consumer Reports*
   b. Stadtlander Drug Company (the company that makes Crixivan)
   c. the owner of your local health food store
   d. the U.S. Food and Drug Administration
   e. your local pharmacist

▲ 2. Issue: Should possession of handguns be outlawed?

   a. a police chief
   b. a representative of the National Rifle Association
   c. a U.S. senator
   d. the father of a murder victim

▲ 3. Issue: What was the original intent of the Second Amendment to the U.S. Constitution, and does it include permission for every citizen to possess handguns?

   a. a representative of the National Rifle Association
   b. a justice of the U.S. Supreme Court
   c. a constitutional historian
   d. a U.S. senator
   e. the president of the United States

4. Issue: Is decreasing your intake of dietary fat and cholesterol likely to reduce the level of cholesterol in your blood?

   a. *Time* magazine
   b. *Runner's World* magazine
   c. your physician
   d. the National Institutes of Health
   e. the *New England Journal of Medicine*

5. Issue: When does a human life begin?
   a. a lawyer
   b. a physician
   c. a philosopher
   d. a minister
   e. you

## Exercise 4-13

Each of these items consists of a brief biography of a real or imagined person, followed by a list of topics. On the basis of the information in the biography, discuss the credibility and authority of the person described on each of the topics listed.

 1. Anne St. Germain teaches sociology at the University of Illinois and is the director of its Population Studies Center. She is a graduate of Harvard College, where she received a BA in 1985, and of Harvard University, which granted her a PhD in economics in 1988. She taught courses in demography as an assistant professor at UCLA until 1992; then she moved to the sociology department of the University of Nebraska, where she was associate professor and then professor. From 1997 through 1999, she served as acting chief of the Population Trends and Structure Section of the United Nations Population Division. She joined the faculty at the University of Illinois in 1999. She has written books on patterns of world urbanization, the effects of cigarette smoking on international mortality, and demographic trends in India. She is president of the Population Association of America.

**Topics**

  a. The effects of acid rain on humans
  b. The possible beneficial effects of requiring sociology courses for all students at the University of Illinois
  c. The possible effects of nuclear war on global climate patterns
  d. The incidence of poverty among various ethnic groups in the United States
  e. The effects of the melting of glaciers on global sea levels
  f. The change in death rate for various age groups in all Third World countries between 1980 and 2000
  g. The feasibility of a laser-based nuclear defense system
  h. Voter participation among religious sects in India
  i. Whether the winters are worse in Illinois than in Nebraska

2. Tom Pierce graduated cum laude from Cornell University with a BS in biology in 1980. After two years in the Peace Corps, during which he worked on public health projects in Venezuela, he joined Jeffrey Ridenour, a mechanical engineer, and the pair developed a water pump and purification system that is now used in many parts of the world for both regular water supplies and emergency use in disaster-struck areas. Pierce and Ridenour formed a company to manufacture the water systems, and it prospered as they developed smaller versions of the system for private use on boats and motor homes. In 1988, Pierce bought out his partner and expanded research and development in hydraulic systems for forcing oil out of old wells. Under contract with the federal government and several oil firms, Pierce's company was a principal designer and contractor for the Alaskan oil pipeline. He is now a consultant in numerous developing countries as well as chief executive officer and chair of the board of his own company, and he sits on the boards of directors of several other companies.

**Topics**

  a. The image of the United States in Latin America
  b. The long-range effects of the leftward turn in Venezuela on South America
  c. Fixing a leaky faucet

d. Technology in Third World countries
e. The ecological effects of the Alaskan pipeline
f. Negotiating a contract with the federal government
g. Careers in biology

## Exercise 4-14

According to certain pollsters, quite a number of people vote for candidates for president not because they especially like those candidates' policies and programs or their idea of where the country should be going, but because they like (or dislike) the candidates personally. Discuss what features a candidate from the recent past may have that might cause such people to vote for (or against) him or her. Which of these features, if any, might be relevant to how good a job the candidate would do as president?

## Exercise 4-15

From what you know about the nature of each of the following claims and its source, and given your general knowledge, assess whether the claim is one you should accept, reject, or suspend judgment on due to ambiguity, insufficient documentation, vagueness, or subjectivity (e.g., "Sam Claflin is cute"). Compare your judgment with that of your instructor.

1. "Campbell Soup is hot—and some are getting burned. Just one day after the behemoth of broth reported record profits, Campbell said it would lay off 650 U.S. workers, including 175—or 11% of the workforce—at its headquarters in Camden, New Jersey."

   —Time

2. [The claim to evaluate is the first one in this passage.] Jackie Haskew taught paganism and devil worship in her fourth-grade classroom in Grand Saline, Texas, at least until she was pressured into resigning by parents of her students. (According to syndicated columnist Nat Hentoff, "At the town meeting on her case, a parent said firmly that she did not want her daughter to read anything that dealt with 'death, abuse, divorce, religion, or any other issue.'")

3. "By 1893 there were only between 300 and 1,000 buffaloes remaining in the entire country. A few years later, President Theodore Roosevelt persuaded Congress to establish a number of wildlife preserves in which the remaining buffaloes could live without danger. The numbers have increased since, nearly doubling over the past 10 years to 130,000."

   —*Clifford May, in the* New York Times Magazine

4. Lee Harvey Oswald, acting alone, was responsible for the death of President John F. Kennedy.

   —*Conclusion of the Warren Commission on the assassination of President Kennedy*

5. "[N]ewly released documents, including the transcripts of telephone conversations recorded by President Lyndon B. Johnson in November and December 1963, provide for the first time a detailed . . . look at why and how the seven-member Warren [Commission] was put together. Those documents, along with

a review of previously released material . . . describe a process designed more to control information than to elicit and expose it."

—*"The Truth Was Secondary,"* Washington Post National Weekly Edition

6. "Short-sighted developers are determined to transform Choco [a large region of northwestern Colombia] from an undisturbed natural treasure to a polluted, industrialized growth center."

—*Solicitation letter from the World Wildlife Fund*

7. "Frantic parents tell shocked TV audience: space aliens stole our son."

—Weekly World News

8. "The manufacturer of Sudafed 12-hour capsules issued a nationwide recall of the product Sunday after two people in the state of Washington who had taken the medication died of cyanide poisoning and a third became seriously ill."

—Los Angeles Times

9. "In Canada, smoking in public places, trains, planes or even automobiles is now prohibited by law or by convention. The federal government has banned smoking in all its buildings."

—*Reuters*

10. "In October 2012, People for the Ethical Treatment of Animals petitioned Irvine, California, to create a roadside memorial for the truckload of live fish that perished in a recent traffic accident."

—Orange County Register

11. "Maps, files and compasses were hidden in Monopoly sets and smuggled into World War II German prison camps by MI-5, Britain's counter-intelligence agency, to help British prisoners escape, according to the British manufacturer of the game."

—*Associated Press*

12. "Cats that live indoors and use a litter box can live four to five years longer."

—*From an advertisement for Jonny Cat litter*

13. "The collapse of WTC Building 7 represents one of the worst structural failures in modern history. The official story contends that fires weakened the structures, resulting in a gravitational collapse. The evidence, obvious to so many researchers but omitted from NIST's Final Report, supports a very different conclusion—one that points squarely to explosive controlled demolition. If WTC 7 was intentionally brought down, then clearly it becomes a 'smoking gun' that must be investigated."

—*http://www.ae911truth.org/news/41-articles/344-building-7-implosion-the-smoking-gun-of-911.html*

14. "Because of cartilage that begins to accumulate after age thirty, by the time . . . [a] man is seventy his nose has grown a half inch wider and another half inch longer, his earlobes have fattened, and his ears themselves have grown a quarter inch longer. Overall, his head's circumference increases a quarter inch every decade, and not because of his brain, which is shrinking. His head is fatter apparently because, unlike most other bones in the body, the skull seems to thicken with age."

—*John Tierney (a staff writer for* Esquire*)*

15. "Gardenias . . . need ample warmth, ample water, and steady feeding. Though hardy to 20°F or even lower, plants fail to grow and bloom well without summer heat."

—The Sunset New Western Garden Book *(a best-selling gardening reference in the West)*

16. "It's stunningly beautiful. The weather is near perfect. The community of locals and expats is welcoming and friendly. The road here is good and you don't want for any modern conveniences or amenities. But hardly anyone knows about it—and real estate is still affordable.

"Once the word gets out about this place, the real estate market is set to explode. But right now . . . you can get lake view lots perched above the boat dock, with a down payment of $1,900 and monthly payment of just $143."

—International Living *(an online advertiser for foreign real estate), about Costa Rica*

17. "On Tuesday, Dec. 4, DJs Mel Greig and Michael Christian phoned the King Edward VII hospital pretending to be Prince Charles and Queen Elizabeth in order to get information about the Duchess of Cambridge. Saldanha, [a nurse] who had been tending to Middleton during her stay, fell victim to the prank and passed the callers on to another employee, who then proceeded to give confidential details about the pregnant royal's condition.

Three days later, Saldanha, known to friends and colleagues as 'Jess,' was found dead of an apparent suicide."

—US Weekly

18. "In our new print issue, which begins hitting newsstands today, the superstar's [John Travolta's] former gay lover breaks his long silence to reveal the shocking details of an intimate six-year sexual relationship. In a bombshell world exclusive ENQUIRER interview, former pilot DOUG GOTTERBA discloses that Travolta's Hollywood image as a big-screen heartthrob throughout the '80s was a total sham."

—National Enquirer, *online*

19. "The Encinitas (California) Union School District is facing the threat of a lawsuit as it launches what is believed to be the country's most comprehensive yoga program for a public school system. Parents opposed to the program say the classes will indoctrinate their children in Eastern religion and are not just for exercise."

—*Associated Press*

20. "Taliban terrorists have a secret weapon to destroy the infidel American enemy—monkey marksmen. According to the *People's Daily* in China, the Taliban in Afghanistan is 'training monkeys to use weapons to attack American troops.' . . . Islamic insurgents have drafted macaques and baboons to be all that they can be, arming them with AK-4 rifles, machine guns and trench mortars in the Waziristan tribal region near the border between Pakistan and Afghanistan. The monkeys, being rewarded with bananas and peanuts, are being turned into snipers at a secret Taliban training base."

—New York Post, *July 13, 2010*

## Exercise 4-16

The following appeared in a local newspaper, criticizing the position on global warming taken by local television weather forecaster and political activist Anthony Watts.

Read it carefully and decide whether anything the newspaper alleges should affect the credibility of Watts or the project he endorsed. Compare your judgment with those of your classmates.

"[Anthony] Watts endorsed the 'Petition Project,' which refutes man-made global warming. Besides many fictitious names submitted, only about one percent of the petition signers had done any climate research.

"The petition was prepared by Frederick Seitz, a scientist who, from 1975 to 1989, was paid $585,000 by the tobacco industry to direct a $45 million scientific effort to hide the health impact of smoking. Does Watts agree that cigarettes are not harmful, as Seitz's studies showed?"

—Chico News & Review

## Exercise 4-17

Find five *ethos* or *pathos* advertisements. Explain how each ad attempts to make the product seem attractive.

## Exercise 4-18

Watch Fox News, MSNBC, and CNN news programs on the same day. Compare the three on the basis of (1) the news stories covered, (2) the amount of air time given to two or three of the major stories, and (3) any difference in the slant of the presentations of a controversial story. Make notes. Be prepared to discuss in class the differences in coverage on the basis of the three criteria just mentioned.

## Writing Exercises

1. Although millions of people have seen professional magicians like David Copperfield and Siegfried and Roy perform in person or on television, it's probably a safe assumption that almost nobody believes they accomplish their feats by means of real magical or supernatural powers—that is, that they somehow "defy" the laws of nature. But even though they've never had a personal demonstration, a significant portion of the population is said to believe that certain psychics are able to accomplish apparent miracles by exactly such means. How might you explain this difference in belief?

2. In the text, you were asked to consider the claim "Charlie's eighty-seven-year-old grandmother swam across Lake Michigan in the middle of winter." Because of the implausibility of such a claim—that is, because it conflicts with our background information—it is reasonable to reject it. Suppose, however, that instead of just telling us about his grandmother, Charlie brings us a photocopy of a page of the *Chicago Tribune* with a photograph of a person in a wet suit walking up onto a beach. The caption underneath reads, "Eighty-Seven-Year-Old Grandmother Swims Lake Michigan in January!" Based on this piece of evidence, should a critical thinker decide that the original claim is significantly more likely to be true than if it were backed up only by Charlie's word? Defend your answer.

3. Are our schools doing a bad job educating our kids? Do research in the library or on the Internet to answer this question. Make a list (no more than one page long) of facts that support the claim that our schools are not doing as good a job as they should. Then list facts that support the opposite view

(or that rebut the claims of those who say our schools aren't doing a good job). Again, limit yourself to one page. Cite your sources.

Now, think critically about your sources. Are any stronger or weaker than the others? Explain why on a single sheet of paper. Come prepared to read your explanation, along with your list of facts and sources, to the class.

4. Jackson says you should be skeptical of the opinion of someone who stands to profit from your accepting that opinion. Smith disagrees, pointing out that salespeople are apt to know a lot more about products of the type they sell than do most people.

   "Most salespeople are honest, and you can trust them," Smith argues. "Those who aren't don't stay in business long."

   Take about fifteen minutes to defend either Smith or Jackson in a short essay. When everyone is finished, your instructor will collect the essays and read three or more to the class to stimulate a brief discussion. After discussion, can the class come to any agreement about who is correct, Jackson or Smith?

5. Search the Internet for answers to one or more of the following questions. Write an essay in which you take a position on the question and defend your position with an argument, and explain which Internet source you came across is most credible and why.

   a. Can smoking stunt bone growth?
   b. Is it safe to smoke tobacco using a hookah?
   c. Should toasters be unplugged when not in use?
   d. Will regular, vigorous exercise make you live longer?
   e. Are sea levels rising?
   f. How harmful is it to get too little sleep?
   g. Is it better to feed dogs raw meat than dog food?
   h. Are psychics really able to solve crimes?
   i. Why do hands and feet get wrinkled if you are in a bath for a long time?
   j. Do smoking laws improve public health?

6. Raise a question you are interested in, research it on the Internet, take a position on it and support it with an argument, and explain which Internet source you came across is most credible and why.

# Rhetoric, the Art of Persuasion

# 5

Rhetoric, the venerable art of persuasive writing and speaking, has been one of the twin anchors of Western education since the days of Aristotle. The other, which also dates from Aristotle, is logic. You use rhetoric to win someone to your point of view; you use logic to demonstrate a claim or support it. These are separate enterprises. You can use logic to persuade people, but all too often they are persuaded by poor logic and unmoved by good logic. This is why education increasingly emphasizes critical thinking, to help people improve their logic and to help them distinguish between proof and persuasion.

In this chapter we do three things. First, we introduce the important concept of rhetorical force. Then we explain several rhetorical devices. Good writers and speakers employ many of these devices to make their cases as persuasive as possible. None of the devices, however, have logical force or probative weight ("probative" means tending to prove). We, as critical thinkers, should be able to recognize them for what they are—devices of persuasion.

Last, after we examine the various devices, we examine four principal techniques of demagoguery. Demagogues use inflammatory rhetoric to win acceptance for false and misleading ideas. They appeal to the fears and prejudices of an audience, and depend on its inability to see through their tricks. Famous demagogues include Adolf Hitler, Joseph McCarthy, and others, including the occasional candidate for the U.S. presidency. Spotting demagoguery and resisting it is perhaps the most important skill a critical thinker can have.

## RHETORICAL FORCE

Words and expressions have more than a literal or "dictionary" meaning. They also have what is known as **emotive meaning** or **rhetorical force** (these being the same thing). This is their power to express and elicit various psychological and emotional responses. For example, "elderly gentleman" and "old codger" evoke different emotions, the first pleasing and the second less so. To say that someone's opinion is "mistaken" is one thing; to refer to it as "bull" is quite another. The two expressions have the same literal meaning, but the second has a negative emotive meaning. Read this statement from a famous speech by Barack Obama, in which he conceded a primary election to Hillary Clinton. Then compare it with the paraphrase that immediately follows:

> Political language is designed to make lies sound truthful . . . and to give the appearance of solidity to pure wind.
>
> —GEORGE ORWELL

And so tomorrow, as we take this campaign South and West; as we learn that the struggles of the textile worker in Spartanburg are not so different than the plight of the dishwasher in Las Vegas; that the hopes of the little girl who goes to a crumbling school in Dillon are the same as the dreams of the boy who learns on the streets of LA; we will remember that there is something happening in America; that we are not as divided as our politics suggests; that we are one people; we are one nation; and together, we will begin the next great chapter in America's story with three words that will ring from coast to coast; from sea to shining sea—Yes. We. Can.

—*Barack Obama speech, January 8, 2008*

Paraphrase:

Let us continue campaigning.

The message conveyed by the two passages is essentially the same. The difference between them is due entirely to the powerful rhetorical force of the first passage, which is inspirational and uplifting, and exhorts listeners toward a common shining goal. The passage illustrates the point made above about rhetoric: It may be psychologically compelling, but by itself it establishes nothing. It has no probative weight. If we allow our attitudes and beliefs to be formed solely by the rhetorical force of words, we fall short as critical thinkers.

Now, before we get in trouble with your English professor, let's make it clear once again that there is nothing wrong with someone's trying to make his or her case as persuasive as possible. Good writers use well-chosen, rhetorically effective words and phrases. But we, as critical thinkers, must be able to distinguish the argument (if any) contained in a passage from the rhetoric; we must distinguish between the logical force of a set of remarks and its psychological force. You won't find much rhetoric of the sort we discuss here in science journals because it carries no probative weight. Scientists may hope readers accept their findings, but it's risky for them to try to sell their findings by couching them in the language of persuasion. It's not that rhetoric weakens an argument; it just doesn't strengthen it.*

*A body of scholarly work known as the "Rhetoric of Science," views science *as* a species of rhetoric. However, if you are looking for examples of the kind of rhetorical devices and techniques explored in this chapter, you won't find many in (for instance) the *Journal of Cell Biology* or the *Journal of the Royal Statistical Society*.

CHAPTER 5: RHETORIC, THE ART OF PERSUASION

## RHETORICAL DEVICES I

The first group of **rhetorical devices** are usually single words or short phrases designed to give a statement a positive or negative slant. For this reason, they are sometimes called **slanters**.

### Euphemisms and Dysphemisms

Euphemisms are unpleasant truths wearing diplomatic cologne.

—QUENTIN CRISP, *Manners from Heaven*

A **euphemism** is a neutral or positive expression used in place of one that carries negative associations. "Detainee" means what most of us call "prisoner," but it seems more benign. At first glance, "waterboarding" sounds like something you'd expect to see young people doing on a California beach, not a torture technique. "Collateral damage" is a sanitized way of saying "civilian casualties."

Euphemisms obviously can be used to whitewash wrongdoing; but they have positive uses as well. It would be insensitive to tell friends you were sorry they killed their dog. Instead, you say you were sorry they had to put their dog to sleep.

A **dysphemism** is used to produce a negative effect on someone's attitude about something, or to tone down the positive associations it may have. It sounds worse to be obscenely rich than to be very wealthy. Eating animal flesh sounds worse than eating meat. The tax imposed on an inheritance is sometimes called a death tax, which leaves a bad taste because it suggests the deceased rather than the inheritors is being taxed. Dismissing a legislative proposal as a "scheme" also qualifies as a dysphemism. We would be hard pressed to explain the difference between "conservative" and "far-right" or between "liberal" and "ultra-liberal," but the second of each of these pairs sounds worse than the first, and they both qualify as dysphemisms. "Wing nut" qualifies as a dysphemism for either end of the political spectrum.

You naturally expect to find a generous sprinkling of dysphemisms when a speaker or writer tries to get us to dislike someone or something. (During political campaigns, they crop up everywhere.) Of course, what counts as a euphemism or a dysphemism is, to some extent, in the eyes of the beholder. One person's junkyard is another person's automotive recycling business; one person's sanitary land fill is another person's garbage dump.

Finally, there is this: Some facts are just plain repellent, and for that reason, even neutral reports of them sound appalling. "Lizzie killed her father with an ax" is not a dysphemism; it simply reports a horrible fact about Lizzie.

### Weaselers

Great Western pays up to 12 percent *more interest on checking accounts.*

—Radio advertisement

Even aside from the "up to" weaseler, this ad can be deceptive about what interest rate it's promising. Unless you listen carefully, you might think Great Western is paying 12 percent on checking accounts. The presence of the word "more" changes all that, of course. If you're getting 3 percent now, and Great Western gives you "up to 12 percent more" than that, they'll be giving you about 3½ percent—hardly the fortune the ad seems to promise.

When inserted into a claim, **weaselers** help protect it from criticism by watering it down somewhat, weakening it, and giving the claim's author a way out in case the claim is challenged.

Without doubt you've heard the words "up to" used as a weaseler a thousand times, especially in advertising. "Up to five more miles per gallon." "Up to twenty more yards off the tee." "Lose up to ten pounds a week." None of these guarantee anything. Sure, you might lose ten pounds, but you might lose nothing. The statement still stands, thanks to "up to."

Let's make up a statistic. Let's say that 98 percent of American doctors believe that aspirin is a contributing cause of Reye's syndrome in children, and that the other 2 percent are unconvinced. If we then claim that "some doctors are unconvinced that aspirin is related to Reye's syndrome," we cannot be held accountable for having said something false, even though our claim might be misleading to someone who did not know the complete story. The word "some" has allowed us to weasel the point. Remember: A claim does not have to be false in order to be misleading.

Words that sometimes weasel—such as "perhaps," "possibly," "maybe," and "may be," among others—can be used to produce innuendo (to be explained below), to plant a suggestion without actually making a claim that a person can be held to. We can suggest that Berriault is a liar without actually saying so (and thus without saying something that might be hard to defend) by saying that Berriault *may be* a liar. Or we can say it is *possible* that Berriault is a liar (which is true of all of us, after all). "*Perhaps* Berriault is a liar" works nicely, too. All of these are examples of weaselers used to create innuendo.

*Not every use of words and phrases like these is a weaseling one,* of course. Words that can weasel can also bring very important qualifications to bear on a claim. The very same word that weasels in one context may not weasel at all in another. For example, a detective who is considering all the possible angles on a crime and who has just heard Smith's account of events may say to an associate, "Of course, it is *possible* that Smith is lying." This need not be a case of weaseling. The detective may simply be exercising due care. Other words and phrases that are sometimes used to weasel can also be used legitimately. Qualifying phrases such as "it is arguable that," "it may well be that," and so on have at least as many appropriate uses as weaseling ones. Others, such as "some would say that," are likely to be weaseling more often than not, but even they can serve an honest purpose in the right context. Our warning, then, is to be watchful when qualifying phrases turn up. Is the speaker or writer adding a reasonable qualification, insinuating a bit of innuendo, or preparing a way out? We can only warn; you need to assess the speaker, the context, and the subject to establish the grounds for the right judgment.

## Downplayers

**Downplayers** attempt to make someone or something look less important or less significant. Stereotypes, rhetorical comparisons, rhetorical explanations, and innuendo (all discussed later) can all be used to downplay something. The remark "Don't mind what Mr. Pierce says; he thinks he is an educator" downplays Mr. Pierce and his statements. (What educator doesn't think he or she is one?) We can also downplay by careful insertion of certain words or other devices. Let's amend the preceding example like this: "Don't mind what Mr. Pierce says; he's just another educator." Notice how the phrase "just another" downplays Mr. Pierce's status still further.

Perhaps the words most often used as downplayers are "mere" and "merely." If Kim tells you her sister has a mere green belt in Pujo (a Tibetan martial art), she is downplaying her sister's accomplishment.

The term "so-called" is another standard downplayer. We might say, for example, that the woman who made the diagnosis is a "so-called medical professional," which downplays her credentials. Quotation marks can be used to accomplish the same thing:

> She got her "degree" from a correspondence school.

Use of quotation marks as a downplayer is somewhat different from their use to indicate irony, as in this remark:

> John "borrowed" Hank's umbrella, and Hank hasn't seen it since.

The idea in the latter example isn't to downplay John's borrowing the umbrella; it's to indicate that it wasn't really a case of borrowing at all.

"Fifteen minutes could save you fifteen percent or more on car insurance."

—GEICO car insurance advertisements

Then again, it might not.

Many conjunctions—such as "nevertheless," "however," "still," and "but"—can be used to downplay claims that precede them. Others, like "although" and "even though," can downplay claims that follow them. Such uses are more subtle than the first group of downplayers. Compare the following two versions of what is essentially the same pair of claims:

> (1) The leak at the plant was terrible, but the plant provided good jobs to thousands of people.
>
> (2) Although the plant provided good jobs to thousands of people, the leak there was terrible.

The first statement downplays the leak; the second statement downplays the good the plant produces.

The context of a claim can determine whether it downplays or not. Consider the remark "Chavez won by only six votes." The word "only" may or may not downplay Chavez's victory, depending on how thin a six-vote margin is. If ten thousand people voted and Chavez won by six, then the word "only" seems perfectly appropriate: Chavez won by just the skin of his teeth. But if the vote was in a committee of, say, twenty, then six is quite a substantial margin (it would be thirteen votes to seven, if everybody voted—almost two to one), and applying the word "only" to the result is clearly a slanting device designed to give Chavez's margin of victory less importance than it deserves.

Downplayers really can't—and shouldn't—be avoided altogether. They can give our writing flair and interest. What *can* be avoided is being unduly swayed by them. Learning to appreciate the psychological and emotional nuances of language decreases your chances of being taken in by the manipulations of a writer or speaker.

---

**Exercise 5-1**

Identify rhetorical devices you find in the following from the previous section of the text (euphemisms, dysphemisms, weaselers, downplayers). *Not every example may contain such a device.*

▲—See the answers section at the back of the book.

▲ 1. There, there; it could be worse.

2. You should install solar panels. They could save you a lot of money.

3. Smithers might have visited a gentleman's club once or twice, but that hardly could disqualify him from the race.

▲ 4. This president wakes up every morning and pretends to speak for the people.

5. Whistle-blower? Dude's a snitch.

6. These self-appointed experts have nothing better to do with their time than tell us what we should do with ours.

▲ 7. Excuse me, Dear. I must powder my nose.

8. I suppose we could go listen to her speech. No doubt some people think she is an expert.

9. We have to take poor Fido to the animal shelter.

▲ 10. "It doesn't say anywhere in the Constitution this idea of the separation of church and state."

*—Sean Hannity*

11. You say you are in love with Oscar, but are you sure he's right for you? Isn't he a little too . . . uh, mature for you?

12. He was at the bar for two hours, officer, but I know he had only four drinks during that time.

▲ 13. "The key principle is 'responsible energy exploration.' And remember, it's NOT drilling for oil. It's responsible energy exploration."

*—Republican pollster Frank Luntz*

14. Of course, it may be that Aaron Hernandez didn't even commit the assaults he was accused of.

15. Try the Neutron Diet for just four weeks, and you can lose as many as twenty pounds!

▲ 16. Republicans stand on principle against the schemes of the environmental extremists.

17. Despite the downplaying by bought-off scientists, climate change is very real.

18. Obama and his Democrat–Communist party bloated the already bloated federal bureaucracy by 25 percent in ONE YEAR.

▲ 19. Charles, be sure to tinkle before we leave!

20. Him? Oh, that's just my brother.

## RHETORICAL DEVICES II

These next three slanting devices rely, in one way or another, on unwarranted assumptions. We have to depend on unstated assumptions all the time, but as you'll see, we can get into trouble when those assumptions are not trustworthy.

### Stereotypes

A **stereotype** is a cultural belief or idea about a social group's attributes, usually simplified or exaggerated. It can be positive or negative. Americans are sometimes stereotyped as friendly and generous, other times as boorish and insensitive. Southern Caucasian males are sometimes stereotyped as genteel or mannerly; other times as bigoted rednecks. Of course, a moment's thought tells us that none of these characteristics could reasonably apply to all the members of these groups. Stereotypes are unreliable characterizations of people; and when speakers or writers use them to try to win us to their point of view, we must be on guard. For example, if someone used the idea of a "welfare queen" (a pejorative stereotype of a lazy mother who prefers collecting welfare checks to finding a job) to persuade us that taxpayers are spending too much money on welfare, we should be aware that the speaker is trying to persuade us with an image rather than with data.*

But stereotyping can work in the other direction as well. If we hear that so-and-so "tells it like it is," we have been given a positive stereotype, that of the outspoken truthteller. Linking people with a stereotype we like can create a favorable impression of them.

Stereotypes come from multiple sources, many from popular literature or the entertainment or recording industries, and are often supported by a variety of prejudices and group interests. Native American tribes of the Great Plains were portrayed

> Mention the *strict regulations*—not protocols or rules—governing nuclear power plants.
>
> —Republican pollster FRANK LUNTZ, in "An Energy Policy for the 21st Century," advising Republicans how to sell nuclear energy

---

*In 2012, welfare accounted for less than one-half of 1 percent of the federal budget.

## Do Blondes Make Us Dumber? Cognitive Functioning in the Presence of Stereotypes

According to research reported by Shelley Emling of the Cox News Service, when subjects (both men and women) were shown photos of women with blonde hair, their ability to answer Trivial Pursuit game questions declined. This did not happen when they saw women with other hair colors. The authors of the study said that it confirmed other findings that people's cognitive functioning is affected by exposure to stereotypes. "The mere knowledge of a stereotype can influence our behavior," one researcher said. One example given for this was that, when people are exposed to elderly people, they tend to walk and talk more slowly.

■ Maybe seeing a picture of German Chancellor Angela Merkel, a very bright blonde woman, who has a PhD in quantum chemistry, would improve subjects' abilities on Trivial Pursuit.

—*Shelley Emling, Cox News Service,* http://thesituationist.wordpress.com/2008/01/22/.

favorably in the popular literature of white Americans until just before the mid-nineteenth century. But as the westward expansion of the United States continued, and conflicts with white settlers escalated, depictions became increasingly pejorative.

Bottom line: Undeniably, some stereotypes carry much rhetorical force, but they have no evidentiary or probative (tendency to prove) force. Rhetoric that contains them may be persuasive psychologically, but it is neither strengthened nor weakened logically.

Incidentally, does the fact that members of a group utter negative stereotypes about themselves make it okay for others to use those stereotypes? We are not aware of an argument to that effect that can withstand scrutiny. "They say bad things about themselves; therefore those things are true" is illogical; and so is "since they say bad things about themselves, it is okay for us to do so too."

### Innuendo

**Innuendo** uses the power of suggestion to disparage (say something bad about) someone or something. Unlike dysphemisms—expressions having obvious negative rhetorical force—innuendo relies on neutral (or even positive) phrasing to insinuate something derogatory. Consider for example this statement:

> Ladies and gentlemen, I am proof that at least one candidate in this race doesn't make stuff up.

*The city voluntarily assumed the costs of cleaning up the landfill to make it safe for developers.*

—Opponents of a local housing development

Oops, the opponents didn't mention that the law required the city to assume the costs. The omission of course suggests that the city was in cahoots with the developers. Leaving out important information in order to convey a negative message about someone or something is another form of innuendo.

### Innuendo with Statistics

> Taxpayers with incomes over $200,000 could expect on average to pay about $99,000 in taxes under [the proposed] plan.
>
> —*Wall Street Journal*
>
> This statement plants the suggestion that the tax proposal will soak anyone who makes over $200,000. But, in the words of the *New Republic* (February 3, 2003), "The *Journal's* statistic is about as meaningful as asserting that males over the age of six have had an average of three sexual partners." Bill Gates and many billionaires like him are among those who make over $200,000.

As you can see, the statement does not say that the speaker's opponent makes stuff up. But it conveys that message nevertheless. Another example:

> Jim: Is Ralph is telling the truth?
> Joe: Yes, this time.

Joe is insinuating that Ralph doesn't usually tell the truth. Yet another example, maybe our all-time favorite, is this remark from W. C. Fields.

> I didn't say the meat was tough. I said I didn't see the horse that is usually outside.

Another example would be:

> She's just the aerobics instructor, at least that's what he tells his wife.

Saying, "He may think he made a good speech" would also count as innuendo, because it insinuates that his speech wasn't very good. So would, "I bet he actually thinks he made a good speech." What we bet is that most people who make good speeches actually think they made good speeches.

Some examples of innuendo are known as **significant mention.** This occurs when someone states a claim that ordinarily would not need making. Here's an example:

> I noticed that Sueanne's latest rent check didn't bounce.

It's clear that the speaker mentions this fact because there was some expectation that the check *would* bounce. Thus the idea that she bounces checks regularly is clearly insinuated.

The key to recognizing innuendo is that it relies entirely on suggestion and implication, rather than on wording that has overtly negative associations. "His speech was vaporous and stupid" is not innuendo.

### Loaded Questions

A **loaded question,** like innuendo, implies something without coming out and saying it. For example, the question "Why does the president hate rich people?" implies without quite saying it that the president hates rich people. "Have you always loved being in debt?" implies without quite saying it that you love being in debt.

Here is how this works. Every question rests on assumptions. Even an innocent question like "What time is it?" depends on the assumptions that the hearer speaks English and probably has means of finding out the time. A loaded question, however, rests on one or more *unwarranted* (unjustified) assumptions. The world's oldest example, "Have you stopped beating your wife?" rests on the assumption that the person asked has beaten his wife in the past. If there is no reason to think that this assumption is true, then the question is loaded.

Loaded questions thus count as a form of innuendo if they imply something negative about someone. However, they can be used to carry a positive message as well, as in the example: "How did Melanie acquire such a wonderful voice?"

■ Photographs, like rhetoric, have suggestive power. For example, what does this picture of Russian President Vladimir Putin suggest about him? Is it favorable or unfavorable, or does it depend entirely on your point of view?

## Exercise 5-2

1. Watch an episode of *Big Bang Theory, Two and a Half Men,* or *Shades of Blue* and see how many stereotyped characters you can identify.
2. Watch an episode of *Good Morning America* or one of the network or cable news programs and see how many stereotyped characters you can spot in the commercials.

## Exercise 5-3

Identify any stereotypes, innuendo, or loaded questions you find in the following text.

1. Devon is a total jock. Don't go making him your study partner.
2. Went to my philosophy class today. The professor showed up sober.
3. At least his wife isn't rude.
4. Don't you have anything better to wear than that?
5. Give the work to Brockston. He's a real man. He'll get it done.
6. You're going to go see what? That's such a chick flick!
7. Who do like better, me or Sydney?
8. For some reason, President Obama has never shown his birth certificate.
9. An attorney questioning a witness: "So, if you were awake when you crossed the bridge, just when did you go to sleep at the wheel?"
10. No, I'm sure you'll enjoy playing tennis with Jerome. He gets around pretty well for a guy his age.
11. Frankly, I believe that flash memory will make any kind of moving-part memory, such as hard drives, completely obsolete.

12. Larry Kudlow, on CNBC (in an *American Spectator* interview): "[Former Treasury secretary] Bob Rubin's a smart guy, a nice man, but he hates tax cuts. To listen to Rubin on domestic issues, you could just die. He's a free-spending left-winger."

13. Has Harry been a faithful husband? Well, he's not been through a Tiger Woods phase.

14. Why is it, do you suppose, that pit bulls are all mean and vicious?

15. I wouldn't worry about the train being late. This is Germany, you know.

16. Keep your kid away from that dog! Didn't you know that's a pit bull?

17. It goes without saying that his kid will do well in school. His kind always do.

18. There is no proof the president deals drugs. On the other hand, there's no proof he doesn't, either.

19. Does Sydney still drink like a fish?

20. Of course Christie had nothing to do with shutting down the lanes on the George Washington Bridge. He's only the governor of New Jersey, after all.

## RHETORICAL DEVICES III

Humor and a bit of exaggeration are part of our everyday speech. But they can also be used to sway opinions if the listener is not being careful.

### Ridicule/Sarcasm

Also known as the **horse laugh,** this device includes ridicule and vicious humor of all kinds. Ridicule is a powerful rhetorical tool—most of us hate being laughed at. So it's important to remember that somebody who simply gets a laugh at the expense of another person's position has not raised any objection to that position.

One may simply laugh outright at a claim ("Send aid to Egypt? Har, har, har!"), tell an unrelated joke, use sarcastic language, or simply laugh at the person who is trying to make the point.

The next time you watch a debate, remember that the person who has the funniest lines and who gets the most laughs may be the person who *seems* to win the debate, but critical thinkers should be able to see the difference between argumentation on one hand and entertainment on the other.

Notice that we are not saying there's anything *wrong* with entertainment, nor with making a valid point in a humorous way.

### Hyperbole

**Hyperbole** is extravagant overstatement, or exaggeration. "The Democrats want everyone to be on welfare" is hyperbole. So is "Nobody in the Tea Party likes African Americans." Describing your

■ Stephen Colbert's stock in trade is making fun of celebrities and politicians.

> A feminazi is a woman to whom the most important thing in life is seeing to it that as many abortions as possible are performed.
>
> —RUSH LIMBAUGH
>
> **A rhetorical definition with hyperbole. (A straw man, too, but that's for a later chapter.)**

parents as "fascists" because they don't want you to major in art also counts. People exaggerate—we all exaggerate—not only to express how strongly we feel about something but also, sometimes, to persuade our listeners of a lesser claim. For example, to persuade your son not to text while driving, you might tell him he's likely to kill half the population of Los Angeles. To convince his girlfriend he really loves her, a young man may state that he loves her more than anyone has ever loved anyone. And so on.

Therefore, the thing to remember when you encounter hyperbole is that, even if you reject it as exaggeration, you might be moved in the direction of a lesser claim even in the absence of argument. If a server tells you that the salmon is the best you will ever eat, you may end up ordering it. If somebody tells you that Clara thinks of nobody but herself, you might be tempted to think that Clara is a little self-centered. If you hear somebody you respect confidently predict "*nobody* will vote for Jackson," you might find yourself surprised when Jackson actually is elected.

It may almost go without saying that other rhetorical devices often involve hyperbole. For example, when we describe a member of the opposing political party as traitorous, we are using a dysphemism that involves hyperbole. And negative stereotyping always involves exaggerating how often some undesirable characteristic is found in the targeted social group.

Exercises for these last two rhetorical devices can be found in Exercise 5-8.

## RHETORICAL DEVICES IV

Definitions, explanations, analogies, and comparisons are all used in straightforward ways most of the time. But, as we'll see, they can also be used in rhetorical fashion to slant a point one way or another.

### Rhetorical Definitions and Rhetorical Explanations

As explained in Chapter 3, **rhetorical definitions** employ rhetorically charged language to express or elicit an attitude about something. Defining abortion as "the murder of an unborn child" does this—and stacks the deck against those who think abortion is morally defensible. Restricting the meaning of "human being" to an organism to which a human has given birth stacks the deck the other way.

In Chapter 3, we explained that when we define a concept by providing an example of it, we are "defining by example." It's worth noting here that even definitions by example can slant a discussion if the examples are prejudicially chosen. Defining "conservative" by pointing to a white supremacist would be a case in point. If one wants to see all sides of an issue, one must avoid definitions and examples that slant a discussion.

**Rhetorical explanations** use the language of standard explanations to disguise their real purpose, which is to express or elicit an attitude.

For example, consider this "explanation" we found in a letter to an editor:

> I am a traditional liberal who keeps asking himself, why has there been such a seismic shift in affirmative action? It used to be affirmative action stood for equal opportunity; now it means preferences and quotas. Why the change? It's because the people behind affirmative action aren't for equal rights anymore; they're for handouts.

This isn't a dispassionate scholarly explanation of causation, but a way of expressing an opinion about, and trying to evoke anger at, affirmative action policies.

## Legislative Misnomers

Several polls have reported that voters sometimes indicate approval of a measure when they hear its title but indicate disapproval after they've heard an explanation of what the measure actually proposes. This isn't surprising, given the misleading proposal titles assigned by members of Congress and state legislatures, and by authors of ballot measures. Here are a few examples of recent laws, initiatives, and so on, the names of which don't exactly tell the whole story:

Healthy Forests Initiative (federal)—Reduces public involvement in decision making regarding logging, reduces environmental protection requirements, and provides timber companies greater access to national forests

Clear Skies Act (federal)—Loosens regulation of mercury, nitrous oxide, and sulphur dioxide, and puts off required reductions of these substances for several years beyond the limits of the current Clean Air Act; allows companies to trade off "pollution credits" so that some communities would get cleaner air and others dirtier air

Defense of Marriage Act (federal)—Does nothing to preserve traditional marriages, but does outlaw same-sex marriages; many parts have been declared invalid

Limitations on Enforcement of Unfair Business Competition Laws (California)—Makes it impossible for consumer groups of all types to sue corporations and businesses to prevent fraud, false advertising, and other deceptions before they take place

Right to Work (many states)—Prevents unions from collecting fees from nonmembers of bargaining units

Prohibition of Discrimination and Preferential Treatment (California)—Weakens or eliminates affirmative action programs

### Rhetorical Analogies and Misleading Comparisons

A **rhetorical analogy** likens two or more things to make one of them appear better or worse than another. This may lead us to change our opinions about something even though we have not been given an argument. For example, hearing Social Security likened to a Ponzi scheme (a Ponzi scheme is a pyramid scheme designed to bilk people who fall for it) might make us suspicious of Social Security. Constant likening of Saddam Hussein to Adolf Hitler may have influenced some people's attitudes about the Iraq invasion. In late 2015 and 2016, we heard Donald Trump compared to Benito Mussolini, the facist dictator of Italy in the early 1940s, in an attempt to paint Trump as a facist.

Of course, people use analogies for straightforward explanatory purposes. If a friend knows nothing about rugby, you might promote his understanding by noting its similarity to football. But when Joseph Goebbels likened intellectuals to "bubbles of fat that float on the surface without affecting the liquid below" (see page 144), it is clear that his intent was to denigrate intellectuals—and lead his listeners to do so as well. On the other hand, when humorist Dave Barry likens having kids to having a bowling alley in your brain, he is simply trying to entertain us.

Rhetorical analogies also include comparisons, like "You have a better chance of being struck by lightning than of winning the lottery." But some comparisons can lead us into error if we are not careful. A female smoker has a much better chance of surviving lung cancer than does a male, but that would not be a good reason for

**Doonesbury**                                                    BY GARRY TRUDEAU

a female smoker not to quit. Advertising sometimes offers vague comparisons, such as "Now 25 percent larger," "New and improved," and "Quietest by far." Unless both sides of a comparison are made clear, the comparison isn't worth much.

Here are a few questions that you could keep in mind when considering comparisons. They include reference to omissions and distortions, which can be among the more subtle forms of rhetorical devices.

1. *Is the comparison vague?* What do you mean, James is a *better swimmer* than Ray? In what way is Sarah *happier* than Santana? What specifically do you have in mind, when you assert that women are *better equipped to deal with grief?* The appropriate question for comparisons like these is not," What makes you think that is true," but rather, "What do you mean?"

2. *Is important information missing?* It is nice to hear that the unemployment rate has gone down, but not if you learn the reason is that a larger percent of the workforce has given up looking for work. Or, suppose someone says that 90 percent of heroin addicts once smoked marijuana. Without other information, the comparison is meaningless, since 90 percent of heroin addicts no doubt ate carrots, too.

3. *Is the same standard of comparison used?* Are the same reporting and recording practices being used? A change in the jobless rate doesn't mean much if the government changes the way it calculates joblessness, as sometimes happens. In 1993, the number of people in the United States with AIDS suddenly increased dramatically. Had a new form of the AIDS virus appeared? No; the federal government had expanded the definition of AIDS to include several new indicator conditions. As a result, overnight 50,000 people were considered to have AIDS who had not been so considered the day before.

4. *Are the items comparable?* It is hard to compare professional golfers Jack Nicklaus and Tiger Woods, since they played against different competitors and had different types of equipment. It's hard to derive a conclusion from the fact that this April's retail business activity is way down as compared with last April's, if Easter came early this year and the weather was especially cold. That more male than female drivers are involved in traffic fatalities doesn't mean much by itself, since male drivers collectively drive more miles than do female drivers. Comparing share values of two mutual funds over the past ten years won't be useful to an investor if the comparison doesn't take into account a difference in fees.

5. *Is the comparison expressed as an average?* The average rainfall in Seattle is about the same as that in Kansas City. But you'll spend more time in the rain in Seattle because it rains there twice as often as in Kansas City. If Central Valley Components, Inc. (CVC), reports that average salaries of a majority of

## Misleading Graphic Comparisons

Comparisons displayed on graphs should be viewed with caution, as this graph illustrates.

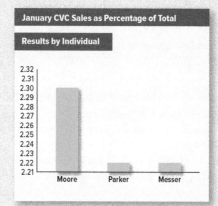

If you just glance at the bars, you might think Moore's sales at CVC (a fictitious company) are many times greater than Parker's or Messer's. That's because Moore's bar is much taller than Parker's or Messer's. But if you look closely at the scale on the vertical axis, you can see that, in fact, the sales of all three salespeople are only about eight one-hundredths of a percent different.

its employees have more than doubled over the past ten years, it sounds good, but CVC still may not be a great place to work. Perhaps the increases were due to converting the majority of employees, who worked half-time, to full-time and firing the rest. Comparisons that involve averages omit details that can be important, simply because they involve averages.

Averages are measures of central tendency, and there are different kinds of measures or averages. Consider, for instance, the average cost of a new house in your area, which may be $210,000. If that is the *mean,* it is the total of the sales prices divided by the number of houses sold, and it may be quite different from the *median,* which is an average that is the halfway figure (half the houses cost more and half cost less). The *mode,* the most common sales price, may be different yet. If there are likely to be large or dramatic variations in what is measured, one must be cautious of figures that represent an unspecific "average."

Never try to wade a river just because it has an average depth of four feet.

—MILTON FRIEDMAN

The wrong average can put you under.

## Cause for Alarm?

According to the National Household Survey on Drug Abuse, cocaine use among Americans twelve to seventeen years of age increased by a whopping 166 percent between 1992 and 1995. Wow, right?

Except that the increase *in absolute terms* was a little less spectacular: In 1992, 0.3 percent of Americans aged twelve to seventeen had used cocaine; in 1995, the percentage was 0.8 percent of that population.

Be wary of comparisons expressed as percentage changes.

**Exercise 5-4**

Identify each of the following as either a rhetorical explanation, rhetorical analogy, or rhetorical definition.

1. "The *New York Times* editorial page is like a Ouija board that has only three answers, no matter what the question. The answers are: higher taxes, more restrictions on political speech and stricter gun control."

   —*Ann Coulter*

2. "Listening to him is like trying to read *Playboy* magazine with your wife turning the pages."

   —*Barry Goldwater, describing fast-talking Hubert Humphrey*

3. A Democrat is a person who likes to take your money and give it to lazy people.

4. Three people are dividing a pie. The Conservative is someone who takes all but one piece of the pie and then asks the other two, "Why is that guy trying to take your piece of pie?"

5. "Good Conservatives always pay their bills. And on time. Not like the Socialists, who run up other people's bills."

   —*Margaret Thatcher*

6. "Yeah, I'm obnoxious, yeah, I cut people off, yeah, I'm rude. You know why? Because you're busy."

   —*Bill O'Reilly*

7. "Republicans believe every day is the 4th of July, but Democrats believe every day is April 15."

   —*Ronald Reagan*

8. "Liberals would rather see a child aborted than a tree chopped down."

   —*Ann Coulter*

9. Philosophers love to argue because they don't have anything better to do with their time.

10. "Liberal soccer moms are precisely as likely to receive anthrax in the mail as to develop a capacity for linear thinking."

    —*Ann Coulter*

11. "A liberal interprets the Constitution. A conservative quotes it."

    —*Rush Limbaugh*

12. "New Rule: Gay marriage won't lead to dog marriage. It is not a slippery slope to rampant inter-species coupling. When women got the right to vote, it didn't lead to hamsters voting. No court has extended the Equal Protection Clause to salmon."

    —*Bill Maher*

**Exercise 5-5**

Explain how rhetorical definitions, rhetorical comparisons, and rhetorical explanations differ. Find an example of each in a newspaper, magazine, or other source.

**Exercise 5-6**

Critique these comparisons, using the questions about comparisons discussed in the text as guides.

**Example**

You get much better service on Air Atlantic.

**Answer**

> Better than on what? (One term of the comparison is not clear.)
>
> In what way better? (The claim is much too vague to be of much use.)

1. New improved Morning Muffins! Now with 20 percent more real dairy butter!
2. The average concert musician makes less than a plumber.
3. Major league ballplayers are much better than they were thirty years ago.
4. What an arid place to live. Why, they had less rain here than in the desert.
5. On the whole, the mood of the country is more conservative than it was in the last decade.
6. Which is better for a person, coffee or tea?
7. The average GPA of graduating seniors at Georgia State is 3.25, as compared with 2.75 twenty years ago.
8. Women can tolerate more pain than men.
9. Try Duraglow with new sunscreening polymers. Reduces the harmful effect of sun on your car's finish by up to 50 percent.
10. What a brilliant season! Attendance was up 25 percent over last year.

## PROOF SURROGATES AND REPETITION

These last two devices don't fit comfortably into any of the other groups, so we've made a group of just the two of them.

### Proof Surrogates

A **proof surrogate** suggests there is evidence or authority for a claim without actually citing such evidence or authority. When someone can't prove or support something, he or she may hint that proof or support is available without being specific as to what it is. Using "informed sources say" is a favorite way of making a claim seem more authoritative. "It's obvious that" sometimes precedes a claim that isn't obvious at all. "It's clear to anyone who has thought the matter through carefully that blahblahblah" is another example, one that by its sheer length might silence push-back.

A more general strategy speakers and writers use to win acceptance for a claim without providing actual proof or evidence is to insinuate themselves into our confidence. If a salesperson can establish common personal ground with a potential buyer, he or she may be more likely to make a sale. The same strategy may be followed by someone trying to sell us an idea—we may be more inclined to accept claims made by people we feel bonded with. As discussed in Chapter 1, it is a part of in-group bias to be more favorably disposed to a spokesperson who belongs to our own tribe; we naturally are inclined to assign him or her high marks for credibility. And it might be hard to question someone who says "As we all know" because it might sound disrespectful, and nobody wants to show disrespect to a fellow member of the club.

Other proof surrogates are less subtle: "Studies show" crops up a lot in advertising. Note that this phrase tells us nothing about how many studies are involved,

In 2003, the administration proposed a tax cut that, it was said, would give the average taxpayer $1,083.

The "average" here is the mean average. However, most taxpayers, according to the Urban Institute–Brookings Institution Tax Policy Center, would have received less than $100 under the administration's proposal.

There is no other country in the Middle East except Israel that can be considered to have a stable government. . . . Is Saudi Arabia more stable? Egypt? Jordan? Kuwait? Judge for yourself!

—"Facts and Logic About the Middle East"

Proof surrogates often take the form of questions. This strategy can also be analyzed as switching the burden of proof (see Chapter 6).

The Great Depression of the 1930s was needlessly prolonged by government policies now recognized in retrospect as foolish and irresponsible.

—Syndicated columnist Thomas Sowell

The phrase "now recognized in retrospect" is a proof surrogate, which hides the fact that the writer has done nothing more than offer his personal opinion.

how good they are, who did them, or any other important information. Here's another example, from *The Wall Street Journal:*

> We hope politicians on this side of the border are paying close attention to Canada's referendum on Quebec. . . .
>
> Canadians turned out en masse to reject the referendum. There's every reason to believe that voters in the United States are just as fed up with the social engineering that lumps people together as groups rather than treating them as individuals.

There may be "every reason to believe" that U.S. voters are fed up, but nobody has yet told us what any of them are.

Bottom line: Proof surrogates are just that—surrogates. They are not proof or evidence. Such proof or evidence may exist, but until it has been presented, the claim at issue remains unsupported.

## Repetition

> The most brilliant propagandist technique will yield no success unless one fundamental principle is borne in mind constantly—it must confine itself to a few points and repeat them over and over.
>
> —*Joseph Goebbels*
>
> A lie told often enough becomes the truth.
>
> —*Vladimir Lenin*

The technique of **repetition,** simply making the same point over and over at every opportunity, is a widely used rhetorical device, and not just in the propaganda of people like Joseph Goebbels and Vladimir Lenin. It may be found in advertising and

■ Putting campaign signs up everywhere is a form of repetition. Everything else being equal, we'd bet the winning candidate is the one who puts up the most visible signs. (Of course, usually everything else isn't equal.)

in everyday politics. The constant repetition of a theme seems eventually to have a dulling effect on our critical faculties, and we can become lulled into believing something simply because we've become used to hearing it. This is attributable to the availability heuristic, discussed in Chapter 1. A critical thinker needs to remember: it takes evidence and argument to provide believability; if a claim is not likely to be true on the first hearing, simple repetition does not make it more likely on the hundredth.

List as many proof surrogates (e.g., "It is very clear that . . . ") as you can.    **Exercise 5-7**

Identify these passages as ridicule/sarcasm, hyperbole, or proof surrogates.    **Exercise 5-8**

1. "Everything about the Left is perception, manipulation, and lies. Everything. Everything is 'Wag the Dog.' Everything is a structured deception."

      —*Rush Limbaugh*

2. "Mr. Obama has an ingenious approach to job losses: He describes them as job gains."

      —*Karl Rove*

3. "How come liberals never admit that they're liberal? They've now come up with a new word called 'progressive,' which I thought was an insurance company but apparently it's a label."

      —*Marco Rubio*

4. "Obviously there is global warming; no responsible climate scientist disputes that."

      —*Al Gore*

5. "I might be in favor of national healthcare if it required all Democrats to get their heads examined."

      —*Ann Coulter*

6. "We had a national tragedy this week, and the President of the United States and Sarah Palin both made speeches on the same day. Obama came out against lunatics with guns, she gave the rebuttal."

      —*Bill Maher*

7. "Rick Santorum doesn't like sex. He doesn't like the pill. He really doesn't like condoms. He said if men are going to pull something on to prevent procreation, nothing works better that a sweater vest."

      —*Bill Maher (Rick Santorum, a GOP presidential contender in 2008, 2012, and 2016, was frequently seen wearing a sweater vest)*

8. "The idea that being black and being gay is the same is simply not true. There are all sorts of studies out there that suggest just the contrary and there are people who were gay and lived the gay life style who aren't any more."

   —*Rick Santorum, addressing the question whether being gay is a matter of heredity like being black*

9. "So the majority of Americans are conservatives. They believe in things like the Constitution. I know that's weird to some people, but they believe in it."

*—Marco Rubio*

▲ 10. "You want to have two guys making out in front of your 4-year-old? It's OK with them. A guy smoking a joint, blowing the smoke into your little kid's face? OK with them. And I'm not exaggerating here. This is exactly what the secular movement stands for."

*—Bill O'Reilly*

**Exercise 5-9**

Identify these passages as ridicule/sarcasm, hyperbole, or proof surrogates.

▲ 1. Medical school, huh? Right. You and your fancy 2.9 grade point are going to get into a fine medical school all right.

2. Laboratory tests have shown that Cloyon produces a sweeter taste than any other artificial sweetener.

3. My wife is nuts. When we go shopping she buys out the entire store.

▲ 4. Anybody who drinks can tell you that three drinks are enough to make that guy seriously impaired.

5. *Rachet & Clank* is the best video game ever made. Try it. You can't stop playing.

6. The only thing you hear on Fox News is right-wing rants, and the only thing you hear on MSNBC are left-wing rants.

▲ 7. That the president is a Marxist simply cannot be denied by any serious observer of contemporary politics.

8. In the 1988 U.S. presidential election, campaigners for Democrat Michael Dukakis took a photograph of Dukakis in an M1 Abrams Tank. The photo was supposed to make Dukakis look strong on defense. Unfortunately, Dukakis had a silly grin and was wearing a helmet too large for his head, and the effect of the photograph was to make him appear diminutive and goofy. The photo was widely shown in the months preceding the election—but not by the Dukakis people. Instead, it was picked up and shown by his opponent, George H. W. Bush. After looking at the photo at the following link, state which technique was being used by the Bush campaign: http://en.wikipedia.org/wiki/File:Michael_Dukakis_in_tank.jpg.

9. If you want to work your way up from being a host to being a server at The Cheesecake Factory, it'll take forever.

▲ 10. The proposal isn't bad when you consider it comes from a group of knuckle-dragging morons.

## PERSUASION THROUGH VISUAL IMAGERY

Images affect emotions profoundly. Pictures of lakes and meadows make us feel good. Videos of chuckling babies cause us to laugh. Pictures of kind faces soothe us. Photos of suffering people or animals lead us to make donations.

Imagery affects emotions, and emotions are the wellsprings of actions. Advertisers and political campaigners know this. They use focus groups and other empirical methods to find out which pictures and videos sell the most beer or cars, or generate the most enthusiastic response among potential voters. When it comes to selling a product, political candidate, or even an idea, imagery seems to work better than reasoned argument. At least it is more common.

Apparently, which images work best to motivate behavior is not fully understood and may actually be surprising. Are people more apt to buy a product when they see a beautiful person using it or when they see someone they can relate to using it? Many Superbowl ads are funny visually, but it's not clear that humor works well if you want to sell a laxative.

Adding the right music or other sounds to a video only enhances its power to persuade. Watch an ad produced by a presidential campaign while muting the soundtrack. It will not seem as compelling.

What, then, is the defense when imagery—with or without sound—is enlisted to persuade us to buy a product or vote for a candidate or enlist in the military? After all, nobody wants to be led blindly by emotions; we all want to make intelligent decisions about political candidates, ballot initiatives, and even household products.

One solution might be simply not to watch. The TV remote has made this easier than it used to be, except that online advertising is now pervasive and hard to click your way out of.

Our recommendation is pretty elementary, though not as foolproof as we would like. It begins with remembering that an image is *not* an argument (see Chapter 2). It is not a premise, and it is not a conclusion. A picture is *nonpropositional:* it's neither true nor false. Of course, a picture can be the basis of an argument. A surveillance camera can provide unimpeachable photographic evidence that a car went through a red light. Pictures of mistreated chickens might give officials an excellent reason for shutting down a poultry farm. News photos keep us informed and help us make better decisions. Looked at in this light, a photograph can be informational. And if it is, it is the *information* documented in it that carries weight, not the emotions it generates. Emotions may be the springs of actions, but information alone can be the basis of a reasoned argument. The best defense against being swayed by "photographic rhetoric," if we may call it that, is to focus on the informational content of the photograph or video—assuming the photograph isn't fraudulent. These days sophisticated photo-editing software makes it easy to alter photos to achieve almost any effect. But this is no different from written records and other forms of information, because they can be faked and altered, too.

## Don't Get Carried Away!

Once you're familiar with the ways rhetorical devices are used to try to influence us, you may be tempted to dismiss a claim or argument *just because it contains strongly rhetorical language.* But true claims as well as false ones, good reasoning as well as bad, can be couched in such language. Remember that rhetoric *itself* gives us no reason to accept a position on an issue; that doesn't mean that there *are* no such reasons.

■ These days there are more ways than ever before to deceive us with images. It is often hard to determine whether an image is Photoshopped, which this one, from a Ted Cruz campaign ad, was.

Of course, reasonable people can disagree about what information actually is provided by a visual. In 2005, a Florida woman named Terri Schiavo, became the center of a nationwide controversy regarding whether she was in a "persistent vegetative state" and could ever be expected to regain consciousness. A videotape made by family members appeared to show her responding to the presence of her mother. Some doctors saw the tape and said that Schiavo seemed to be responding to visual stimuli; other doctors said that her facial expressions were not signs of awareness. The first group of doctors thought life support should not be withdrawn; the second group felt that it should. But there is nothing unique about photographic evidence in this regard; other forms of evidence too mean different things to different people. Thus, when you see compelling imagery—meaning imagery that has been used to promote an idea—focus on the information that may or may not be contained within the images, and evaluate it relative to the issue at hand.

## THE EXTREME RHETORIC OF DEMAGOGUERY

No account of rhetoric in a book on critical thinking could be complete without a discussion of the rhetoric of demagoguery. Demagogues fan the flames of fanaticism, and use extreme rhetoric to propagate false ideas and preposterous theories—even among people who might otherwise be generous, kind, and honorable. In this section, we highlight four broad rhetorical techniques that demagogues persistently employ.

*Otherizing,* which is pervasive in demagoguery, divides people into two groups—*us* and *them*—and portrays *them* as suspicious, dangerous, or repulsive. *Them* includes ideological opponents and other social groups who can be blamed for *our* problems. Minorities with their "unreasonable demands" make easy targets. The following passage will illustrate the technique. It is from a speech by Joseph Goebbels, the head of the Nazi Ministry of Information. Goebbels, who had a PhD in literature, once boasted that you can convince people that 2 + 2 is 5 if you know how to do it. In this passage, Goebbels otherizes intellectuals and critics of the Nazi regime:

> One cannot make history with such quivering people [intellectuals and dissenters]. They are only chaff in God's breath. Thankfully, they are only a thin intellectual or social upper class, particularly in the case of Germany. They are not an upper class in the sense that they govern the nation, but rather more a fact of nature like the bubbles of fat that always float on the surface of things.
>
> The people want nothing to do with them. These Philistines are the 8/10 of one percent of the German people who have always said "no," who always say "no" now, and who will always say "no" in the future. We cannot win them over, and do not even want to . . . . One does not need to take them all that seriously. They do not like us, but they do not like themselves any better. Why should we waste words on them?

If you think about it, this is pretty obvious. Reading this, whose side would you want to be on, the side of "the people," or on the side of "them," who are so contemptible "we" should not even "waste words on them"? The *fundamental attribution error* and *in-group bias,* which you read about in Chapter 1, have obvious connections with otherizing.

The second pervasive rhetorical technique used by demagogues is *demonizing—* trying to induce loathing of someone or something by portraying the person or thing as evil. Demonizing is often used with otherizing, and the two are frequently blended together so completely that they are impossible to separate out. In 1962, many white Alabamians thought that George Wallace was insufficiently opposed to racial integration to warrant their vote for governor of Alabama. To shore up his credentials as a hardline segregationist, Wallace hired the head of the Ku Klux Klan to write his speeches—and won election. In the following excerpt from his 1963 inaugural address, referred to as his "Segregation Now, Segregation Forever" speech, Wallace demonized the U.S. Supreme Court and the U.S. president, Dwight D. Eisenhower:

> It is this theory that led the Supreme Court for the first time in American history to issue an edict, based not on legal precedent, but upon a volume, the editor of which said our Constitution is outdated and must be changed, and the writers of which admitted belonging to as many as half a hundred communist-front organizations. It is this theory that led the same group of men to briefly bare the ungodly core of that philosophy, in forbidding little school children to say a prayer. And we find evidence of that ungodliness even in the removal of the words "In God we trust" from some of our dollars. . . . It is the spirit of power thirst that caused a president in Washington [Eisenhower] to take up Caesar's pen and with one stroke of it make a law . . . that tells us that we can or cannot buy or sell our very homes except by HIS conditions and except at HIS discretion. It is the spirit of power thirst that led the same president to launch a full offensive of twenty-five thousand troops against a university of all places in his own country and against his own people.

George Wallace attempts to block the integration of the University of Alabama in 1963.

As Wallace portrayed them, the members of the Supreme Court were atheistic communists who removed God from our currency and even forbade little school children from praying; and Eisenhower, according to Wallace, was a dictator who told people when they could buy or sell their own homes. He (Eisenhower) even launched an assault against one of our own universities. Notice that Wallace demonized his targets without resorting to many dysphemisms. And without looking too hard, you can find demonizing statements like these on political blogs today.

*Fostering xenophobia* is the third pervasive rhetorical strategy employed by demagogues, and it goes hand-in-hand with otherizing and demonizing. Xenophobia is the fear or dislike of what is foreign or strange. When we are suspicious of people simply because they dress or talk differently from "us," are from a foreign country, or simply are not "from around here," we are being xenophobic. Demagogues use xenophobia to elicit the worst in human nature. Excerpts from people like Joseph Goebbels and Adolf Hitler are so repugnant that we decline to provide examples.

Fourth, demagogues invariably try to stimulate an audience's fear, resentment, and hatred. *Fear and hate mongering* are used in conjunction with otherizing, demonization, and xenophobia, and you can see how they all work together. Here is

The innocent-looking Joseph Goebbels, PhD, shown here accepting an award from a youngster, used stock propaganda techniques to sell the vile and malignant concepts of the Third Reich.

a passage from another Goebbels' speech, which uses fear and hate mongering to support the other demagogic techniques discussed.

> When Mr. Bramsig or Mrs. Knöterich [names of everyday Germans] feel pity for an old woman wearing the Jewish star, they should also remember that a distant nephew of this old woman by the name of Nathan Kaufmann sits in New York and has prepared a plan by which all Germans under the age of 60 will be sterilized. They should recall that a son of her distant uncle is a warmonger named Baruch or Morgenthau or Untermayer who stands behind Mr. Roosevelt, driving him to war, and that if they succeed, a fine but ignorant U.S. soldier may one day shoot dead the only son of Mr. Bramsig or Mrs. Knöterich. It will all be for the benefit of Jewry, to which this old woman also belongs, no matter how fragile and pitiable she may seem.

Goebbels used fear and hate to prime his audience, something like loading a gun for further use, so that at the right time they would be willing or able to harm the "other," even if the "other" was a helpless old woman.

The four techniques we have just discussed—otherizing, demonization, fostering xenophobia, and fear and hate mongering—are persistently used by demagogues to manipulate the opinion of an audience. Here's the lesson: When you feel yourself enthralled by a speaker, with your blood pumping and your pulse rising—and, in particular, if you are being turned against some person or group of people this is when you most need to think critically. Step back and analyze what is being said. Set aside the temptation to strike out at someone or something. Dial down the anger. Look hard for arguments. You might find there aren't any. This is the only way, short of censorship, to make sure there is never another Joseph Goebbels.

## Recap

Things to remember from this chapter:

- Persuasion attempts to win someone to one's own point of view.
- Rhetoric seeks to persuade through the rhetorical force of language and other devices.
- Although it can exert a profound psychological influence, rhetoric has no logical force or probative value.
- There are a multitude of rhetorical devices in common use; they include:
    - **Euphemisms:** seek to mute the disagreeable aspects of something or to emphasize its agreeable aspects
    - **Dysphemisms:** seek to emphasize the disagreeable aspects of something
    - **Weaselers:** seek to protect a claim by weakening it
    - **Downplayers:** seek to tone down the importance of something
    - **Stereotypes:** a cultural belief about a social group's attributes, usually simplified or exaggerated
    - **Innuendo:** using the power of suggestion to disparage someone or something

- **Loaded questions:** questions that depend on unwarranted assumptions
- **Ridicule and sarcasm:** widely used to put something in a bad light
- **Hyperbole:** overdone exaggeration
- **Rhetorical definitions and explanations:** definitions and explanations used to express or influence attitudes or affect behavior by invoking images with emotional associations
- **Rhetorical analogies:** analogies used to express or influence attitudes or affect behavior by invoking images with emotional associations
- **Proof surrogates** suggest there is evidence or authority for a claim without actually saying what the evidence or authority is
- **Repetition:** hearing or reading a claim over and over can sometimes mistakenly encourage the belief that it is true

▨ These devices can affect our thinking in subtle ways, even when we believe we are being objective.

▨ Although photographs and other images are not claims or arguments, they can enter into critical thinking by offering information bearing on an issue. They can also affect us psychologically in the same way that emotional language affects us, and often even more powerfully.

▨ Demagogues use extreme rhetoric to spread false ideas and to gain power over people. Four rhetorical techniques persistently used by demagogues are otherizing, demonizing, fostering xenophobia, and fear and hate mongering. One of the most important tasks of critical thinking is to recognize these techniques for what they are.

# Additional Exercises

Identify each of the following passages as otherizing, demonizing, fear or hate mongering, or fostering xenophia. Some passages may fit more than one category. One passage does not fit any of these categories.

 1. "They aren't from around here. You know that just by looking at them."

—*Overheard conversation*

2. "Whether they are defending the Soviet Union or bleating for Saddam Hussein, liberals are always against America. They are either traitors or idiots, and on the matter of America's self-preservation, the difference is irrelevant."

—*Ann Coulter*

3. "It [Poland] was a State built on force and governed by the truncheons of the police and the military. The fate of Germans in this State was horrible. There is a difference between people of low culture being governed by a culturally significant people and people of high cultural significance having forced upon them the tragic fate of being oppressed by an inferior."

—*Adolf Hitler*

 4. "Barack *Hussein* Obama."

—*Emphasis on middle name, used by some Obama opponents to refer to him*

5. The fact is that public schools in this country have become nothing better than government indoctrination centers. Teachers look constantly for ways to brainwash our students and make them incapable of independent thought or critical judgment. Our children spend their lives in government prison camps where their heads are filled with propaganda. They are told what to think, not how to think. No wonder high school students seem so dumb. Why would anyone want to subject their children to this?

   —Adapted from *The American Dream* http://endoftheamericandream.com/ archives/category/commentary

6. "These people don't care about our country."

   —*Charles Rangel, referring to Republicans*

7. "Our intellectual, cultural, and political elites are today engaged in one of the most audacious and ambitious experiments in history. They are trying to transform a Western Christian republic into an egalitarian democracy made up of all the tribes, races, creeds, and cultures of planet Earth. They have dethroned our God, purged our faith from public life, and repudiated the Judeo-Christian moral code by which previous generations sought to live."

   —*Patrick Buchanan*

8. Ew. Don't play with *her.*

9. "Once the Republicans get rolling, they assume they're going to win everything. They are zealots, and zealots assume the last five percent of whatever their plan is will be taken care of by their own greatness or momentum or divinity."

   —*Keith Olbermann*

10. "Let us therefore brace ourselves to our duties, and so bear ourselves that, if the British Empire and its Commonwealth last for a thousand years, men will still say, 'This was their finest hour!'"

    —*Winston Churchill*

11. "What's really funny is seeing these [gay] activists supporting Muslim governments. They don't want us to bomb them. . . . Do they know what would happen to them outside of the United States? Do they know what would happen to them if Islamists took over this country? They are lucky that they live in a privileged country . . . a country which gives them every right to do whatever they want no matter how much they happen to hate it. It's all very ironic."

    —*Sarah Palin*

12. "As a mom, I was vigilant about food safety. Right, moms? I mean, if you could depend on the government for one thing, it was you had to be able to trust the water that our kids drank and the food that they ate. But this [the Republican Party] is the *E. coli* club. They do not want to spend money to do that."

    —*Nancy Pelosi*

13. "They keep coming."

    —*1996 reelection campaign ad for California governor Pete Wilson, in reference to undocumented immigrants*

14. "Mitt Romney. He's not one of us."

*—2012 Obama Ohio campaign ad*

15. "When Mexico sends its people, they're not sending their best. They're sending people who have lots of problems, and they're bringing those problems to us. They're bringing drugs. They're bringing crime. They're rapists. And some, I assume, are good people."

*—Donald Trump*

## Exercise 5-11

In the first ten examples, identify which, if any, of the listed rhetorical strategies are being employed. In the second ten, identify which, if any, of the listed slanting devices are being employed.

1. "Yes, a lot of innocent civilians are being killed by the bombing in both North and South Vietnam, but do remember that Asians do not believe in the importance of individual lives like we do. Life just doesn't mean as much to them."

   *—Overheard conversation during the Vietnam War*

   a. demonizing
   b. fostering xenophobia
   c. otherizing
   d. fear or hate mongering
   e. no rhetorical import

2. No, we should not raise the minimum wage for agricultural workers. Many of those people are illegal, and besides, they're happy to work for low wages or they would not have come to this country to begin with.

   a. demonizing
   b. fostering xenophobia
   c. otherizing
   d. fear or hate mongering
   e. no rhetorical import

3. Immigrants, legal and illegal, are coming over here by the thousands and taking jobs away from us—and jobs are already hard enough for us to find.

   a. demonizing
   b. fostering xenophobia
   c. otherizing
   d. fear or hate mongering
   e. no rhetorical import

4. About 47 percent of the American public receive benefits from the government and about the same percentage pay no income tax. They are takers, not like you and me.

   a. demonizing
   b. fostering xenophobia
   c. otherizing
   d. fear or hate mongering
   e. no rhetorical import

5. The motorcycle gangs that come through here regularly are like nothing you've ever seen. They are filthy, they dress like wild people, they are foul-mouthed, and their motorcycles make such a racket it drives you crazy. Decent folk can hardly go out in the street while they're here. We have got to get the city council to do something to stop this terrible invasion of our town.

   a. demonizing
   b. fostering xenophobia
   c. otherizing
   d. fear or hate mongering
   e. no rhetorical import

6. It is indeed an unintended consequence of the new voting laws here in our state that a few people who do not have government-issued photo identification will have trouble voting. The purpose of the laws was to help discourage voter fraud, although nobody is certain whether that has been a problem in our state.

   a. demonizing
   b. fostering xenophobia
   c. otherizing
   d. fear or hate mongering
   e. no rhetorical import

▲ 7. Planned Parenthood is badly named. "Planned Population Control" is more like it. The head of that outfit said she's for killing any infant that survived an abortion. That's murder! These are fiends! They give hundreds of presentations a year in Los Angeles schools. They are insinuating their foul views of humanity into our own children!

   a. demonizing
   b. fostering xenophobia
   c. otherizing
   d. fear or hate mongering
   e. no rhetorical import

8. An upper-class British woman around the turn of the last century: "Working people are supposed to work; what could they possibly want with a day off?"

   —*Paraphrase of Bertrand Russell, from* In Praise of Idleness

   a. demonizing
   b. fostering xenophobia
   c. otherizing
   d. fear or hate mongering
   e. no rhetorical import

9. It isn't just the *numbers* of illegals that are streaming across our borders. It's the fact that they are universally poor, mainly illiterate, and without real means of self-support. That means our welfare system, the one you and I pay dearly to support, will be clogged with these invaders.

   a. demonizing
   b. fostering xenophobia
   c. otherizing
   d. fear or hate mongering
   e. no rhetorical import

▲ 10. Crime is going to get nothing but worse with the growth in population, and neither your family nor your property is safe anymore. There have been break-ins, home invasions, and muggings right here in our town. Get an alarm system. Better yet, get a gun.

    a. demonizing
    b. fostering xenophobia
    c. otherizing
    d. fear or hate mongering
    e. no rhetorical import

11. "Making a former corporate CEO the head of the Securities and Exchange Commission is like putting a fox in charge of the henhouse." This is best seen as an example of

    a. rhetorical analogy
    b. rhetorical explanation
    c. innuendo
    d. dysphemism
    e. not a slanter

12. "Right. George Bush 'won' the election in 2000, didn't he?" The use of quotation marks around "won" has the effect of

    a. a weaseler
    b. a dysphemism
    c. a downplayer
    d. a rhetorical explanation
    e. not a slanter

▲ 13. "The obvious truth is that bilingual education has been a failure." In this statement, "the obvious truth" might best be viewed as

    a. a proof surrogate
    b. a weaseler
    c. innuendo
    d. a dysphemism
    e. not a slanter

14. After George W. Bush announced he wanted to turn a substantial portion of the federal government operation over to private companies, Bobby L. Harnage Sr., president of the American Federation of Government Employees, said Bush had "declared all-out war on federal employees." Would you say that the quoted passage is

    a. a rhetorical explanation
    b. a euphemism
    c. a weaseler
    d. hyperbole/a rhetorical analogy
    e. not a slanter

15. "Harry and his daughter had a little discussion about her outfit . . . one that left her in tears." This statement contains

    a. a loaded question
    b. a euphemism
    c. both a and b
    d. neither a nor b

16. "Before any more of my tax dollars go to the military, I'd like answers to some questions, such as why are we spending billions of dollars on weapons programs that don't work." This statement contains

    a. a downplayer
    b. a dysphemism
    c. a proof surrogate
    d. a loaded question
    e. hyperbole and a loaded question

17. "Can Governor Evans be believed when he says he will fight for the death penalty? You be the judge." This statement contains

    a. a dysphemism
    b. a proof surrogate
    c. innuendo
    d. hyperbole
    e. no slanters

18. President Obama promised change, but he continued to turn government operations over to private companies, especially in Iraq and Afghanistan, just like his predecessor did.

    a. hyperbole
    b. a dysphemism
    c. a loaded question
    d. a proof surrogate
    e. a downplayer

19. "Studies confirm what everyone knows: smaller classes make kids better learners."

    —*Bill Clinton*

    This statement is

    a. a proof surrogate
    b. a weaseler
    c. hyperbole
    d. an innuendo
    e. no slanter

20. MAN SELLING HIS CAR: "True, it has a few dents, but that's just normal wear and tear." This statement contains

    a. a loaded question
    b. innuendo
    c. a dysphemism
    d. a euphemism

## Exercise 5-12

Determine which of the numbered, italicized words and phrases are used as rhetorical devices in the following passage. If the item fits one of the text's categories of rhetorical devices, identify it as such.

The National Rifle Association's campaign to *arm every man, woman, and child in America*[1] received a setback when the president came out for gun control. But *the gun-pushers*[2] know this is only *a small skirmish in a big war*[3] over guns in America. They can give up some of their more *fanatical*[4] positions on such things as protecting the *"right"*[5] to possess *cop-killer bullets*[6] and still win on the one that counts: regulation of manufacture and sale of handguns.

## Exercise 5-13

Follow the directions for Exercise 5-12.

The *big money guys*[1] who have *smuggled*[2] the Rancho Vecino development onto the November ballot *will stop at nothing to have this town run just exactly as they want.*[3] *It is possible*[4] that Rancho Vecino will cause traffic congestion on the east side of town, and *it's perfectly clear that*[5] the number of houses that will be built will overload the sewer system. *But*[6] a small number of individuals have taken up the fight. *Can the developers be stopped in their desire to wreck our town?*[7]

## Exercise 5-14

Follow the directions for Exercise 5-12.

The U.S. Congress has cut off funds for the superconducting super-collider that the *scientific establishment*[1] wanted to build in Texas. The *alleged*[2] virtues of the supercollider proved no match for the *huge*[3] *cost overruns*[4] that had piled up *like a mountain alongside a sea of red ink.*[5] Despite original estimates of five to six billion dollars, the latest figure was over eleven billion and *growing faster than weeds.*[6]

## Exercise 5-15

Read the passage below, then answer the questions that follow it. Your instructor may have further directions.

"There is something called 'carried-interest' that occupies a peculiar spot in the U.S. tax code; it represents one of the most glaring injustices in a tax law that is chock full of injustice. While most of the people who make a substantial income—and I include here surgeons, stockbrokers, baseball players, and corporate lawyers—will have to pay the new higher marginal rate of 39.6% on the top part of their earnings, there are a few who are exempted from the higher rate.

"The beneficiaries of this tax giveaway are private equity and hedge fund managers, venture capitalists, and partners in real estate investment trusts. Their income, which comes from managing other people's money—they do not have to invest a dime of their own money, mind you, to get this benefit— is taxed as 'carried-interest' at a rate of only 20%. So, a tiny group of individuals who are already stupendously wealthy, manage to get away with a tax burden 19.6% lower than others who earn their money in some other way. For a million-a-year single filer, that could make a difference in taxes of almost a quarter of a million dollars, and all because one made his money by managing other people's money.

"The unfairness of this loophole, which was crafted in large part by Senator Charles Schumer (Democrat of New York), should be obvious to anyone. The New York Times referred to it as 'crony capitalism,' since it favors certain kinds of work over others. Myself, I call it cheating."

—*From a speech by Joel Trajan, at the Northstate Economic Forum, March 2013*

1. What issue is the author addressing?
2. What is the author's position on that issue?
3. Does the author support that position with an argument (or arguments)? If you think so, state that argument (or one of those arguments) in your own words.
4. Are there rhetorical devises or strategies employed in the passage? If so, identify any that fall into the categories described in this chapter.

## Exercise 5-16

Follow the directions for Exercise 5-15, using the same list of questions.

Schools are not a microcosm of society, any more than an eye is a microcosm of the body. The eye is a specialized organ which does something that no other part of the body does. That is its whole significance. You don't use your eyes to lift packages or steer automobiles. Specialized organs have important things to do in their own specialties. So schools, which need to stick to their special work as well, should not become social or political gadflies.

—*Thomas Sowell*

## Exercise 5-17

Follow the directions for Exercise 5-15, using the same list of questions.

The core of the Judeo-Christian tradition says that we are utterly and distinctly apart from other species. We have dominion over the plants and the animals on Earth. God gave it to us, it's ours—as stated succinctly in the book of Genesis. Liberals would sooner trust the stewardship of the Earth to Shetland ponies and dung beetles. All their pseudoscience supports an alternative religion that says we are an insignificant part of nature. Environmentalists want mass infanticide, zero population growth, reduced standards of living, and vegetarianism. The core of environmentalism is that they hate mankind.

—*Ann Coulter,* Godless: The Church of Liberalism

## Exercise 5-18

Follow the directions for Exercise 5-15, using the same list of questions.

Asked whether he would be resigning, [U.N. Secretary General Kofi] Annan replied, "Hell, no. I've got lots of work to do, and I'm going to go ahead and do it." That's doubtful. His term is up at the end of 2006, and few—after the mess he's caused—take him seriously. He may have a lot of "work" he'd like to do, but he won't be permitted to do it. All around Annan is the wreckage of the U.N.'s spirit of high-level cronyism.

—*Editorial in the* National Review Online, *April 1, 2005*

## Exercise 5-19

Follow the directions for Exercise 5-15, using the same list of questions.

> "It is not the job of the state, and it is certainly not the job of the school, to tell parents when to put their children to bed," declared David Hart of the National Association of Head Teachers, responding to David Blunkett's idea that parents and teachers should draw up "contracts" (which you could be fined for breaching) about their children's behavior, time-keeping, homework and bedtime. Teachers are apparently concerned that their five-to-eight-year-old charges are staying up too late and becoming listless truants the next day.
>
> While I sympathize with Mr. Hart's concern about this neo-Stalinist nannying, I wonder whether it goes far enough. Is it not high time that such concepts as Bathtime, Storytime and Drinks of Water were subject to regulation as well? I for one would value some governmental guidance as to the number of humorous swimming toys (especially Hungry Hippo) allowable per gallon of water. Adopting silly voices while reading *Spot's Birthday* or *Little Rabbit Foo-Foo* aloud is something crying out for regulatory guidelines, while the right of children to demand and receive wholly unnecessary glasses of liquid after lights-out needs a Statutory Minimum Allowance.
>
> —*Walsh, John,* "I say there, are you absolved?" The Independent, August 30, 1998. Copyright © 1998 by The Independent. All rights reserved. Used with permission.

## Exercise 5-20

Choose which answer is best from among the alternatives provided.

   1. "The Clintons have indeed employed elite accountants to help limit their own family's tax liability. Because they're so very concerned about the wealth gap, you see."

—*Guy Benson, Town Hall.com, January 5, 2016*

This contains

a. a downplayer
b. sarcasm, ridicule
c. hyperbole

2. "Liberals need to understand the global health argument for abortion is deeply offensive. It is like fighting disease by killing everyone who has a disease."
This contains

a. a euphemism
b. a dysphemism
c. a rhetorical definition
d. none of the above

3. "Why does Senator Schmidt collect child pornography? Only the Senator can answer that." This contains

    a. a loaded question
    b. a euphemism
    c. a dysphemism
    d. none of the above

▲ 4. "Does Senator Schmidt collect child pornography? Only the Senator can answer that." This contains

    a. innuendo
    b. a downplayer
    c. a euphemism
    d. a stereotype

5. "Better lock up your whisky before Patrick gets here. Didn't you know he is Irish?" This contains

    a. a loaded question
    b. a rhetorical definition
    c. a stereotype
    d. a euphemism.
    e. none of the above

6. "Ecology? I will tell you what ecology is. Ecology is the Marxist 'science' that tries to shove bogus facts about global warming down everyone's throat." This contains

    a. a rhetorical definition
    b. a rhetorical explanation
    c. a rhetorical analogy

▲ 7. "Ecology? I will tell you what ecology is. Ecology is the Marxist 'science' that tries to shove bogus facts about global warming down everyone's throat." The quotation marks around "science" are

    a. hyperbole
    b. a proof surrogate
    c. a downplayer
    d. a stereotype

8. "Ecology? I will tell you what ecology is. Ecology is the Marxist 'science' that tries to shove bogus facts about global warming down everyone's throat." "Marxist" and "bogus" are

    a. proof surrogates
    b. dysphemisms
    c. hyperbole
    d. rhetorical comparisons
    e. none of the above

9. "The reason Republicans oppose health care is that they don't care about anyone except their friends in the insurance industry." This sentence contains

    a. a rhetorical definition
    b. a rhetorical explanation
    c. a rhetorical analogy
    d. none of these

▲ 10. "Rush Limbaugh doesn't make things up? C'mon, it's been shown over and over that he makes things up." This contains

   a. a stereotype
   b. hyperbole
   c. ridicule
   d. a proof surrogate

## Exercise 5-21

Identify any rhetorical devices you find in the following selections, and classify those that fit the categories described in the text. For each, explain its function in the passage.

▲ 1. I trust you have seen Janet's file and have noticed the "university" she graduated from.

2. The original goal of the Milosevic government in Belgrade was ethnic cleansing in Kosovo.

3. Obamacare: The compassion of the IRS and the efficiency of the post office, all at Pentagon prices.

▲ 4. Although it has always had a bad name in the United States, socialism is nothing more or less than democracy in the realm of economics.

5. We'll have to work harder to get Representative Burger reelected because of his little run-in with the law.

6. It's fair to say that, compared with most people his age, Mr. Beechler is pretty much bald.

▲ 7. During World War II, the U.S. government resettled many people of Japanese ancestry in internment camps.

8. "Overall, I think the gaming industry would be a good thing for our state."

   —*From a letter to the editor,* Plains Weekly Record

9. Capitalism, after all, is nothing more or less than freedom in the realm of economics.

▲ 10. I'll tell you what capitalism is: Capitalism is Charlie Manson sitting in Folsom Prison for all those murders and still making a bunch of bucks off T-shirts.

11. Clearly, Antonin Scalia was the most corrupt Supreme Court justice in the history of the country.

12. If MaxiMotors gave you a good price on that car, you can bet there's only one reason they did it: It's a piece of serious junk.

▲ 13. It may well be that many faculty members deserve some sort of pay increase. Nevertheless, it is clearly true that others are already amply compensated.

14. "The only people without [cable or satellite TV] are Luddites and people too old to appreciate it."

   —*Todd Mitchell, industry analyst*

15. I love some of the bulleting and indenting features of Microsoft Word. I think it would have been a nice feature, however, if they had made it easy to turn some of them off when you don't need them.

## Exercise 5-22

Identify any rhetorical devices you find in the following passages, and explain their purposes. *Note:* Some items may contain *no* rhetorical devices.

▲ 1. "The Obama administration is shamelessly rolling Homeland Security Secretary Janet Napolitano out this week to make sure Americans everywhere know that terrorists will be crawling through their children's bedroom windows as early as next week if the Republicans don't back down on this budget thing."

—*Matt Taibbi*, Rolling Stone Magazine

2. "If the United States is to meet the technological challenge posed by Japan, Inc., we must rethink the way we do everything from design to manufacture to education to employee relations."

—Harper's

3. According to UNICEF reports, several thousand Iraqi children died each month because of the UN sanctions.

▲ 4. I did see someone sleeping through her lecture, but of course that could have been just a coincidence.

5. I can't find it in myself to sympathize with people with drug problems. I mean, I didn't have anything to do with causing their "problem"; I don't see why I should have anything to do with getting them over it. Let the do-gooders help these druggies. These addicts are like pets—they accept care from others but they can't do anything for themselves.

6. Maybe Professor Stooler's research hasn't appeared in the first-class journals as recently as that of some of the other professors in his department; that doesn't necessarily mean his work is going downhill. He's still a terrific teacher, if the students I've talked to are to be believed.

7. Let's put it this way: People who make contributions to my campaign fund get access. But there's nothing wrong with constituents having access to their representatives, is there?

—*Loosely paraphrased from an interview with a California state senator*

8. In the 2000 presidential debates, Al Gore consistently referred to his own tax proposal as a "tax plan" and to George W. Bush's tax proposal as a "tax scheme."

9. George Bush got us into two wars, and Jeb is his brother after all. . . .

10. "They'll have to pry my gun out of my cold, dead hands."

—*Charlton Heston*

11. Wayne Lapierre? Hah! He's worse than Charlton Heston. He's at the point now where he believes that the only—the *only*—solution to the country's problems is more guns! That the solution to *all* the country's problems is more guns!

12. I pulled my child out of school because I learned that his teacher is an atheist. I was amazed that they'd hire an atheist to teach small children. Those people are not satisfied to condemn themselves in the eyes of God; they want to bring our children along with them with their Godless teachings. These are really the most dangerous people in the world, when you think about it. Let's get them out of the schools!

▲  13. All I know is that they started reporting small amounts of money missing not too long after she started working in their house.

14. [*Note:* Dr. Jack Kevorkian was instrumental in assisting a number of terminally ill people in committing suicide during the 1990s.] "We're opening the door to Pandora's Box if we claim that doctors can decide if it's proper for someone to die. We can't have Kevorkians running wild, dealing death to people."

     —*Larry Bunting, assistant prosecutor, Oakland County, Michigan*

15. "LOS ANGELES—Marriott Corp. struck out with patriotic food workers at Dodger Stadium when the concession-holder ordered them to keep working instead of standing respectfully during the National Anthem. . . . Concession stand manager Nick Kavadas . . . immediately objected to a Marriott representative.

     "Marriott subsequently issued a second memo on the policy. It read: 'Stop all activities while the National Anthem is being played.'"

     "Mel Clemens, Marriott's general manager at the stadium, said the second memo clarified the first memo."

     —*Associated Press*

▲  16. These so-called forfeiture laws are a serious abridgment of a person's constitutional rights. In some states, district attorneys' offices have only to claim that a person has committed a drug-related crime to seize the person's assets. So fat-cat DAs can get rich without ever getting around to proving that anybody is guilty of a crime.

17. "A few years ago, the deficit got so horrendous that even Congress was embarrassed. Faced with this problem, the lawmakers did what they do best. They passed another law."

     —*Abe Mellinkoff, in the* San Francisco Chronicle

18. "[U]mpires are baseball's designated grown-ups and, like air-traffic controllers, are paid to handle pressure."

     —*George Will*

▲  19. "Last season should have made it clear to the moguls of baseball that something still isn't right with the game—something that transcends residual fan anger from the players' strike. Abundant evidence suggests that baseball still has a long way to go."

     —*Stedman Graham,* Inside Sports

20. "As you know, resolutions [in the California State Assembly] are about as meaningful as getting a Publishers' Clearinghouse letter saying you're a winner."

     —*Greg Lucas, in the* San Francisco Chronicle

21. The entire gain in the stock market in the first four months of the year was due to a mere fifty stocks.

▲  22. "The climate has changed considerably over the last few decades, with the last two years being the hottest on record in several places around the globe and we've seen the hottest overall global temperatures recently as well. There is every reason to believe that this trend is going to continue, with the result that the planet will gradually become more and more unlivable."

     —*Jim Holt,* Slate *online magazine*

23. "[Supreme Court Justice Antonin] Scalia's ideology is a bald and naked concept called 'Majoritarianism.' Only the rights of the majority are protected."

*—Letter to the editor of the* San Luis Obispo Telegram-Tribune

24. When the government has finished taking over health care—and believe me,
the so-called "Affordable Care Act" is just the first step—government bureau-
crats will be deciding who gets treated for what. You'll wait while you're
dying while some clerk with a rubber stamp figures out whether you get
treated or not. Oh yes, and if treatment and death are the alternatives, there
will be death squads to make that decision for you. A bunch of government
goons will be deciding whether you're worth saving or not. It's going to be
wonderful, just like these "progressives" say. You betcha.

▲ 25. "We are about to witness an orgy of self-congratulation as the self-appointed
environmental experts come out of their yurts, teepees, and grant-maintained
academic groves to lecture us over the impending doom of the planet and
agree with each other about how it is evil humanity and greedy 'big business'
that is responsible for it all."

*—Tim Worstall, in* New Times

26. "In the 1980s, Central America was awash in violence. Tens of thousands of
people fled El Salvador and Guatemala as authoritarian governments seeking
to stamp out leftist rebels turned to widespread arrests and death squads."

*—USA Today*

## Exercise 5-23

Discuss the following stereotypes in class. Do they invoke the same kind of images
for everyone? Which are negative and which are positive? How do you think they
came to be stereotypes? Is there any "truth" behind them?

1. soccer mom
2. Religious Right
3. dumb blonde
4. tax-and-spend liberal
5. homosexual agenda
6. redneck
7. radical feminist
8. contented housewife
9. computer nerd
10. Tea Partier
11. interior decorator
12. Washington insider
13. old hippie
14. frat rat
15. Barbie doll
16. trailer trash

### Exercise 5-24

Your instructor will give you three minutes to write down as many positive and negative stereotypes as you can. Are there more positive stereotypes on your list or more negative ones? Why do you suppose that is?

### Exercise 5-25

Write two brief paragraphs describing the same person, event, or situation—that is, both paragraphs should have the same informative content. The first paragraph should be written in a *purely* informative way, using language that is as neutral as possible; the second paragraph should be slanted as much as possible either positively or negatively (your choice).

### Exercise 5-26

Explain the difference between a weaseler and a downplayer. Find a clear example of each in a newspaper, magazine, or other source. Next find an example of a phrase that is sometimes used as a weaseler or downplayer but that is used appropriately or neutrally in the context of your example.

### Exercise 5-27

Critique these comparisons, using the questions discussed in the text as guides.

1. You've got to be kidding. Paltrow is much superior to Blanchett as an actor.
2. Blondes have more fun.
3. The average chimp is smarter than the average monkey.
4. The average grade given by Professor Smith is a C. So is the average grade given by Professor Algers.
5. Crime is on the increase. It's up by 160 percent over last year.
6. Classical musicians, on the average, are far more talented than rock musicians.
7. Long-distance swimming requires much more endurance than long-distance running.
8. "During the monitoring period, the amount of profanity on the networks increased by 45–47 percent over a comparable period from the preceding year. A clear trend toward hard profanity is evident."

   —*Don Wildmon, founder of the National Federation for Decency*

9. As a company, Google is a greater benefit to the country than Amazon.
10. Which is more popular, the movie *Gone With the Wind* or Bing Crosby's version of the song "White Christmas"?

### Exercise 5-28

In groups, or individually if your instructor prefers, critique these comparisons, using the questions discussed in the text as guides.

1. A course in critical thinking will make you smarter.
2. Students are much less motivated than they were when I first began teaching at this university.

3. Offhand, I would say the country is considerably more religious than it was twenty years ago.

▲ 4. In addition, for the first time since 1960, a majority of Americans now attend church regularly.

5. Science is not appreciated in this country like it was 50 years ago.

6. Hire Ricardo. He's more knowledgeable than Annette.

▲ 7. Why did I give you a lower grade than your roommate? Her paper contained more insights than yours, that's why.

8. Golf is a considerably more demanding sport than tennis.

9. Yes, our prices are higher than they were last year, but you get more value for your dollar.

▲ 10. So, tell me, which do you like more, fried chicken or Volkswagens?

## Writing Exercises

1. The illustration below is for an article on banks and bankers in *Rolling Stone Magazine* online. After seeing the illustration but before reading the article, how sympathetic to bankers would you expect it to be? Try to come up with a couple of sentences that you think the image illustrates—you'll probably need some forceful language.

Juhasz, Victor, Cartoon from The Rolling Stone, April 15, 2010. Copyright © 2010 by Victor Juhasz. All rights reserved. Used with permission.

2. Over the past decade, reportedly more than 2,000 illegal immigrants have died trying to cross the border into the Southwestern United States. Many deaths have resulted from dehydration in the desert heat and from freezing to death

on cold winter nights. A San Diego–based nonprofit humanitarian organization now leaves blankets, clothes, and water at stations throughout the desert and mountain regions for the immigrants. Should the organization do this? Its members say they are providing simple humanitarian aid, but critics accuse them of encouraging illegal activity. Take a stand on the issue and defend your position in writing. Then identify each rhetorical device you used.

3.  Until recently, tiny Stratton, Ohio, had an ordinance requiring all door-to-door "canvassers" to obtain a permit from the mayor. Presumably, the ordinance was intended to protect the many senior citizens of the town from harm by criminals who might try to gain entry by claiming to be conducting a survey. The ordinance was attacked by the Jehovah's Witnesses, who thought it violated their First Amendment right to free speech. The Supreme Court agreed and struck down the law in 2002. Should it have? Defend your position in a brief essay without using rhetoric. Alternatively, defend your position and use rhetorical devices, but identify each device you use.